Teachers of the Foothills Province

In 1967 the Alberta Teachers' Association published, in honour of Canada's Centennial, a history of the public school system in Alberta entitled *Schools of the Foothills Province.* This informative book published for the Association by University of Toronto Press is now followed by a companion volume written by the same author, which tells the story of the Association itself, and its long and sturdy efforts to improve the position of teachers and the quality of education in the province. After providing the background to the formation of the ATA (which officially began on July 24, 1918) the author goes on to describe the growth of the organization from its beginnings as a spare-time activity for teachers to a strong and influential union. From its earliest years it was affiliated with the labour movement of the Twenties, and fought with increasing strength for the rights of Alberta teachers. Throughout this study, the ATA'S concern is evident not only for the economic aspects of teaching, for higher salaries and pension schemes, but also for other features: departmental examinations and curricula, preparation and certification of teachers, and educational research.

The ATA'S mercurial relations with the provincial government are related, its struggle through the depression years and its blossoming in the first decade after 1935 under a Social Credit Government. Leading personalities move through this story against the turbulent background of a growing young province, contributing an air of vigorous controversy and achievement to the story of the ATA.

DR. JOHN W. CHALMERS has been engaged in some aspect or other of Alberta public education almost continually since he entered the third class of the fledgling School of Education, University of Alberta, in 1931. He has been a high school teacher, superintendent of schools, and educational administrator with both provincial and federal government departments. Even his wartime service in the RCAF was spent largely in the teaching of navigation. Preparation for his profession he obtained at the universities of Manitoba and Alberta, and at Stanford University. Dr. Chalmers is at present the Superintendent of the St. Albert Protestant Separate School District No. 6.

Dr. Chalmers' previous writing includes *Schools of the Foothills Province* (1967), companion volume to this one, and numerous educational, historical, and general articles in Canadian and American publications. He has collaborated in the preparation of several secondary school literature textbooks, has written a number of works based on Canadian history, and has co-edited a Canadian historical atlas.

JOHN WALKER BARNETT

from a portrait by Don Frache hung in Barnett House

Teachers of the Foothills Province

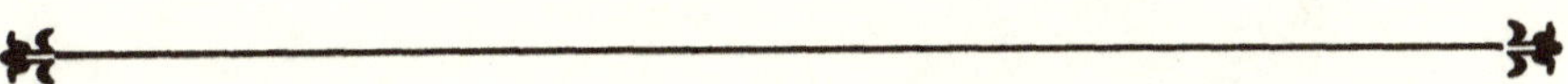

THE STORY OF
THE ALBERTA TEACHERS'
ASSOCIATION

JOHN W. CHALMERS

Published for The Alberta Teachers' Association
by University of Toronto Press, 1968

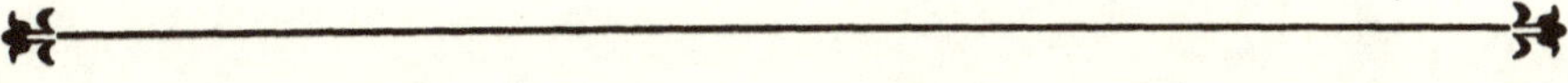

Reprinted in paperback 2015

ISBN 978-0-8020-3220-1 (cloth)
ISBN 978-1-4426-3904-1 (paper)

In memory of John
Walker Barnett

Prelude

TO JOHN BARNETT

He was strong—
The strong are many.
He was wise
But many men are wise.
His wisdom and his strength
Were rare
Only in this,
That both were used for others.

He was, of all men, fearless,
Yet knew
So well
The fears of little men
Caught fast
In the tyrant-grip
of Yesterday.

He did not fear Tomorrow,
And Today
He used
For wider sowing.
Up to the last he toiled
For our growing.
Let us, who stay for the harvest—
In our yearning—
Still follow in the furrow
Of his turning.

John Burke

Foreword

AS THE 1917 Easter convention of the Alberta Education Association in Calgary was drawing to a close and all business activity had been cleared away in preparation for the address of the final speaker, a young high school teacher secured the floor and presented three motions which caused considerable consternation among members of the educational establishment of that era. These called for the creation of a provisional Alberta teachers' organization, designated its officers, and provided from the AEA treasury sufficient funds to launch the new venture. A year later the Alberta Teachers' Alliance held its first annual meeting. On July 24, 1918, now regarded as the ATA's birthday, it received its charter from the Alberta government.

Thus 1968 marks the golden anniversary of the Alberta Teachers' Association. To commemorate the occasion it has authorized the preparation and publication of this work, the story of the ATA's first fifty years. It is altogether fitting that it should be dedicated to the memory of John Walker Barnett, LL.D., one of the founding fathers of the Alliance, now Association, for nearly thirty years its executive secretary, a man who spent half his life in single-minded devotion to the cause of Alberta's teachers.

In preparation of this book the author is happy to acknowledge his debt to the members of the ATA's Liaison Committee, consisting of Miss L. Jean Scott, Messrs. R. V. Mundell (chairman), A. M. Arbeau, W. Moysa, and H. G. Ward, of the Association, and Messrs. F. J. C. Seymour and W. W. McConaghy, Assistant Executive Secretary and Editor respectively of the ATA. Their comments, suggestions, and even questions have helped more than they can probably ever realize, as has the assistance of Miss Marian Allison, of the ATA staff.

It was with a profound sense of shock and loss that the author and the remaining members of the committee learned in February, 1968, of the sudden and untimely death of their friend and colleague Fred Seymour. For more than twenty years he had served the Alberta Teachers' Association as member of the provincial executive council, president, and assistant executive secretary.

Edmonton, March 1968 J.W.C.

Contents

Illustrations

I

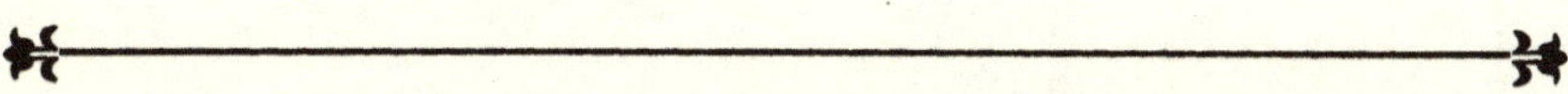

The Alliance

Necessity Most Imperious

AT ITS 1916 MEETING, the Alberta Education Association, of which more anon, passed a resolution directing School Inspector George Gorman to take initial steps towards the formation of a provincial teachers' association. Predictably, at least from the vantage point which hindsight provides, nothing came of this timid gesture, nor did anything deserve to. For Gorman was part of the very establishment against which any organization of classroom teachers would inevitably find itself arrayed: an establishment which included the professors of the provincial university and its president, Protestant clergymen, especially of the status of bishop or better, and officers of the Department of Education. Others in the Association less visibly a part of the power structure were the trustees of the large urban school systems and such cabinet ministers and other government members of the provincial legislature as concerned themselves with education.

No doubt these worthy gentlemen were puzzled as to why the humble classroom practitioners of the pedagogical craft were anxious to have their own organization when in the Alberta Education Association they were able to enjoy the fruits of their superiors' greater learning, experience, and wisdom, while the erection of a body limited in membership to practising teachers would exclude them from such manifold advantages.

There were many reasons why teachers in 1916 were disenchanted with the way the school systems' establishment was looking after their interests. Basically, their reasons fell into two categories: economic and educational. The first, of course, was the more urgent. In 1916, Alberta teaching salaries ranged between $450 and $3,000 per year. The latter figure was not inconsiderable—but was earned only by principals of large city systems. The beginning teachers' stipend was usually much nearer the lower figure, and the average for all the 3,963 teachers in the province in 1916 was only $828.69—hardly more than the $800 which the Edmonton public school district had paid its first instructor away back in 1885. Furthermore, at the time of the 1916 Easter convention of the Alberta Education Association, salaries were still falling because of the immense dislocation of the Great War which had erupted in 1914. In 1913, average salaries reached the figure of $819.71 per annum; within two years they had dropped to $792.72. Only by the end of 1916 had they reached the pre-war high. Nor was the nominal remuneration the same as the take-home pay, even in that innocent pre–income tax era. For example, the Edmonton public school board, motivated by a perhaps laudable patriotism, volunteered for its teachers a sizeable percentage of their pay for patriotic purposes. In their wisdom the trustees did not feel it necessary to consult their staff before taking such nefarious action. Other school boards took similar measures to promote the war effort without cost to themselves or their districts.

In the rural areas especially, annual salaries and amounts which the teachers received often bore little relation to each other. Virtually dependent on local resources, school boards found themselves ground between the upper millstone of operational costs and the lower one of uncollectable taxes. In those unhalcyon days, rural school boards were their own tax-collecting authorities. Thus a decision by school trustees to sell a farm for taxes often meant taking punitive action against friends and neighbours, never a popular activity. Furthermore, if the taxes were unpaid because the taxpayer was serving in the Canadian Army overseas at $1.10 a day, then it was quite unthinkable to put his farm up for sale.

Since the major part of the cost of operating a rural one-room school consisted of the teacher's salary, relief to the taxpayer could be found only by reducing expenditures in this direction. There were several ways of doing so. One, of course, was by reducing the incumbent's annual salary. Thus minimum salaries dropped from $480.00 in 1914 to $300.00 a year later, although the corresponding figure had risen to $450.00 in 1916. Average salaries dropped $28.00 per year in the 1913-1915 biennium. Another method of cutting expenditures for salaries was simply not to pay them, and many a young schoolmarm finished the school year and left the district with her employers owing her hundreds of dollars—not to mention what they owed her predecessors.

Still another technique was to appoint teachers with sub-marginal qualifications—they came cheaper. In 1916, almost exactly half of the 1,184 teachers' licences issued by the Department of Education were provisional certificates, granted to young men and women who could not qualify even for a third class teacher's certificate. In other words, they had absolutely no preparation whatsoever in the art or craft of teaching. This proportion of provisional certificates was the highest since 1908. Their holders may not have done much for Alberta education, but they surely helped to keep school expenditures down.

Finally, the simplest and perhaps the most honest device was just to close the school when the money ran out. In 1916, 48,000 of Alberta's school pupils attended ungraded (i.e., one-room) schools; 51,000 were in more pretentious multi-room institutions. But the latter group attended for a school year averaging 193.89 school days; the former were present for only 165.15. The average ungraded school operated only 8¼ months; as many were below as above that figure. The doors of some rural schools stood open for only three months in the year; their teachers were not counted among Alberta's most affluent residents.

Perhaps teachers might have found their penury tolerable had the whole province been in the grip of a war-born depression. However, they were almost unique in their straitened circumstances. Crops had never been better, war-stimulated markets were excellent, grain prices were high. In a word, farmers never had it so good. Teachers wondered why they, and apparently they alone, could not share in the general prosperity, especially as the war-time inflation meant that each month their meagre wages constituted less and less buying power.

Nor did they enjoy any fringe benefits to protect them from the slings and arrows of outrageous fortune. They had no tenure, not even during the school year. Any teacher could be–and was–dismissed on thirty days' notice, with or without cause. Competition from unqualified (and low-cost) personnel was an ever present threat, as is indicated by the number of provisional certificates issued each year. Salaries were determined by individual negotiation between the hard-nosed school trustees, on the one hand, and the often immature and inexperienced teacher, on the other. Usually, of course, such negotiation consisted of an offer by the school board, and acceptance or rejections thereof by the teacher. Outside of the cities, qualifications and experience were considered immaterial if not downright irrelevant although most school boards would give preference to the holder of a first class certificate over one who had the second class credential, other things (usually salary) being equal. Pensions for teachers, of course, were far in the future. Normally their absence did not worry the nubile young ladies in search of husbands or the young men aiming at careers in business or one of the learned professions. But the absence of any retirement benefits did not help to persuade any young pedagogues to consider teaching as a life-time career. And the absence of superannuation provisions meant that for many years to come a number of aged arthritic, deaf, and otherwise handicapped classroom veterans had to continue in service, long after they should have been able to enjoy a life of serene leisure.

Living and working conditions often fell far short of what beginning teachers had been accustomed to. In the time of Alberta's first dawning, sewers, running water, and electricity could be found only in the cities; even quite large towns did not know these amenities. But, as always, the great bulk of Alberta's teaching force was drawn from solid middle-class people; they enjoyed relatively high standards of food and housing. The fortunate rural teacher found a boarding place comparable to the environment he had come from, and enjoyed the comfort, privacy, and even the fellowship and affection he had known in his own home. Many others found themselves living in tiny dwellings where privacy was impossible, the food inferior to or at least different from what they were used to, the language spoken in the household a completely alien tongue.

Some, of course, enjoyed the tenancy of teacherages, often and deservedly called shacks, each boasting not more than two rooms, totalling perhaps 300 square feet in area, bereft of basement and storm windows, and, as January blizzards emphasized, quite innocent of any kind of insulation. The tenant of such an edifice, however, did enjoy a modicum of privacy, whose other names were loneliness and isolation.

Today the teacher of a one-room school might understandably feel a bit sorry for himself. Of course, in Alberta there are only about 100 of these tiny institutions still in existence, two-thirds of which are in Hutterite Colonies and most of the remainder in forest or frontier districts. But in 1916, when half the province's pupils attended such schools, they constituted the norm for rural education. By the standards of the day, they were not bad buildings. Although many were log structures, most were frame-built edifices, well-lighted (occasionally), usually less than ten years old. However, like teacherages, they commonly lacked storm windows and basements, and in the winter months the pot-bellied stove produced an indoor climate ranging from torrid to frigid, depending on the distance from the source of heat. Commonly also, the school was dirty, the walls begrimed from the coal or (more usually) wood stove; muddy weather left its enduring deposit on the floor, which was usually scrubbed not more often than once or twice a year. Daily caretaking services, including firelighting, were never satisfactory, often being performed by one of the pupils. Quite occasionally the school's incumbent combined the offices of teacher and janitor. Unless there was a well in the school yard—by no means invariably the case—water for both ablutions and libations was generally in short supply. Often its provision was another responsibility delegated to one of the young acolytes at the temple of learning, and was conveyed to school in a cream can riding in a buggy driven by a youthful Jehu.

In brief, living and working conditions for rural teachers were not very good, even by the undemanding standard's of Alberta's salad days. It is therefore not surprising that the province's teachers felt the need for an organization of their own to work for their material betterment. Yet the cutting edge of the thrust for organization came not from the young rural schoolmarms on the bottom of the ladder, but rather from the mature, well-qualified, experienced and relatively secure principals and high school teachers in the big city systems, big at least in relation to the others in the province. These people, with the least to gain from the formation of an aggressive and demanding association, and the most to lose should they become known as trouble-makers likely to upset the educational establishments' *canot du maître*, were driven by considerations other than material. They were sincerely disturbed by what they considered to be the faults and inadequacies of the educational system.

For one thing, they were concerned with the constant turn-over of teaching personnel, not simply as a result of transfer from one school to another, but of movement in and out of the profession, if a prestigous word can be used for such a sometime calling. By the end of 1916, there were 3,143 classrooms operating in Alberta, yet from the formation of the province in 1905, 11,761 new teaching certificates had been issued, enough to staff every teaching station almost four times over—and this without considering the number of credentials issued previously by the government of the North-West Territories. Of course, the brief tenure of the rural teacher was a by-word in western Canada during and previous to World War I. Some teachers left their little schools after a few months, because their school districts ran out of funds and were no longer able to pay them. Some pert young school mistresses departed because they married local farmers—and others because they didn't. If a girl hadn't acquired an engagement ring by the end of her first year of teaching, she usually left for pastures greener. Nor did the young men in the one-room schools have any deeper commitment to their calling. Sometimes engaged only for the summer months, they were often taking time out from their own studies in order to earn and save enough money to continue towards their chosen careers in agriculture, business, law, medicine, or the Christian ministry.

In 1916 another factor, the war itself, was contributing to teacher turn-over. The armed services and war industry were making devastating inroads on the school staffs, members of which left their classrooms for pelf, death and/or glory, with the complete approbation of their neighbours, as though carnage were a more necessary and honourable calling than was teaching.

Another matter of concern to leaders in the field of education was the deplorably low standard exacted of those to whom the children and therefore the future of the country were being entrusted. Thus in the 1905-1916 period, over one-third, and in some years almost one-half of the teaching certificates issued were provisional, that is, mere permits granted to persons with absolutely no professional preparation whatsoever. At the other end of the scale, only 11.6 per cent of the new certificates were at the highest, or first class level, which required complete Grade XII or better for admittance to training. Nor was the programme of preparation all that impressive. The third class certificate course was no longer being offered in 1916, and the course for the first and second class credentials required only four months. Two classes a year usually were graduated. In actuality, the diplomas were sometimes little more than attendance certificates, as it was almost impossible to fail the programme if one attended classes with a fair degree of regularity and stayed the required time. Failures in one or two subjects could be erased through the writing of supplemental examinations, but they did not hinder one from applying for and accepting a position. Lack of success in more subjects might result in the issuance of a third class certificate, a stigma which could be removed only through further training. However, it was still a valid licence to teach.

In 1916, many of Alberta's leading teachers believed that education could be improved as a result of better salaries, less turn-over in teaching staff, better living and working conditions, some security of tenure, pensions and better teaching preparation, and that these laudable aims could best be achieved through a strong organization of teachers.

However, there were other aspects of the educational scene that were as unpleasing as those which surrounded the classroom practitioner. The shortness of the rural school year—8¼ months—has already been mentioned. But coupled with this fact was the poor attendance during the time the school was actually operating. In 1916 it amounted to only 56.44 per cent, to give an average attendance for the school year of a mere 92.7 days, about half of what would be considered as a minimum acceptable standard in 1968. In the graded schools the school year was one and one-half months longer at 193.89 days, but regularity of attendance at 64.76 per cent was not excitingly better, even though the longer school year implied an average annual attendance of 125.5 days.

Nor was the retentivity of the schools overly impressive. Only 5.49 per cent of Alberta's 99,000 school children were to be found above the eighth grade, that is, in high school, and of course virtually none of these 5,763 senior scholars were discernible in the rural ungraded schools. Only 541 students, 0.55 per cent, attended at the Grade XII level. Fifty years later, 1966, the proportion of Alberta students in Grades IX to XII was 25.53 per cent; in Grade XII it had reached 6.01 per cent.

Another source of concern was the inherent inferiority of the one-room school, regardless of the modernity of the school building or the excellence of the teacher. Since its enrolment of twenty to thirty-five pupils ran the gamut of six to eight grades, pupils spent but a short while each day under the teacher's direct instruction. Most of the time they read or studied by themselves, or spent their priceless minutes in busy-work, plasticine modelling, raffia-work, paper mat weaving, or like make-work projects. The teacher, or jack of all pedagogical trades, could be a specialist in none of them. The school, because of the limited resources of the district, boasted of but a rudimentary library, and other instructional equipment, save for a torn wall map or two and a terrestial globe, was quite absent.

If only, the master teachers thought, these farm children could be gathered together in big schools, not more than one or two grades in each classroom, then each class could receive more instructional time from teachers who could specialize in teaching Grade I or IV or VIII or whatever, or who would have special training and competence in particular fields such as music, art, physical training, domestic science, or manual training. Provision of more attractive and stable teaching situations, and payment of higher salaries, would enable such schools to attract more highly qualified teachers. A better physical environment and transportation services for pupils would make their attendance more regular and more effective. With a larger tax base, school systems could remain open for a full year, not just a few months. They would also be able to provide high school services, heretofore almost unobtainable by rural boys and girls. Larger schools would also be able to provide better instructional and recreational equipment, and more of it. The larger schools would provide more sophisticated, more challenging situations for their pupils than could the one-room institutions with perhaps only two or three pupils per grade or class.

Thus Alberta teachers quite approved of the emerging movement towards school consolidation. The Alberta legislature had amended the School Ordinance in 1913 so as to permit two or more districts to form an organic union, operate a single school with services to at least Grade XI, i.e., entrance to normal school or the provincial university, and keep the school open for the full year. During the first calendar year of operation, only one consolidated school district had been established, and only one in 1914. However, by the beginning of 1916, ten more had come into existence, and during that year another fifteen were erected. This movement was the brightest feature of Alberta education during the war years, and even gave promise, illusory as it ultimately proved, of eventually embracing all rural districts.

Besides the demonstrable need for an organization to further the interests both of teachers and of education in general, the social climate of the early war years was conducive to such a movement. By and large, the people of North

A Meeting of the School Trustees by Robert Harris
courtesy of National Gallery, Ottawa

Weedon School, built near Cochrane, Alberta, in 1910 and donated to Heritage Park, Calgary, as an educational museum. (Photo by Jack DeLorme, Calgary)

America were both idealists and optimists, with an abiding faith in the perfectibility of man and the effectiveness of reason to achieve improvement in the human condition. In fact, they—or their ancestors—could hardly have emigrated to the New World without such a faith. (Negroes, of course, didn't really count.) That the war which was being bitterly waged in 1916 was a denial of the whole thesis of human perfectibility was quite overlooked. Young Canadians in their hundreds of thousands were joining the army and navy from the most idealistic of motives. And within a few months the United States would enter the fray to end war forever and make the world safe for democracy.

However, across North America there were many people who were or recently had been advocating less grandoise and more realizable social objectives. These included provision of workmen's compensation for on-job injuries, abolition of child labour, female suffrage, pension schemes, slum clearance, passage or improvement of pure food and drug laws, homes for working girls and working mothers, and of course total prohibition. In the realm of political thought, agrarian radicalism was sweeping across the plains of western United States and to a lesser extent the Prairie Provinces. The movement was predicated, in part, on the theory that the political parties which controlled the various state, provincial, and federal governments were captives of the Eastern vested interests, commercial and industrial, and it was a vain hope to expect them to do anything for the betterment of labour, small farmers and ranchers, or indeed anyone in the West. What was needed was a system whereby legislators would be not so much representatives as delegates of the electors, taking direction from and being responsible to their constituents. This delegation of authority would be reinforced and emphasized by such devices as to recall, whereby intransigent legislators could be removed simply because of their intransigency. Another device of direct democracy which claimed attention was the referendum. By this process, a legislative proposal is placed before all the voters, and, upon its passage, it automatically becomes law. In this respect, it differs from a plebiscite, which simply provides direction to the legislature, direction which need not be followed. The initiative in both is somewhat similar, except that in the plebiscite it lies not with the legislature but with the electorate, usually in the form of a petition. Adoption of such changes would result in a non-partisan form of government and the destruction of the political system as it has developed north and south of the Forty-Ninth Parallel. Many students of political science feel that the Prairie Provinces have in effect operated under non-partisan governments most or all of the years since about 1921.

In any event, in 1916 the need was apparent and the social climate was propitious for the formation of a teachers' association in Alberta. The fact that as a result of poor strategy the first moves proved abortive could not long turn back the wave of the future.

Before we begin the chronicle of future organization, we might look back to the past, to the traditions of teaching, which have their origin in antiquity.

Indeed, teaching, as a purposeful and deliberate transmission of society's wisdom and culture, its lores and folkways, is an activity so venerable that its origins are lost in the mists of time. If it is not the oldest profession, it is certainly one of the most ancient. In the most primitive societies, anthropologists have found evidence of puberty rites, the purpose of which is to instil in a boy those essentials of knowledge and wisdom and understanding which he requires to be a man. Pictorial records from ancient Egypt show cross-legged priests and their acolytes facing each other as the unhappy young students struggle to master the mysteries of Isis and Osiris. Classical Greece had both amateur teachers such as Socrates and Plato, and professionals like the Sophists. These latter, with their emphasis on the practical application of the skills they taught, and the fact that they accepted money for their services, were held in low esteem by the pure-minded philosophers who believed that wisdom was priceless and therefore no money could or should ever be charged for its transmission. Their objectives and even their status were not unlike those of vocational teachers in some parts of Canada even to this day.

In the centuries since the glory that was Greece, the teacher has been found in a whole range of social positions, from that of the Roman slave (pedagogue) who accompanied the young scholar creeping like a snail unwillingly to school to the confidant of princes and kings, like Aristotle. With the spread of Christianity, to a large extent the function of the teacher became absorbed into that of the priest—shades of ancient Egypt—a partnership which continues to a greater or less degree to the present.

The Middle Ages saw the development of skilled trades through the guild system with its organization of apprentices, journeymen, and master craftsmen. Had teaching not been incorporated into the church, it might have become a skilled trade like the crafts of the fletcher, the glovemaker, the silversmith. As it was, a somewhat parallel development occurred in the rising universities, with their degrees of bachelor, master (implying master teacher), and doctor, which word derives from the Latin *docere,* to teach.

During comparatively recent times, say within the last two hundred years, a teaching force might include such disparate practitioners as a housewife operating her dame school in a corner of her kitchen for the benefit of her neighbours' children, a half-literate army veteran driven into teaching because of service-incurred disabilities which prevented him from making a more comfortable living, a monitor in a Manchester-type mass-production educational institution, learning his lessons one day and teaching them the next, or a rural curate preparing his young parishioners for entrance to a private secondary school or to a university. Only recently, despite the antiquity of their calling, have teachers had their own organizations.

Probably the first one in Europe to represent most of the teachers in a legally constituted system of schools was the Educational Institute of Scotland, which dates back to 1847, even though it was not chartered until four years later. Some twenty years afterwards, in 1870, there appeared the National Union of Teachers of England and Wales (the world famous N.U.T.), as it is now known. But even earlier, in 1861, an educational organization was founded in Canada West. From 1867 this body was known as the Ontario Teachers' Association, and after 1892 as the Ontario Educational Association. However, this pioneer organization, which became the prototype for many others in western Canada and elsewhere, could hardly be considered an organization by and for teachers. Its ranks included university professors, department of education personnel, clergymen, and interested laymen, who tended to gravitate to positions of control. Its early presidents were usually civil servants, professors, anybody but classroom teachers.

In Canada East (Lower Canada) local teachers' organizations began to appear by the late 1850's. The first truly provincial teachers' organization in Canada was probably that now known as the Provincial Association of Protestant Teachers of the Province of Quebec, founded in 1864, which continues to this day with virtually the same name and under a set of aims and by-laws very similar to those which it had in the beginning. Such continuity of nature, name, and purposes was by no means the rule for nineteenth-century teachers' organizations. Despite its name, however, as J. M. Paton indicates, "Principals of McGill . . . and of Bishop's, the Director of Protestant Education, and the occasional clergyman, judge, and departmental inspector supplied much of the leadership and held the top posts for the first thirty or forty years, just as they did in the Ontario Educational Association."[1] In 1899 the organization received the first provincial charter granted any teachers' organization in Canada, and by 1894 it began electing classroom teachers to its presidency.

Farther east, a provincial teachers' association was established in Prince Edward Island in 1880 and secured an act of incorporation from the provincial legislature in 1895. However, Paton notes, "It may be assumed that this body did not give the teachers the organized voice they needed, because a different organization bearing the name 'Union' succeeded it after the First World War."[2] On the mainland, the Nova Scotia Teachers' Union was organized in 1896 as a part of a grab-bag educational association. The Union did not achieve its present structure until 1920. The New Brunswick Teachers' Association emerged about 1902 from a union of county bodies, lapsed into inactivity shortly afterwards, and finally became active in 1917. The Newfoundland Teachers' Association almost got under way in 1889-1890, held its first convention in 1898, then went into hibernation for a full decade.

In the North-West Territories, local teachers' organizations were becoming visible by the late 1890's. Typical of these was the Northern Alberta Teachers' Association—how contemporary that name sounds—which met at Edmonton in 1903 for its seventh annual convention, with the ringing declaration, according to the printed program, "Let's meet, and either do or die."[3] Meet they did, for that was the name of the game, the primary purpose of that association, whose members taught, not in the northern half of the foothills province, but in the corresponding part of the North-West Territories of Alberta.

The two-day session opened with preliminary business under the admonition that "Order is heaven's first law." (The final such session carried the reminder that "Despatch is the soul of business.") President D. C. McEachren, a classroom teacher like the other executive officers, delivered his presidential address, although his topic was not noted and no doubt has long been forgotten by any survivors of that gathering.

[1]J. M. Paton, *The Rôle of Teachers' Organizations in Canadian Education* (Quance Lectures, 1962), p. 28.

[2]*Ibid.*, p. 31.

[3]Northern Alberta Teachers' Association, Convention program, 1903.

Most of the presentations were delivered by teachers, on such subjects as "Classification in the Public Schools," and "Measurements." One teacher's subject was "The Globe." That this probably did not refer to Shakespeare's theatre is suggested by the accompanying quotation: "Make me no maps, sir; my head is a map, a map of the whole world." However, there were orators other than teachers. His Worship Mayor Short spoke on "The Teacher as a Citizen," and Dr. H. L. McInnis dealt with "Hygiene, Its Place and Importance in Schools." The incumbent Northern Alberta school inspector, T. E. Perrett, no doubt referred to his little black book when he attacked the topic entitled "Field Notes." Probably he commended teachers for their collective achievements and chided them for their shortcomings. His colleague, Inspector J. F. Boyce from Red Deer, spoke on "Practical Composition."

The Association elected, as its next president, teacher W. Rea, who in a few short years was to become a force in the young Alberta Teachers' Alliance. He had delivered an address entitled "The Value of Language" ("But, for mine own part, it was Greek to me.") Following the election of officers, the Northern Alberta Teachers' Association no doubt relapsed into a state of dormancy until its next convention in October, 1904.

The last page of the 1903 programme carries a list of the officers—four vice-presidents, even—who had "allured to brighter worlds and led the way." Yet the brighter worlds, at least as realized in a comprehensive and effective teachers' organizations, were very slow in coming. Before 1905, there had been a Territorial Teachers' Association, which in 1907 became the Saskatchewan Education Association. A body with a parallel name appeared in Alberta shortly afterwards, probably in 1911. But, as with the Ontario Educational Association, these bodies could by no means be considered teachers' organizations, and for the same reasons. As this writer has indicated in another context:

> They were dominated by university personnel, clergymen (the church had long had a vested interest in western education), and officers of the Department of Education; in fact, the associations might even be considered captives of these departments. They usually operated through a convention. often held during the Easter holidays. At such gatherings, teachers listened to inspirational addresses, received information on departmental and government policies from their school inspectors and others, and heard a few talks on teaching techniques from normal school instructors and other such experts. They were also subject to assorted criticisms on the way they were keeping school. Occasionally they passed a few innocuous and ineffective

resolutions on such matters as salaries, pensions, and teacher training and certification.[4]

First of what may be regarded as the second-generation teachers' organizations was the Saskatchewan Union of Teachers, founded in 1914. Although its early records have been lost, apparently it was established as a result of a refusal by the minister of education to consider a teachers' presentation of grievances which included requests for more adequate salaries, security of tenure, and a pension scheme. In view of the factors discussed earlier, it is not surprising that this pioneering organization should appear on the prairies, nor even that it should contain the word "Union" in its name. However, in view of the Russian revolution of 1917, with the resultant continent-wide fear of Bolshevism, and of the post-war industrial unrest, it is understandable that in 1919 the Union changed its name to Saskatchewan Teachers' Alliance.

Returning to the Alberta scene, we find that the teacher members of the Alberta Education Association were not to be put off by the failure of Inspector George Gorman to implement the 1916 directive to take initial steps towards the formation of a teachers' organization. For the 1917 AEA convention the teachers planned their strategy much more carefully. George D. Misener, an Edmonton school principal, managed to gain the floor of the convention and, despite cries for the last scheduled speaker, he introduced three resolutions which set the stage for the formation of the Alberta Teachers' Alliance. The timing of his action appears fortuitous; just possibly it was Machiavellian. Had his resolutions been introduced earlier in the convention, there would have been time for the minions of the minister of education to apply pressure for their recission. Whether or not this was a likelihood, certainly the teachers' strategy made it impossible. According to A. Kratzmann, an organizational structure was also managed:

> G. D. Misener of Edmonton and C. E. Leppard of Calgary were appointed acting president and vice-president of the Alliance; a small sum of money to cover necessary initial expenses was voted from the treasury; and the two nominees were given authority to choose a general secretary-treasurer. As well, these two elected officers were assigned the task of drafting a suitable constitution for the Alliance. To assist them with this task, they chose John W. Barnett, teacher at Strathcona high school, Edmonton, as Secretary-Treasurer.[5]

[4]J. W. Chalmers, *Schools of the Foothills Province* (Toronto: 1967), p. 435.

[5]A. Kratzmann, "The Alberta Teachers' Association: A Documentary Analysis of the Dynamics of a Professional Association," unpublished doctoral dissertation, University of Chicago, 1963, p. 32.

It is part of the irony of Alberta's educational history that the AEA not only condoned the formation of a body which in the end would lead to its own demise, thus acquiescing, as it were, in its own obsequies, but even provided the money to pay the undertaker. Probably, in view of the opposition to Misener's climatic presentation, the educational establishment felt some forebodings of the shape of things to come. But the teacher members of the AEA would not be denied; since they formed an overwhelming majority of the voting participants at that 1917 convention, they ignored the vociferous opposition and speedily passed Misener's resolutions.

The Alberta Teachers' Alliance was on its way.

Where Your Beginnings Are

THE PROVISIONAL EXECUTIVE of the infant organization acted quickly and decisively. It chose as secretary-treasurer a young Edmonton high school teacher. G. D. Misener has told us how this man was persuaded to accept this assignment. "The writer met the late John W. Barnett while he, like Cincinnatus of old, was cultivating a plot of ground," he relates, "and spent the greater part of the afternoon persuading him to assume the duties of general secretary-treasurer of the new organization."[1] Barnett had been a local president of the British National Union of Teachers, a man experienced in the business of a teachers' organization, its structure, functions, problems, benefits, a pedagogue completely dedicated to the idea of the rightness of such an association. With his assistance the newly chosen officers drafted a constitution for adoption at the 1918 meeting of the Alberta Educational Association and prepared plans for the new body's guidance.

The first annual general meeting of the new organization was held as a session of the AEA in First Presbyterian Church, Edmonton, on April 2, 1918. The proposed constitution was adopted with only minor changes. It envisaged a federation of "Local Unions," although their designation was changed to

[1]G. D. Misener, "The Alberta Teachers' Association," *The ATA Magazine,* XXI, 4 (Dec. 1950), 4-5.

"Local Alliances," an arrangement which has been followed ever since. To describe the new Alliance as a federation, however, seems to imply a rather narrow definition of the word, for the local units did not send delegates to a provincial council or governing body. Rather, the executive, with the exception of the secretary-treasurer, was to be chosen by direct franchise of the members. President and vice-president were to be elected at large; other elected members were to be chosen by geographical districts, the only function of which was to serve as their constituencies. The Locals, however, did have a function other than that of dealing with strictly local matters. They were to send representatives each year to the annual general meeting (AGM), which has been termed "the parliament of the ATA." The purposes of this yearly gathering were to hear reports from the Alliance's officers and committees, formulate policy through resolutions, and give instructions to the executive council. However, if the council chose not to follow the direction of the AGM, there was no way in which the latter could impose its will, since the council members were responsible neither to the AGM nor to the Locals, but only to the membership of the whole organization. In general, these characteristics of the ATA's constitution have continued to the present day with but minor changes. For example, the number of vice-presidents elected by the membership as a whole has increased to two, the number of districts (and councillors) has also increased, and the AGM is now known as the annual representative assembly (ARA).

Qualifications for membership in the new Alliance differed in very important respects from those of the AEA. In fact, it was precisely these differences—the possession of a valid Alberta teaching credential and employment by a public or separate school system—that justified the establishment of the new organization when an estimated 80 per cent of the AEA were already teachers. The AGM modified the provisional constitution, which opened membership to "any person directly interested in education." At one stroke all the do-gooders, the amateurs, the permit-holders, the clergymen, professors, departmental officials, and other stalwarts of the educational establishment were removed from positions where, from the best of motives and with the best (or worst) of intentions, they could impede the welfare of the teaching profession as the teachers conceived it. Unqualified personnel were not thereby automatically and permanently removed from the classroom, but ever since the formation of the Alberta Teachers' Alliance their presence has been regarded only as an emergency measure and not as a normal condition. Nor did the birth of the association forever end the proclivity of certain self-appointed spokesmen, such as school superintendents, ministers of education, and inspectors to claim that they knew better than did the teachers themselves where the teachers' interests lay. But thereafter such claims were never meekly accepted. That only their own organization could speak for the profession has been one of the ATA's foundation stones.

There have been a few modifications to the letter but not the spirit of the requirement that membership is open only to certificated teachers employed in public education. Teacher-trainees have been accepted as student members, and qualified teachers practising their profession in institutions other than public or separate schools (e.g. the provincial correspondence school) have also been made eligible for membership. But not for several decades was a formula devised to permit school administrators such as superintendents to join the organization.

Another basic and enduring concept of the ATA's founders was that there should be but one teaching organization in the province, and that it should include within its ranks all teachers regardless of status, sex, religion, grade level taught, or language of instruction. The concept of a unitary organization embracing all classroom personnel was typical of the West. If there was at least a superficial resemblance to the industrial One Big Union (OBU) and the radical American-based International Workers of the World (IWW), in the opinion of many the similarity was more than coincidental. Certainly in Canada's heartland—Ontario and Quebec—such monolithic institutions as the western teachers' organizations were slow in emerging. There, separate organizations for men and women, for elementary and secondary teachers were the rule, or for Protestant or Roman Catholic, or English or French-speaking teachers but not both, or for principals on the one hand, classroom teachers on the other. Even in Alberta such divisiveness lingered in Edmonton and Calgary, where separate Locals for public and high school teachers endured for many years. But with these relatively minor exceptions the ATA has always been an organization based on the idea that teachers had more common than separate and individual concerns. This principle has been one of the great strengths of the association: that no attack could be made on a single teacher without the whole membership closing ranks to protect the threatened individual.

The first AGM did much more than approve a constitution for the new

Alliance and set the qualifications for membership; it resolved to seek incorporation (achieved on June 24, 1918) and ordered that a delegation be sent to the government to press for publication of a directory of schools and teachers in the province. The council was to seek a standard teacher's contract which would provide a modicum of security of tenure, and a pension scheme. The AGM also arranged for the preparation of a code of honour of professional etiquette to be presented at the second AGM. Finally, it sought and obtained financial support from the Alberta Educational Association, which approved a grant not exceeding $300, finances permitting. (By the time of the next AEA meeting two years later, the AEA had subsidized the ATA to the extent of $450.) On the financial side, the meeting raised the annual membership fee from 35c to 75c per year, approved an honorarium of $50 to the secretary-treasurer for the previous year, and of exactly twice that for the 1918-19 term of office.

Alberta's professional teachers—those with a commitment to their calling and a mastery of their craft achieved through study and experience—well realized that in 1918 their occupation could not yet be called a profession other than by courtesy. Many criteria of the professional as opposed to the non-professional person have been published. Paton describes the professional in the following terms:

1. *He has specialized knowledge.* This means that his work makes intellectual demands upon him; that he must retain a scholarly, inquiring attitude; and that he must constantly take responsibility for important decisions affecting the personal lives of people.
2. *He uses specialized skills and techniques.* Despite the foregoing emphasis upon the ability to conceptualize and to generalize, a profession has a practical side involving techniques that can be taught to others, provided they already have the basic intellectual equipment.
3. *He serves society and people.* A professional person is motivated by a desire to help people and to serve important social ends. Because of this, and in view of the two characteristics already mentioned, he works best independently, with a minimum of supervision from fellow-professionals and without interference from laymen.
4. *He has a corporate voice.* Professionals are strongly organized in order to attain and to maintain high standards of admission to, and competence in the practice of their chosen profession.[2]

[2]J. M. Paton, *The Rôle of Teachers' Organizations in Canadian Education* (Quance Lectures, 1962), pp. 19-20.

To these, A. Kratzmann adds two other criteria:

5. The professional person achieves authority over, and is guaranteed respect from his clientele by their confidence in his expertness in such knowledge and in his technical competence.
6. The professional performs his service for a clientele for an established fee or salary.[3]

Determined to achieve professional status according to these or similar standards, the ATA formulated a set of "Initial Objects." Again according to Kratzmann, these were to:

(*a*) advance and safeguard the cause of education in the Province of Alberta.
(*b*) raise the status of the teaching profession in the Province of Alberta.
(*c*) unite members for their mutual improvement, protection and general welfare.
(*d*) effect united action to the common interest in educational institutions in the Province of Alberta.
(*e*) Co-operate with teachers' organizations in other Provinces having the same or like aims and objects.[4]

Actually, three constellations of aspirations soon became evident in the activities of the fledgling Alliance. These were a drive towards professionalization of the calling, a demand for official recognition of the ATA as the official voice of profession by the provincial government, the school boards, the provincial university, and the public, and finally an unremitting push for economic betterment of the individual teachers.

This purposefulness was to become a distinct contrast to the atomistic nature of the craft of teaching shortly before the formation of the Alberta Teachers' Alliance. The previous aimlessness was recalled by G. D. Misener, its first president, some years later. In 1950 he wrote:

In 1915, the administration of education in Alberta headed by the Department of Education was a strictly paternalistic system with an occasional trend towards dictatorship. The spring and fall conventions were presided over by officials of the Department, and when a senior principal was finally nominated and elected to head an Edmonton fall convention, his advancement was noted to be a distinct innovation. There was no continuity of business. Resolutions, rather in the form of petitions, were passed from year to year and never heard of again. The purpose of the con-

[3]A Kratzmann, "The Alberta Teachers' Association: A Documentary Analysis of the Dynamics of a Professional Association," unpublished doctoral dissertation, University of Chicago, 1963, p. 18.

[4]*Ibid.*

ventions appeared to be to listen respectfully to speakers and to start from scratch each year.[5]

Within three years of its highly tentative and provisional beginnings in 1917, the ATA had grown to the point where it could no longer operate as a provincial body on the basis of spare-time activities of its officers, particularly those of its secretary-treasurer. That his job was more than nominal is indicated by the fact that in April 1919 the executive council voted him an honorarium of $125 for services rendered the previous year. At the same time it formally appointed him General Secretary-Treasurer at $400 per year, and raised membership fees to the following schedule:

Annual salary	*Annual fee*
Less than $1,000	$2
$1,000 but less than $2,000	4
$2,000 or more	5

A far cry from 35c in 1917 and 75c the following year!

Changes in the organization of the Alliance continued in the fall of the same year, when, subject to approval of the Locals, it was decided to organize the province into seven districts: the cities of Edmonton and Calgary, and five districts centered in Medicine Hat, Lethbridge, Stettler, Red Deer, and Wainwright. With a representative from each, plus the president and vice-president, the elected members of the executive council would total nine rather than five as previously. At the same meeting it was decided to employ an organizer for three months at $500 per month, this figure no doubt to include his expenses.

By April 1920, less than two years after the first executive meeting, it had become apparent that the appointment of a full-time executive secretary was of paramount urgency. A committee was struck to interview John Barnett with a view to persuading him to accept the position. Two days later the committee reported that it had been successful. Barnett agreed to assume the new post on July 1 following at a salary of $325 per month, with travelling expenses at the rates paid by the provincial government. In addition, he was to have $250 per year to provide an office, preferably in his own residence. He was to:

1. Take general charge of office and general administrative work.
2. Assume control of books of accounts.

[5]Misener, *op. cit.*, p. 5.

3. Consult with the Executive on all matters likely to involve a change of policy or initiation of a new policy.

4. Keep the Executive informed on all matters pertaining to important correspondence, interviews, or peculiar conditions affecting Local Alliances.

5. Be responsible for the general organizing work under the direction of the Executive.

6. Attend meetings of teachers from time to time as might be deemed necessary.

7. Be guided at all times strictly in accordance with the policy laid down by the Executive at regularly called meetings.

8. If circumstances should arise which in the opinion of the General Secretary-Treasurer necessitated his leaving headquarters, he was to confer with the Executive before so doing.

It is quite evident from this frame of reference that the executive council members were determined to keep effective control of the Alliance in their own hands. Even though the secretary-treasurer was directed to "attend meetings of teachers from time to time as may be deemed necessary,"[6] he virtually had to secure the executive council's permission to do so if the meetings were held away from headquarters, that is, Edmonton. J. W. Barnett, the incumbent, was tremendously admired and respected by his colleagues, no matter how much he was *persona non grata* with trustees and ministers of education. Nevertheless, the council and not the appointed officer was in charge. This refusal of the elected officers to abrogate their responsibility, a characteristic shared with other similar provincial teachers' organizations, no matter how much confidence they had in their chief of staff, is one more point of difference between these teachers' organizations on the one hand and certain labour unions on the other. Refusal of Barnett's successor, some decades later, to accept direction from the executive council precipitated him on a collision course with that body, ultimately leading to his dismissal and reaffirmation of the council's authority.

The arrangements outlined above served as the basis of a contract. Formal appointment was made on July 7, 1920. The following spring Barnett's salary was raised to $4,000, at a time when the highest teacher's salary in Alberta was only $3,500.

[6]Alberta Teachers' Alliance, unpublished minutes of the Executive Council (hereinafter referred to as ATA Ex.), April 7, 1920.

By December 1919 the executive council of the ATA was giving consideration to a publication of its own, perhaps because with the exception of the Calgary *Albertan* the public press showed an unremitting hostility to the young organization, a hostility which no doubt owed some of its vehemence to such unsettling phenomena as the Winnipeg general strike of that year and the post-war labour unrest fomented by the Wobblies, as the IWW was called, south of the American border. In April 1920 a staff was appointed for the proposed magazine: Editor-in-Chief, H. C. Newland (who was also president of the ATA); Education Editor, T. E. A. Stanley (the Alliance's past president); News Editor, J. T. Cuyler; Business and Advertising Editor, J. W. Barnett, the general secretary-treasurer of the organization. Quite evidently the ATA was not going to entrust this important venture to other than its first-string talent!

It was decided to appeal to the Alberta Educational Association for a grant of $1,000 towards the financing of *The ATA Magazine*. In view of the limited resources of that Association, if such an appeal was made, it probably was unsuccessful.

The ATA executive council members were apparently under the impression, incorrect as it turned out, that the ATA charter did not permit them to engage in the publishing business. Accordingly, the ATA Publishing Company, Ltd., was established to publish the magazine, an unnecessary complication which in the future was to cause endless trouble to the Alliance. However, in the spring of 1920 the first number of the new periodical appeared. Never since that time has it missed a regular publication date, although the number of regular issues has varied from twelve to the present six per year. It was anticipated that the new magazine would be self-supporting, as is evidenced by the fact that in November 1920 the ATA did not grant but advanced $1,000 to its publishing company.

In 1921, H. C. Newland, president of the ATA, dealt with the status of the teachers' own organization in an address to the AEA, in which he referred to a letter from the AEA secretary published in the Calgary *Albertan*, a letter in which "it was made abundantly clear that the Alberta Teachers' Alliance was the official organization of the teachers of this Province."[7] It was relatively easy to secure the recognition of the Alliance as the voice of the teaching pro-

[7]H. C. Newland, "President Newland's Report of the A.T.A. to the A.E.A.," *Report of the Eleventh Annual Convention, Alberta Educational Association*, p. 20.

fession as far as the Alberta Educational Association was concerned; after all, an estimated 80 per cent of the latter body each year consisted of certificated teachers. As will be seen, however, the Department and the trustees granted their recognition much more reluctantly.

Professional status and recognition were without doubt among the ATA's most important long-term objectives: from these all other benefits flowed. But economic betterment was equally important, as well as being the Alliance's most immediate and most urgent problem. How urgent it was appears in a 1924 reminiscence of General Secretary J. W. Barnett:

> The teaching profession was in the deepest despondency. Teachers' salaries were "cut" while other wage-earners were reaping considerable compensation for the increased cost-of-living; teachers felt themselves powerless; they were leaving the profession by hundreds because of the apparent hopelessness of things; "permits" and letters of authority were showered like blessings on the poor; individual teachers were without any form of protection whatever against wrongful treatment; officialdom and autocracy were apparent everywhere; and those outside the profession treated teachers with a most humiliating condescension.[8]

But even before the Alliance could make a frontal attack on the economic problems which beset the school teachers, it had to develop a membership base to work from. This was found in the teaching staffs of the province's four largest cities: Edmonton, Calgary, Lethbridge, and Medicine Hat. Within two or three years nearly all of the teachers in the public systems at least had taken out memberships. Recruitment in the rural areas, however, proceeded much more slowly, and for a number of reasons. Proseltyzing was physically much more difficult, involving long drives by the urban members over uncertain roads, often in open touring cars of proven unreliability, to attend rural conventions and so spread the gospel. Even when these missionaries were successful in securing a hearing, they were not usually successful in converting all their audience. Some teachers were reluctant to pay even the modest annual fee, for proportionately their salaries were even more modest. Others felt that any benefits that ATA achieved they would enjoy without the obligations of membership. Still others felt no real commitment to teaching or to their colleagues. And as the burgeoning Alliance began to make its influence felt, many young, in-

[8]J. W. Barnett, "Seventh Annual Report of the General Secretary-Treasurer," *The ATA Magazine*, III, 12 (May 1924), 7.

experienced, and insecure teachers feared the active animosity of their school boards. Teacher recruitment advertisements reading "No ATA members need apply" did not further the Alliance's membership drive. Nevertheless, by 1920 Barnett was able to report a membership of 1,763, of whom some 350 were normal school enrolees. As there were 4,289 classrooms in Alberta in 1920 in operation, about one-third of the employed teachers had joined the ATA. Of those holding valid teaching certificates the proportion was no doubt higher. About half the members (excluding normal school students) were located in five cities: Edmonton, 320; Calgary, 230; Medicine Hat, more than 70; Lethbridge, 51; Wetaskiwin, 30. Nevertheless, the Alliance was moving into the boondocks; between 79 and 86 Locals had been established not only in the cities but along the railway lines in the hinterland. A year later the president of the ATA was able to claim that the organization's membership included 66 per cent of the province's practising teachers.

From its earliest days the Alberta Teachers' Alliance definitely showed the influence of the vigorous trade union or labour movement. As already mentioned, the general secretary-treasurer had been a local officer of the National Union of Teachers in England. Hundreds of other teachers were also immigrants from the United Kingdom, and as such were familiar with this aggressive organization which, according to Kratzmann, "had established a retirement fund for teachers, had offered protection and free legal advice for members, had exerted considerable influence on the administration of elementary schools, on teacher preparation programmes and on the establishment of professional standards for teachers and undertaken an active programme to improve salaries and raise the status of teachers and teaching in Britain."[9]

Influences from the United States were equally militant. As early as May 1918, the ATA executive council received a strong plea for co-operation and affiliation from the American Federation of Labor, and the following year appointed a fraternal delegate to the convention of the Alberta Federation of Labor. At the 1920 convention of the AEA, W. Hay of Medicine Hat gave an address on "Teachers and Labour Affiliations." Nevertheless, the AEA took no action as a result of Hay's talk, "the opinion prevailing that the teachers were not prepared to affect a direct federation with the labour organizations."[10]

[9]Kratzmann, *op. cit.*, p. 163.
[10]AEA, *Report of the 10th Annual Convention*, p. 3.

From that date, exchange of fraternal delegates between the ATA and the AF of L was a common practice. At its 1921 convention, AEA president (and an elected officer of the ATA) made an eloquent acknowledgment of the contribution of the labour movement to the welfare of workers.

Perhaps if the teachers had confined their admiration of labour to verbal plaudits, all would have been well. It was when the ATA started acting like an aggressive labour union that it aroused the hostility of the government, the trustees, and the public press. Its action took many forms, including a demand for a minimum salary. In 1918 the Hon. J. R. Boyle, Minister of Education, spoke to the AEA. Adverting to the shortage of teachers, he announced, "I have introduced a bill into the legislature establishing a principle which has not heretofore been established on this continent, as far as I know, fixing by statute the minimum salary for teachers in this Province. We are proposing to pay a minimum salary for any teacher in rural schools of seventy dollars per month per ordinance."[11] Yet the ATA members had the temerity to demand protection not only for rural teachers but for town and city ones as well; and not only that but to announce that not $70 per month or $840 per year but $1,200 annually was the tolerable minimum, and to refuse to accept positions at any lower figure —just as if they had the right to deny their services to financially hard-pressed school districts.

They also began to talk about collective bargaining and salary schedules which would eliminate the power that school boards of multi-room systems enjoyed of being able to negotiate with each staff member individually. This claim for many reasons the trustees vigorously rejected. For one thing, it was a limitation on the power granted by the School Ordinance and delegated to the school boards by the voters of their districts. And in Alberta as elsewhere, trustees have always protested at any lessening of their authority, whether it comes from the legislature, the department of education, municipal councils, teachers, or any other source. They resisted the move towards collective bargaining because they correctly regarded as inherent in it a move to higher salaries and therefore higher taxes, and they realized that they would be far less able to browbeat a a committee of mature and experienced teachers than they would a young inexperienced schoolmarm with no commitment to her calling.

Finally, the trustees disliked collective bargaining because, they said, it gave

[11] J. R. Boyle, "Address," AEA, *Report of the 9th Annual Convention*, pp. 3-4.

them no opportunity to reward the good teacher without also bonusing the poor or mediocre one. This claim the teachers rapidly came to regard with profound scepticism. Time after time they found teachers of high reputation not rewarded but dismissed for trivial and irrelevant reasons; on one occasion the whole staff of such a large system as that of the Calgary public school board was dismissed in order that a new and unilaterally determined salary schedule could be implemented.

The young Alliance also began demanding that its members have some security of tenure, minimal though it might be. In 1918 the executive council of the infant organization resolved: "That a teacher, if dismissed at the end of a term, shall receive notice by the first of June or the first of December and that a teacher cannot be fired, except by permission of the Department, at any other date."[12] Another limitation of the school board's authority! At the same meeting the executive council resolved to ask for a self-renewing teacher's contract.

In those days, when teachers frequently taught in one school district for less than a full school year, and often left for reasons beyond their control, their salary was calculated on the basis of the number of days taught divided by 210 and multiplied by the agreed annual salary. This formula assumed a school year to consist of 210 school days, that is, to run from the middle of August to the end of June following if the usual holidays were taken at Christmas and Easter. Yet often a school board could not or would not operate its school for that length of time. The ATA therefore asked that 200 days be considered a full school year and a partial salary be computed accordingly. Yet it was a long time before this request was granted.

Like a trade union, the Alliance also became concerned with its members' working conditions. In December 1918 its executive council noted that one of the matters to be taken up with the minister of education was that maximum class loads in graded schools should not exceed 35 pupils, or 25 in ungraded classrooms.

The Alliance did not stop at simply making requests of the educational establishment, embarrassing though these might be. As early as May 1918, even before it had applied for incorporation, the organization appointed G. H. Van Allen, a young lawyer and former school teacher, as legal adviser. Thereafter his counsel was sought and obtained when members of the Alliance felt that

[12]ATA Ex., July 7, 1918.

they had grievances against their employers. When conditions appeared propitious, the ATA did not hesitate to enter suit against school districts and boards for salary arrears, or for damages for breach of contract by a board or defamation of character by an individual trustee. In one instance, the ATA took a member's case all the way to the Supreme Court of Canada (and won), something which that individual could never have afforded to do if he had been dependent on his own financial resources. The prospect of legal action no doubt served to inhibit many school boards from running rough-shod over the civil rights of their employees, but certainly did not endear the Alliance to individual trustees. Equally, the practice of the government in supplying free legal counsel to embattled school boards—but never to individual teachers—was a source of disenchantment to members of the ATA.

Not all controversies, of course, were taken to the courts. In many cases, teachers were treated unjustly but perfectly legally. In such cases where there was no prospect of success in legal action, the Alliance would usually dispatch a task force of one or more teachers (and often the general secretary-treasurer) to plead a member's case with his school board. Often such disputes were quickly settled to the satisfaction of the parties concerned, sometimes because they arose from a genuine misunderstanding, sometimes because the school boards did not realize that teachers had certain rights, minimal though they were, and probably sometimes because the school boards did not wish to become embroiled with an organization which was gaining in membership and influence every day. Yet they obviously were not happy in having to deal with the approximate equivalent of a labour union's shop steward.

The Alliance had still another weapon in its arsenal to employ against particularly intransigent school boards. This was the well-known "blacklist." It consisted simply of a notice in the public press, and later in the Alliance's own publication, requesting teachers contemplating employment with certain school systems first to get in touch with the ATA office. It did not prevent such systems from appointing teachers, although ATA members who accepted positions with such school boards might be subject to censure or reprimand for unprofessional conduct. But in times of full teacher employment such as prevailed until the depression of the 1930's, blacklisting greatly limited a school board's freedom of choice of teachers. This the trustees knew; for this reason they hated blacklisting.

The Alliance soon realized that the blacklist placed a potent weapon in their hands. In July 1918 the executive council resolved: "That the Secretary be authorized to ask for advice from the Alliance's Solicitor concerning a Black List for Teachers and Trustee Boards."[13] A year later that body passed another resolution: "That the S. C. School Board be asked to settle Mrs. H.'s claim in full and that in the event of their failing to do so, the Alliance places the School Board on the Black List and advertise them."[14] In January of the following year that school board was indeed placed in "Bad Standing," along with the board of Youngstown. Minutes of a law committee meeting held on October 30, 1920, give the sequel to the action against Youngstown, which had dismissed a teacher during the fall term of 1920, but without giving him the usual 30-day notice to become effective at the end of December. He secured another position in Eden, Manitoba, but at a lower salary. The executive council approved a settlement on the following bases: that the school board thereafter give full recognition to the ATA—a reminder of the unremitting drive for such recognition—and that the teacher be paid compensation equal to the difference in salary for December 1919 between the Youngstown rate and the rate he earned in Manitoba. The modest size of the settlement arose from the fact that the school board could have given notice of dismissal on December 1 to become effective at the end of the month and have been perfectly within its rights, even in the eyes of the Alliance.

It is noteworthy that the ATA did not cease to press for a settlement for this teacher, even though he had left the province and was no longer a member of the Alliance.

Not every teacher–school board dispute was minuted by the executive council or the law committee; many were settled before the council or committee would have a meeting. Particularly vexatious in 1920 apparently were disputes involving two of the larger systems, Lethbridge and Ponoka. The executive council dealing with the former reads:

Resolved: That the General Secretary-Treasurer write the Lethbridge School Board deprecating their method of procedure in the matter of the recent dismissals, pointing out that the A.T.A. Executive consider their procedure unjust to the teachers concerned, that the letter call for an explanation as to just how these

[13]*Ibid.*

[14]*Ibid.*, July 14, 1920.

teachers were proven inefficient and, further, ask them if the Board is prepared to institute an enquiry into the affair.[15]

The Lethbridge affair apparently affected only some of the teachers, but in Ponoka the whole staff was involved, as the following minute indicates:

> The General Secretary-Treasurer gave a detailed report of the conditions prevailing in the Ponoka School for the past three years, showing how the Board paid very inadequate salaries and generally showed a lack of appreciation of the susceptibilities of the teachers on their staff as is particularly evidenced by their policy, by minute established, of dismissing every teacher at the end of each school year and re-engaging those whose services they wish to retain.
>
> Resolved: That the Ponoka School Board be placed in 'Bad Standing' pending a reversal of their policy.[16]

Where then was the contention that freedom to hire and fire as they chose gave school boards the opportunity to reward their good teachers?

Although blacklistings in another direction were not so well known, the ATA did not hesitate to chide its own members upon occasion. Thus the executive council minutes reveal that "The General Secretary-Treasurer was authorized to place [a teacher] in 'Bad Standing' by virtue of the fact that his acceptance of a position with the Separate Board is deemed to be an unprofessional act."[17] The nature of his offence is not clear since the Separate School Board referred to in the quotation does not appear to have been in "bad standing" at that time. Possibly it was "contract jumping," that is, accepting a position when a teacher had already signed a valid contract with another school board.

The following year another internal dispute occurred at Castor. Reading between the lines, one can guess that the school board dismissed its principal and that one teacher, possibly because he coveted the position itself, did not support his superior. The pertinent action of the executive council is indicated by the following resolution: "That the lady teachers on the Castor staff be approachced with a view of their supporting Mr. G. and signing the statement and that the final arrangements and action be left in the hands of the Law Committee and that Mr. F. be officially declared in 'Bad Standing.' "[18]

[15]*Ibid.*

[16]*Ibid.*

[17]*Ibid.*, Jan. 18, 1920.

[18]*Ibid.*, April 3, 1921

Nor did the Alliance hesitate to criticize the department of education or even the minister of education himself when occasion seemed so to demand. In 1919 the ATA censured the department for instituting a short (four-month) course for the preparation of teachers almost immediately after it had agreed with departments of education in other western provinces to require a full academic year for such training. More barbed was a resolution passed in 1920, "That the Alberta Teachers' Alliance protest against the Department of Education interfering in cases where a contract favourable to the teacher and mutually agreed upon by teacher and School Board has been signed, provided such contract is not inconsistent with the provisions of the School Ordinance or the Regulations of the Department of Education."[19]

Such unwarranted interference by the department of education, i.e., by its minister, to modify legal contracts mutually acceptable to teachers and school boards was indicative of deteriorating relationships between the ATA on the one hand and the government and the trustees on the other. In 1918 a new minister, the Hon. G. P. Smith, had replaced Boyle in the education portfolio. He apparently adopted the trustees' viewpoint that teachers were no more than hired hands. Their claim that they were professional people and their demands should be so considered apparently puzzled and ultimately infuriated him. Early in 1920 when the Alliance published the first number of *The ATA Magazine*, its cover bore this ringing challenge:

Are you a member of the ATA?
Do you meet persons who express doubts about the propriety of teachers' organizations and who advise you to keep clear of anything so banal or "common" as a "union"?
Mark those persons. They are your *enemies*. They fear organization, much preferring that you remain what you are, an individual powerless to resist domination. Magistri neque servi.[20]

Such defiance the minister could not believe to be the true expression of the sentiments of all the nice, tractable teachers who staffed the province's schools. It and similar statements therefore had to represent the personal biases of the fire-breathing general secretary, John W. Barnett, or of the newly appointed brilliant little editor and president of the Alliance, Hubert C. Newland. Accord-

[19]*Ibid.*, Jan. 18, 1920.
[20]Alberta Teachers' Alliance, *The ATA Magazine*, I, 1 (May 1920), front cover.

ingly, he said as much on the public platform, leading the ATA to the unprecedented action of censuring a minister of education, not for his policies or those of his government but for his actions as an individual. The expression of their displeasure is contained in the following ATA council resolution: "That the Executive send a letter of censure to the Minister of Education for abusing the General Secretary-Treasurer and making disparaging remarks in public places about other members of the Executive of the Alberta Teachers' Alliance."[21]

The minister's next move was to do what many school boards have attempted to do since—go over the heads of the Alliance's duly elected officers and appeal directly to the organization's members. He discovered what the trustees were later painfully to learn—that members of the ATA regard their association as the only body which is entitled to speak for them, and that it speaks only through its chosen officers. The Alliance received numerous letters of support from both individual teachers and from Locals. Smith's tactics had simply served to knit the Alliance closer together and make it stronger than ever.

The Honourable Mr. Smith by his own boast had probably attended more teachers' gatherings than any of his predecessors. It was at such meetings, when his position as minister of education made it imperative to issue him an invitation to speak, that he disparaged the officers of the Alliance; it was at such gatherings that he tried to by-pass the ATA's executive council. But he discovered that teachers were not hired men or hired girls, subject without question to the boss's orders—that, or lose their jobs. He found that a teachers' convention did not provide him with the sounding board which he wanted to promulgate his ideas about education; the enthusiasm of the audience obviously left something to be desired. He probably realized also that the Alberta Educational Association was not suitable, either. To change the metaphor, it was no longer the tame pussycat of prewar days, even though the government grant still constituted an important part of its revenue—$300 out of slightly more than $1,700 in 1918-1919. The educational establishment had lost control of this creature. Its officers were now classroom teachers; not only classroom teachers but the very ones who held executive positions in the Locals of the Alliance which the minister obdurately refused to recognize as the official organization of the teaching profession. The 1920-21 president of the AEA was T. E. A. Stanley, past president of the Alberta Teachers' Alliance itself.

[21]ATA Ex., Nov. 6, 1920.

To get a reliable sounding board for his views, to obtain a rostrum in the educational market-place, Smith turned to the almost moribund trustees' association.

This organization began in 1907 as the "First Provincial School Boards' Convention for Alberta," and met irregularly until World War I broke out in 1914. The disruption caused by that holocaust apparently resulted in no meetings being held until 1920, when a very small gathering, estimated at 35 delegates, assembled. Smith recognized the potentialities of the organization for the dissemination of his own views. He apparently correctly assessed the sentiment of school trustees and systematically encouraged school boards to send delegates to the 1921 convention of what has since that time been known as the Alberta School Trustees' Association. His efforts were so successful that the honourable minister himself estimated that over 1,000 districts were represented by perhaps 1,300 or 1,400 delegates. And they knew why they were there. Their duty was clear: to repel the teachers' attacks on the barque of educational authority. As one delegate said, ". . . the big question before the convention is collective bargaining." The implicit purpose of the gathering was the eradication of the ATA. Smith attended practically all sessions of the convention, sitting on the right hand of the chairman, apparently to ensure the political and legal soundness of the Association's strategy.

The little firebrand of the ATA, H. C. Newland, was president of the teachers' organization in 1921. As such, he was extended the courtesy of an invitation to the trusteees' convention, perhaps in the same spirit that an ancient Hebrew was invited to join the lions in their den. This modern-day Daniel not unwillingly hazarded his cause if not his life in the lair of his enemies. He attacked the matter of the hated blacklist head-on, discussing it in the following terms:

> Whenever one of our members complains of the action of any board and asks for protection, or seeks advice in regard to any dispute with a board, we forthwith endeavour to obtain the board's side of the case by a communication through our General Secretary or our solicitors. Occasionally we have the advantage of a personal interview. Our earnest desire is to have the fullest information on both sides of every case. If, now, the board refuses to answer our communication or to have anything to do with the Alliance or its representatives, we simply report the circumstances to our members for their guidance and protection. That is all.

Craftily the minister's address was scheduled for the evening, *after* Newland's talk. Ostensibly his speech was on the topic "The Future of Our Schools"; actually only about one-third of it was devoted to that subject. Approximately the first 40 per cent was given over to a slanted and emotional attack on the Alliance. He reacted to Newland's explanation regarding the blacklist in these words:

> . . . it then becomes a non-professional act for any teacher in the Province to accept a position with that Board and that school may be closed up and the children may be left on the street and the Board helpless until they bow to the will of the person giving the order. . . . It is a very serious thing and a very serious trespass upon the rights and powers of School Boards, the elected representatives of the people. It is a complete reversal of British institutions. I want to say . . . that some way will be found to prevent this very thing happening. If there is nothing in the present law . . . we shall see if something cannot be put into the law.

Obviously the Honourable G. P. Smith had not the least idea how he could legally deal with the problem; as long as the Alberta Teachers' Alliance avoided libellous and scurrilous attacks on trustees and school districts, the minister was powerless—and he probably knew it. Thus his anger was compounded by frustration.

He also attacked the ATA for its insistence on a teacher's right to a representative of his own choosing in the case of an appeal to a school board over the matter of a dismissal. In 1921 the only champion a teacher could enlist to plead his (or more likely her) cause was either a ratepayer of the district or a member of the teacher's immediate family. The right to representation by counsel of one's own choosing was anathema to the minister. In his view:

> Now, what does the alternative clause require? That the teacher may be represented by an agent or a solicitor. We are told that it is not to be a police court, but it seems to me that the police court is where you find solicitors. I want to say that this thing is as old as the hills. It has been tried out in several of the States to the south of us; it just causes turmoil and trouble and does no good to anybody and it is not going to be introduced here.

Smith was perhaps unfamiliar with Samuel Johnson's aphorism that "Patriotism is the last refuge of a scoundrel"; otherwise he might have been less ready to brand ideas which he disliked as unBritish or (even worse) American.

Among the other desiderata for which the Alliance was striving was a provincial salary schedule with adjustments for both experience and training. This aspiration gave Smith an opportunity to destroy a straw man of his own devising, which he did in these words:

> There are certain things . . . with which I do not agree. One is the matter of urging a dead-level salary . . . without any possibility of enforcing that demand . . . to the practicable possibilities of the school districts concerned . . . to the qualifications of the teacher . . . to the length of experience of the teacher . . . for the efficiency of her work. I think there must be differentiations according to the experience, qualifications, capacity for service, and the certificate held.

One other Alliance aim he treated with derision. The ATA had been pressing for recognition by school boards to the extent that a teachers' representative be permitted to attend all school board meetings and participate fully in all discussions and debates without, of course, the right to vote. Although after the lapse of nearly half a century this demand seems naively presumptuous even to teachers, in 1921 ATA members regarded it so seriously that it was one of the crucial issues that led to a strike of high school teachers in Edmonton that year. A more reasonable demand, in these days of certification and decertification of unions, was that the Alliance be considered as speaking for *all* the members of the profession. But these two related demands the minister of education rejected out of hand. "Certain members of this organization wanted more than recognition," he claimed. "They wanted domination. They wanted the Department to abdicate and the School Boards to follow suit."

As this writer has indicated in another context, Newland's cool, reasoned talk was greeted with a cool, polite vote of thanks. The minister's diatribe, on the other hand, was constantly interrupted: 'Applause,' 'Prolonged applause,' 'Laughter,' 'Voices: hear, hear, and applause,' 'Hear, hear,' 'Prolonged and continued applause.' "[22] Considering that the convention proceedings were published by the department of education, one can only feel grateful to its minister that he did not let his natural modesty conceal from posterity the great enthusiasm with which his talk was received.

Two months later, when Smith met the teachers face to face at the AEA Easter Convention, he was much more conciliatory. He pointed out that he had gone to extraordinary lengths to meet teachers and teacher trainees. "I have attended every teachers' convention that it was possible for me to get to and discussed at length the policies of the Government and the educational problems of this

[22]Alberta School Trustees' Association. *Annual Report of Convention* (Feb. 2-3, 1921). Subsequent questions from speeches given at the Convention are from this source.

Province,"[23] he claimed. "I have visited every Normal School class in the last three years. . . . I don't suppose any other Minister of Education on Canadian soil ever did anything like it."[24] It was, of course, on such occasions that he had made the remarks which members of the ATA executive council found so offensive.

The rest of Smith's address was devoted largely to rebutting some of the criticisms which the ATA had made of the government's educational policies, or at least of its educational achievements. He pointed out that Alberta was no longer offering a normal school programme leading to a third class teacher's certificate, even though the credential was still granted to immigrants to the province and those who failed to qualify for a higher certificate. He mentioned that the government had instituted loans to normal school students, and cut the number of permits issued to unqualified instructors from about 950 in 1918 to less than half that number a year later, "and today there are just one hundred and twenty-eight permits in this province." But the departmental registrar's report showed 729 issued in 1921, 668 in 1920, 447 in 1919. Smith concealed these facts by the statement that "We have never had, since I have been Minister, more than three hundred in the province *at one time.*" (Emphasis added.)

Respecting teachers' claims that salaries should be higher, the minister pointed out that provincial appropriations had increased by more than $1,000,000 in three years and grants to schools had risen, in some cases, from $200 to $800 per classroom per year, enabling school boards to grant substantial salary increases at no cost to their taxpayers.

Concerning the short normal school course to which teachers objected, and which the department had instituted almost as soon as it had embarked on a full year programme, the speaker defended it as strictly an emergency measure. "We cannot take the position that we are going to deliberately, in cold blood, lock up the schools of this Province," he affirmed.

Smith also claimed another credit for his government, its policy of building teacherages. Certainly the government was to be commended on its action in this field, even though its representative neglected to mention that the school districts had to find two-thirds of the cost of the residences. The minister claimed

[23]J. W. Chalmers, *Schools of the Foothills Province* (Toronto, 1967), p. 381.

[24]G. P. Smith, *AEA Annual Report of Convention* (March 29-31, 1921), p. 29.

that a free teacherage and free fuel were worth probably $600 to the teacher. But the day would come when such perquisites would no longer be free.

Smith was careful to deal only with those criticisms where the government's objectives were basically in harmony with those of the Alliance—raising the admission standards for normal schools, lengthening the period of preparation for student-teachers, improving salaries and living conditions. But he said not a word about the controversial issues which had so exercised him at the trustees' convention the previous month: the blacklist, the teachers' demands for recognition, for freedom to choose one's own representative in teacher–school board disputes, for security of tenure, for collective bargaining.

His talk to the AEA was the last significant educational address which the Liberal minister of education ever had an opportunity to deliver. Within a few months his party was defeated at the polls and he was minister of education no longer, to the deep and widespread satisfaction of Alberta's teachers. Poor George Peter Smith! Probably few men had as much influence as he in building up the Alberta Teachers' Alliance, for his savage and unremitting opposition to the young professional organization must have convinced many teachers that only if they stood together could they hope to prevail against such hostility. With enemies like him, what organization needed friends?

The period between 1917, when the ATA's first provisional organization was hammered out, and 1921, when the Liberal government was defeated, was very important in determining the Alliance's characteristics as a members' welfare and self-help organization. The welfare objectives were spelled out—better salaries, security of tenure, collective bargaining, recognition of the ATA as the teachers' agent, implementation of salary schedules, better living and working conditions, right of appeal against dismissals, even cumulative sick leave. Techniques and tactics that were to be used to achieve these objectives were also developed. These included indoctrination of ATA members, appeals to the department of education, to individual school boards, and even to the general public, appeals to courts where indicated, and even such direct action as the use of the blacklist and the strike. Few if any of these aims were achieved, except partially, but the issues were defined, the lines drawn, the objectives clarified.

This four-year period also established a public image of the Alberta Teachers' Alliance as an aggressive, fearless union wholly devoted to the welfare of its members, under the direction of clever, selfless leaders impervious to intimidation, or threats to their own professional security. Basically, this image persists to the present day, although the outlines have become softened and refined by a concept of professionalism, whatever that may mean to the average parent or taxpayer.

Yet, less publicly visible, during the same four-year period the professionalization of teaching was being started. For teaching to become a profession, members of the Alliance believed, a number of changes had to be effected. Qualifications of teachers had to be improved through the raising of admission standards to the normal schools, lengthening of the period of professional preparation, and elimination of unqualified personnel from the classrooms. The Alliance also pressed for the right of the profession to be heard, not only across the bargaining table but in every committee and conference room where decisions affecting education were being made, decisions affecting the development of school curricula, the teacher-training programmes, the issuance of teachers' certificates, the proceedings of the provincial university's senate. Furthermore, its members believed that the Alliance should be recognized as representing the profession and be granted the right to choose the teachers who would fulfil that function. Teachers appointed to curriculum or other assignments by the department of education, without reference to the teachers' own organization, could not, the ATA members believed, be considered as representing their profession, but only the organization which appointed them.

Even though their remuneration came to them in the form of wages or salaries instead of fees, the teachers felt that their relationship to their employers was rather that of practitioner to client than of hireling to boss—a concept which trustees found very difficult to accept. But the ATA's motto has ever been "Magistri Neque Servi," masters not servants.

From the first days, the Alliance members gave attention to the relationships of professional teachers to one another, to their pupils, their employers, and the public generally. They established criteria of professional conduct which have continued with but minor amendments ever since.

Examples of unprofessional action in the inter-member field would be applying for a position which is not vacant, underbidding another teacher for a teaching position, or criticizing a colleague in public or otherwise, except to a superior, and then only after informing him beforehand. With respect to one's employers, unprofessional conduct includes "contract jumping," or leaving employment otherwise than according to legally constituted procedures. It was and is considered unprofessional for a teacher to bargain other than collectively, or to speak on behalf of his profession unless properly authorized by his colleagues so to do. It is also unprofessional to accept remuneration from a parent to coach or tutor one's own pupils in or out of class, or to use the teacher-pupil relationship for his personal benefit, e.g., to sell encyclopaedias to the parents of one's pupils. The most recent codes of professional ethics and etiquette are included in Appendix III.

The establishment of codes and standards without the power to enforce them may appear an empty gesture, may even seem mere window-dressing with no other purpose than to impress the public. Of course, the Alliance did not have any power other than that of moral persuasion. It could not cancel or suspend a teacher's credential; it could not even levy a modest fine for infractions. And a member of the Alliance could apparently escape scot-free from any punitive measures simply by resigning from the ATA.

However, the action of the Alberta Teachers' Alliance in establishing standards of conduct for the profession did have more than purely formal significance. In the first place, it proclaimed to the people of the province, professional and lay alike, that the ATA might be considered a labour union, but it was more than that; its members' aspirations were as high as those of physicians, barristers, clergymen—which last group, incidentally, like teachers, usually received their remuneration in the form of a salary, even though they called it a stipend. Codes of professional behaviour also served as guidelines for the future, when the ATA did acquire legal power to discipline its members.

And even though the Alliance had only powers of persuasion and censure, when it counted two-thirds of the province's teachers, these powers were not inconsiderable. For some people, perhaps most, the censure of one's peers is a traumatic experience, to be avoided if at all possible. When such a censure comes from an organization which includes two out of three of one's colleagues, when it is likely to be accompanied by a withdrawal of professional co-operation, by the isolating of that person from his confrères, it is an experience to be avoided at almost any cost. Teachers on strike did not throw rocks through the windows of strike-breakers or call them scabs to their faces—not in Alberta, at least—but more sophisticated means could be used to convey the same message. It is reported, probably truthfully, that when the Edmonton high school teachers went on strike in 1921, in at least one school their replacements could not find a single classroom register; they had all been carefully put away for safekeeping during the weekend, and no one seemed to remember where. In the same or another school the principal called the students together to inform them of the impending strike. He told the boys and girls that he expected them to co-operate fully with the incoming replacements—while they were there—but added that he would fully understand if they found it difficult to get along with a whole new staff of teachers, none of whom they knew. The result was that for the fortnight's duration of the strike, lack of student discipline reduced the institution to a shambles.

Alarms of Struggle

BY 1921 the future of the Alberta Teachers' Alliance looked promising. The organization's membership filled over half the classroom positions in the province. The hostile Liberal government had been defeated, and the ATA's *bête noir,* the Hon. G. P. Smith, formerly Liberal minister of education, had been banished to the outer darkness of political limbo. Legislation was on the statute books establishing a minimum salary. Even if it was only $840 a year, it was still higher than the minimum of any of the other provinces, some of which had none at all. Alberta had entered into an agreement with other western provinces to discontinue the short teacher-training programmes of less than a full year, and the third class certificate was a thing of the past, in theory at least. Pensions for teachers seemed to be just around the corner. Circumstances augured favourably for advances in all directions. As LaZerte has mentioned, "From its birth . . . the ATA pressed continuously for automatic membership, higher certification standards, larger units of administration; increased school grants, teachers' pensions and the transfer of all teacher training to the University."[1]

But instead of rolling smoothly forward through the Golden Twenties, the Alliance found itself fighting for its life. Crop failures were common, although they did not reach the endemic proportions of those of the Hungry Thirties. The

[1]M. E. LaZerte, "The Development of the A.T.A. during the Presidency of M. E. LaZerte 1937-1938," unpublished and undated memoir, p. 2.

wheat farms north and east of Calgary, wrested from Palliser's semi-arid triangle by the aid of bountiful wartime rains, reverted to type, to short grass rangeland —except that the short grass had been ploughed under. Hundreds of families east of Hanna turned the keys in their buildings and headed for the fabulous Peace River country, or some other El Dorado. At the same time, prices of wheat and cattle, mainstays of Alberta's economy, nose-dived as the forced-draft economy of World War I slowed to a peacetime tempo. School taxes were uncollected and uncollectable.

The teachers discovered something else: that school trustees, especially rural ones, were extremely stubborn about two things: raising tax rates, and surrendering any part of their authority to manage the affairs of their districts as they saw fit. It wasn't that the trustees were opposed to higher salaries for teachers; on the contrary, they were quite in favour of them provided increases could be effected without raising taxes, for instance, through increased grants. However, this was rarely or never possible; other services besides education had claims on the provincial coffers. Besides, the twenties were a period when matching or conditional grants were in their heyday; any increase in provincial funds to school boards was likely to be for specific purposes, for instance, teacherages, school libraries, pupil transportation, and then only if they were matched to a specified proportion by district expenditures. In any event, such funds were not available for salary purposes.

Trustees' exercise of their authority affected a number of people: the supplier of fuel, the janitor, the van driver (in the case of a consolidated school), occasionally a few others. But mainly it affected the board's power to hire or fire a teacher, or to pay him what they chose, or to impose any working or living conditions which they might regard as reasonable. Anything that intervened in any way between the school board and the teacher they regarded as a diminution of their authority.

And the Alliance was touching raw nerves. On the one hand, it was insisting on higher salaries plus such fringe benefits as pensions, and on schools being kept open for a full ten months, and on adequate living and working accommodation and conditions, all of which tended to raise the cost of school operations, and ultimately taxes. On the other hand, it was pushing for continuous contracts, collective bargaining, no dismissals except for cause, appeal tribunals in the case of dismissals, freedom of a teacher to have a representative of his own choice at such tribunals. The Alliance was also attempting to influence teachers, members and non-members alike, to dissuade them from applying for positions which were not vacant, from under-bidding their colleagues for those which were vacant, from applying for positions with school boards which were in bad odour with the ATA, even at rare intervals to strike the schools. All of these actions the trustees regarded as restrictions on the legal authority which their fellow-citizens had elected them to exercise; therefore they were opposed to the ATA.

And so was the newly elected, rural-oriented United Farmers of Alberta government. After all, there were more voters among rural trustees (and more farm voters) than there were among rural teachers. Many of the latter were young schoolmarms or schoolmasters old enough to undertake the responsibility for the education of thirty, forty, sometimes even fifty boys and girls, but not old enough to cast a ballot in protection of their own interests. And those rural pedagogues who had passed their twenty-first birthday were usually disenfranchised anyway. At the provincial level they were voteless because they were usually away from their schools during the summer months when elections were called, and therefore did not meet the residence requirements where they happened to be on voting day. At the local level they were seldom owners or tenants of tax-assessed land, therefore ineligible to exercise a school district or municipal franchise. So the UFA government soon adopted the protective colour of its main supporters; it rapidly became as indifferent to educational progress as its predecessor, and as hostile, or almost so, to the Alberta Teachers' Alliance.

Accordingly, the Alliance discovered that its grand schemes for the betterment of education had to give way, at least temporarily, to two more urgent concerns. One was the continuous building and rebuilding of its membership, a task to which the general secretary had to dedicate himself anew each fall, one to which he had to give himself almost entirely for about four months of every year. He did this in the face of official attitudes which made his job anything but easy, as Powell demonstrates:

> The new UFA Minister of Education was Perren E. Baker, a successful dry farmer from the southern Cypress Hills riding, a former church minister and a graduate of McMaster. His ear was finely tuned to the sentiments of the farming people who would be keeping him in power, and these sentiments did not often harmonize with those of the urban teachers whose voice was most clearly heard in

the ATA. Moreover, Baker did not mistake the feelings of his Deputy about this upstart Alliance. He therefore never allowed himself any expression of warmth or approval towards our organization until the last years of the Brownlee government.

There is a point to this small historical digression. It is quite normal for persons in subordinate positions, with a healthy desire for advancement, to take notice of the likes and dislikes of those above them, and to govern themselves discreetly. This was widely true among teachers and administrators in Alberta. At least one Normal School principal, several inspectors, numerous principals and many teachers took their cue from the top men, and the ATA made little progress among them. Fortunately on the other hand there were many influential men in administration and local leadership who thought for themselves, who had seen professional organization in action back in Ontario or elsewhere, and who were willing to help the young Alliance fight for its life in a fair field.[2]

The monumental lack of enthusiasm of the teaching profession, or at least of the ATA, for the deputy minister is indicated in a letter by Powell. He writes, "In 1930 an honorary doctorate was awarded by the University [of Alberta] to John T. Ross upon his retirement after many years as Deputy Minister of Education. The A.T.A. was informally approached to buy the doctoral robes for him. However, Mr. Ross's demeanour towards the Alliance had been so consistently cold and disdainful that John [Barnett] and Cedric [Hicks] would have none of it, and Mr. Ross got his robe elsewhere."[3] The ATA did have the grace, however, to publish a little complimentary story about the honour in *The ATA Magazine.*

Another factor besides indifference and hostility in high places made the maintenance of membership an arduous task. This was the composition of the teaching body, especially that portion of it which was employed outside Alberta's cities. As Powell notes:

In those early days, while city teaching staffs had become pretty well stabilized, the rural and village teachers were still a very transient lot. They passed through Normal School, taught just long enough to repay their government loan, then married or went into other activities. (In those days it was considered unthinkable for a married woman—unless widowed or divorced—to hold a teaching job.) The average teaching career of those in rural and village areas was thus from two to three years. This meant that the task of indoctrinating the teaching body with professional

[2]A. J. H. Powell, "The Alberta Teachers' Alliance," unpublished memoir (1962), p. 8.
[3]A. J. H. Powell, letter to S. C. T. Clarke, Jan. 25, 1967.

solidarity had to be pursued without pause in order to gain recruits in place of the annual exodus.[4]

Thus the achievement of building a voluntary organization which grew from about 2,000 members at the beginning of the Twenties to approximately 3,000 at the end of the decade was no mean accomplishment. Again to quote Powell, "It is doubtful if so Herculean a task of teacher organization has ever been successfully pulled off elsewhere. In Saskatchewan the effort was made for some years, but the STA died during the Great Depression. In Manitoba the MTF rode on the shoulders of Winnipeg with rural teachers remaining in outer darkness. The BCTF was carried by Vancouver and Victoria, but reached out with much more vigour to the hinterland teachers."[5]

Although the Alliance never really lost sight of its professional objectives or wholly neglected them, it and its leaders had only a limited amount of time, money, and energy. First priority was therefore given to improvement of the teachers' economic position: better salaries, collective bargaining, security of tenure, continuous contracts, right of appeal against dismissal to an independent tribunal, right to an advocate of one's own choice at such tribunals, better living and working conditions, shorter working year.

As opposed to these "trade union" objectives, there were the professional ones dealing with such matters as the schools' curricula, teacher training and certification, educational research—these and many more. But one full-time officer of the association (and later his secretary), operating on a limited budget, could do only so much. Although in the long run, professional advancement was of paramount importance, both for the teachers themselves and for Alberta society as a whole, improvement in welfare of the teachers was the most urgent, both intrinsically and to hold the organization together. Unless the teachers could be persuaded that the Alliance was actually doing something for their material welfare—or they were convinced that without the ATA there could be no progress in this direction—the Alliance was doomed to a slow or sudden death.

Accordingly, from its first organization the ATA strongly pushed for increases in salaries, and pressed the Canadian Teachers' Federation to do likewise, as Paton indicates: "For example, the 1921 CTF slogan, 'Double the 1914

[4]Powell, "The ATA," p. 14.
[5]*Ibid.*, p. 6.

salary,' was a typical Charlesworth-Barnett move, whose effect on provincial salary schedules was probably slight."[6] It is unnecessary to state that in Alberta the objective was not reached, at least not until after World War II. The provincial average salary in 1914 was $810.23; in 1947 it reached $1,652.02. In 1917, when first steps were being taken to organize the ATA, the figure stood at $862.64. The following year the Alberta legislature approved an $840 annual minimum. In 1921, when the CTF was broadcasting its ringing challenge, the Alberta median was $1,180. And there it stayed, almost unchanged, for a full decade, although by 1930 it had inched up to $1,241.60. Then came the disaster known ever since as "the Depression," wiping out the insignificant but hard-won gains of a score of years. In 1935 the average teacher's salary in Alberta had dropped to $970.86. And in 1943 it had reached $1,196.17, almost identical with the figure for 1921.

TABLE I

CLASSES OF NEW ALBERTA CERTIFICATES
1921 and 1943

	1921		1943	
	No.	%	No.	%
University degree plus ½ to 1 yr. professional preparation	29	1.9	23	2.8
Grade XII plus 2–3 yrs. professional preparation	nil	nil	9	1.1
Grade XII	139	9.3	621	76.2
plus 1 yr. professional preparation	1332	88.8	162	19.9
Totals	1500	100	815	100

Source: Alberta, Department of Education, *Annual Reports.*

In effect, every effort that the Alliance had expended from 1921 to 1943—the establishment of its own minimum of $1,200, lowered in 1927 to $1,100, the attempt to label as unprofessional conduct the acceptance of a salary lower than its minimum, the introduction of collective bargaining and salary schedules

[6]J. M. Paton, *The Rôle of Teachers' Organizations in Canadian Education* (Quance Lectures, 1962), p. 45

in rural areas after 1935—all of these seemed in vain. In fact, from 1921 to 1943 the teachers had actually lost ground, for the inflation to which our economy seems chronically afflicted (except during the Thirties) meant that the purchasing power of the 1943 dollar was much less than that of its 1921 counterpart. Furthermore, the teachers' qualifications in 1943 were far higher than those in 1921, as indicated in Table I by the classes of new certificates issued in two significant years. Of course, the proportion of all those teaching in Alberta in 1942-1943 who had at least Grade XII and at least one year of professional training would be much less than 80 per cent, but obviously would be far ahead of the corresponding ratio for 1919-1920.

The ATA was not really successful in raising salary levels during the Twenties and the Thirties; in fact, it was not even able to hold the 1921 levels. Basically, the reason for the Alliance's failure in this direction was the adverse economic climate. Hardly had the province climbed out of the slough of the post–World War I recession than it was plunged into the apparently bottomless muskeg of the Great Depression in the Thirties. A contributing factor, of course, was the willingness of the UFA government to grant exemptions to school districts from paying the $840 minimum. In fact, so widespread did the practice become of paying $700 that many school boards assumed such exemptions were automatic and did not even go through the formality of requesting the necessary permission from the minister of education. Teachers who accepted positions at, say, $700 when they knew that the school board had not received authority to pay less than the statutory minimum, and then sought the ATA's assistance in collecting the difference, presented the Alliance with a thorny dilemma. To press school boards for the minimum salary seemed to condone sharp practice on the part of the teachers concerned, some of whom had in effect secured the positions by underbidding their colleagues. Not to do so would seem an admission that something less than $840 was an acceptable minimum annual salary. In the end, the executive council usually supported the teachers' claims, and successfully so. After all, it was not the Alliance's responsibility to protect school boards from mistakes of their own making, and it was more important to protect the profession as a whole from predatory school boards than to allow individual teachers to get their well-deserved lumps.

What, then, did the ATA accomplish with respect to teachers' salaries during the score of years between 1920 and 1940 or thereabouts? At least, it kept salaries from sliding further into the mire. Certainly in 1933 it was the efforts of the Alliance which, with those of the public press, blocked a bill to reduce the statutory minimum salary from $840 to $600. With respect to the influence of teachers' organizations on salaries, Paton comments: ". . . their annual salary as a per cent of earnings per person in the labour force of the country in receipt of income reached a higher point in 1933 than it has since. This proves two things: first, that teaching is a stable and secure way of earning a living; and second, that teachers' organizations in the depression were strong enough to keep salary cuts to a minimum."[7]

The success of the ATA during the twenties and thirties was essentially a holding operation, in that it was at best a factor in keeping salaries from going even lower than they probably would have otherwise. However, in another area of welfare benefits, it was quite unsuccessful. This was in the matter of pensions or superannuation benefits. As Kratzmann notes, "While Alberta was responsible for, or shared in many firsts in education . . . it was the last geographical unit of the English-speaking British Empire to achieve a state-supported pension fund for teachers."[8]

According to G. E. Phillips, the Royal Institution of Quebec paid generous pensions to at least four teachers as early as 1820, "but the practice ceased when the paternalistic agency, soon afterwards, lost its favoured position."[9] Pension schemes for teachers appeared in Canada West and East in 1854 and 1857 respectively, but one may assume that the recipients did not have to sit up late of nights wondering how to squander their stipends. In Canada West (Upper Canada) the annual pension was $26.54 in 1860. In the other Canada the rate for each year of service had fallen from $4.00 to $1.75 by 1867. The size of these benefits reflected the inadequacy of the two schemes.

Quebec, formerly Canada East or Lower Canada, introduced a more adequate scheme in 1880, based on teachers' contributions of 2 per cent of their salaries plus assistance from the government. No minimum pension was guaranteed, but the scheme did permit increased benefits purchasable by voluntary

[7] *Ibid.*, p. 44.

[8] A. Kratzmann, "The Alberta Teachers' Association: A Documentary Analysis of a Professional Organization," unpublished doctoral dissertation, University of Chicago, 1963, p. 186.

[9] C. E. Phillips, *The Development of Education in Canada*, p. 559.

teachers' contributions, and half-pensions for widows. Ontario teachers in 1881 sought similar benefits. The reply of the minister of education was a masterly bureaucratic *non sequitur*: the minister was opposed to compulsory pensions, especially for women, and he was also against higher benefits for veteran teachers after twenty-five years of service "for fear that teachers who had outlived their usefulness would continue teaching in order to get a larger pension."[10] In any event, the Ontario government ceased to support any pension scheme from 1885 until 1917, when a new plan was adopted.

Considering the meagreness of its developed natural resources until after World War II, it is surprising to discover that Newfoundland's was the earliest superannuation scheme with any pretence of adequacy. In 1892 that province established a teachers' pension fund to provide $100 per year at age 60, but teachers contributed to it for 20 years before the first pensions were paid. Consequently, when they were, in 1912, the fund was in an unusually strong position and teachers' rights were well protected financially.

When the founders of the infant Alberta Teachers' Alliance hammered out its objectives in 1917 and 1918, they included a pension plan as one of their most important. Many of the young men and women who were typical of the craft in those days were quite indifferent to it. No doubt, like young people of every age, they thought they would live forever, and if necessary, they would work as long. Anyway, retirement was thirty or forty years away, and besides, most of them never expected to stay in the classroom long enough to enjoy retirement benefits. Each young schoolmarm expected some Prince Charming on a white charger to ride into the school yard and carry her off to a magic castle on a fertile quarter-section. Each young man dreamed of becoming rich and famous as a landowner, business tycoon, political leader, as a learned judge, wise physician, beloved pastor. Yet the older, wiser, more experienced teachers in the towns and cities knew that for teaching to take its place with the learned professions it had to have stability and continuity of membership, and that an adequate retirement scheme was a prerequisite of such a condition.

In April 1918 the first general meeting of the ATA chose a committee to prepare a Code of Honour and decided to seek a pension scheme from the government. The prospects appeared reasonably bright as, according to D. M. Duggan, the year earlier the minister of education, the Hon. J. R. Boyle, had

[10]*Ibid.*

admitted the rightness of pensions for teachers and promised consideration thereof, and in 1919 the Hon. G. P. Smith, Boyle's successor in the same Liberal government, promised scrutiny and consideration.[11]

So from the first, in season and out, the ATA pressed for a pension scheme. It had its committee of the executive council, which studied scheme after scheme, which prepared one proposal after another for the government's consideration. Through the columns of *The ATA Magazine* the Alliance ever kept the objective before the eyes of its members in editorials, articles, news stories, drafts of proposed plans, etc. In February 1935 the *Magazine* reviewed its own efforts in this direction for the period 1920-1934, and found it had dealt with pensions no fewer than 54 times. The very first issue of the periodical, in July 1920, had given some attention to this matter; the fifty-fourth mention appeared in July, 1934. And the Alberta government had approved not the slightest vestige of a superannuation scheme for the province's classroom practitioners.

Not quite. If the government didn't give the teachers a pension plan, it did make them promises of one. Yes, the government would establish a scheme—but not yet. Typical of the Liberal and UFA reaction was that of the latter government when the same subject kept being raised. In 1921 the Alliance had published its Manifesto, a statement of its immediate objectives in both the professional and the welfare fields, including pensions. This was presented to the Hon. Perren Baker, minister of education, in the winter of 1921-1922. As usual, he promised favourable consideration of the teachers' submissions. In 1923 he indicated that the time for a pension plan was not propitious. Two years later, the general secretary-treasurer reported to the executive council that the government had promised to draft the necessary legislation, but first a survey of the teachers was necessary before a submission could be made to the cabinet. The government therefore undertook to poll teachers in rural areas and in Edmonton and Calgary as well as members of the Alliance. And still nothing happened. Premier Greenfield postponed implementation of his promises until the provincial revenues were in better shape. Therefore in 1927 the ATA came up with its own proposal, which no doubt was carefully filed away—presumably in a wastebasket. But not without an explanation for the unfortunate but strictly temporary delay: Alberta's entire educational system was due

[11]D. M. Duggan, *The Alberta Teachers' Magazine*, X, 8 (April 1930), pp. 13 *et seq.*

for a revision, and any pension scheme would have to fit into the reorganization.

In the meantime, even the other western provinces were leaving Alberta behind—those in the east had done so long before. In 1928 the Saskatchewan government pushed its fine new Retirement Act through the legislature. British Columbia introduced its scheme in 1929. At last Alberta's premier seemed ready to respond to the campaign which the ATA had waged all these years.

A. J. H. Powell has told the story:

> The U.F.A. caucus could not be shown that teachers, any more than farmers, should be taken care of in their old age. It was not until the summer of 1929 that Premier Brownlee, conscious of the conspicuous isolation of Alberta in the matter, took John Barnett aside. He asked John to keep his pension people quiet for a few months, so that the government would not seem to be under pressure. If this were done, he believed he could carry through a teachers' retirement plan at the next [1930] session of the House. . . . The crash on Wall Street came in October, 1929; the fiscal condition of the province immediately became precarious, and in the depression which followed nothing was heard of teachers' pensions. For a few destitute old teachers, Perren Baker was able to secure an indigent allowance of $25 or $30 a month; that was all.[12]

According to *The ATA Magazine* (Feb. 1928), the premier informed ATA representatives that a general revision of the educational system was being seriously considered by the provincial cabinet for action by the legislature at its 1929 session, and pensions for teachers would be seriously considered in relation to that revision. The contemplated changes were probably those connected with the introduction of the divisional or large administrative unit into the system of local school government. A bill for this purpose was in fact presented to the legislative assembly. To give time for its consideration both by the legislators and by the public, it went only as far as the second reading, and in fact, such was the opposition that it never became law.

However, at the 1929 session, a resolution passed by the legislature, with non-partisan support, authorized the minister of education to inquire into the circumstances of indigent ex-teachers and pay them such allowances as he might deem necessary. For ten years this was the only pension legislation on Alberta's statute books, and it certainly could not be considered a superannuation

[12]Powell, "The ATA," p. 21.

scheme. By 1931, Alberta and Prince Edward Island were the only provinces without teachers' pension plans supported by provincial revenues, although in some cases the government contribution was quite small. In this respect, by 1934 the foothills province stood in something less than splendid isolation.

The pension issue did not disappear quite as quickly as Powell has indicated, for *The ATA Magazine* of March, 1930, reported that the government had conferred with the governments of Manitoba and Saskatchewan respecting their superannuation schemes, and that the Alberta authorities were paying $30 a month to at least one teacher. It exercised such generosity only in cases of direct need, but it is comforting to know that at least one teacher, after a lifetime of service to our province's boys and girls, could spend her declining years in the comparative affluence which $30 per month represented—actually about 35 per cent of the minimum salary of the period.

The Alliance kept on trying. In 1933 it came up with a new scheme, one in which: (1) only teachers in the highest categories would contribute; (2) the government costs for the first three years would be for administration only; (3) anticipated profits of $33,000 would be available to the government as a loan. But the UFA party, riven by personal scandals involving some of the cabinet ministers and stranded by the ebb-tide of the Depression, was desperately involved in trying to save itself from oblivion, and had no energy to devote to the rescue of old and broken-down school teachers.

However, if the provincial government felt no responsibility to its veteran pedagogues, a few urban school districts did. In 1931, Calgary school district introduced a scheme whereby retiring teachers with long service to the system were granted a gratuity equal to one year's salary spread over the three years following retirement. Edmonton rapidly followed suit. These allowances would carry a grizzled old veteran to or past his sixty-eighth birthday. And if he hadn't had the grace to die by then, and could hang on until he reached 70, he could then gracefully enjoy security and oblivion on an old age pension of $30 a month.

If during the UFA era (1921-1935) the Alliance had only the most ambiguous success in protecting salaries, and virtually none in securing a pension plan for its members, in another area its attainments were much more respectable. This was in the field of security of tenure. It is, of course, vitally important to teachers as to others that they receive adequate remuneration for their labour, but teachers being the kind of people they are, following as they do a calling without any promise of such glittering rewards as wealth or glory, perhaps even more important than the size of the remuneration is the knowledge that they will continue in quiet enjoyment of it; in short, that they will enjoy security of tenure. This concept seems to be so well known that it is seldom defined. It appears to imply that a teacher (or whoever) will not be dismissed except for cause; not only that he will continue in employment but that he will know, within limits, what his rate of pay will be, and that it will not be capriciously or maliciously altered. It implies, further, that if he receives notice of dismissal, that notice will be subject to review by an independent tribunal at which the dismissed person may be represented by an advocate of his own choice. Finally, it implies that the reviewing tribunal will have the power to sustain or reverse the employer's action of dismissal.

As with pensions, the Alberta Teachers' Alliance never ceased to press for legislation which would give its members security of tenure as a statutory right. However, its members did not confine themselves to efforts to influence the legislature; they also made representations to the individual school boards.

Such representation actually began before the birth of the ATA. The staffs of individual school systems had begun seeking some modicum of tenure security even when the province was being formed in 1905, for example, in Medicine Hat. Within ten or twelve years of that date a number of staffs had persuaded urban school boards to pay salaries according to a schedule of sorts. In 1908, the Medicine Hat teachers were petitioning their trustees for amendments to the salary schedule. In the period 1915 to 1917, teachers in Medicine Hat, Lethbridge, Calgary, and Edmonton were all in communication with their school boards over schedules, usually to request removal of the unilaterally imposed cuts which their patriotic trustees had inflicted on the staffs as a wartime measure, or to ask for increases. However, it was generally recognized by teachers and trustees alike that adoption of a salary schedule was an employer's prerogative, one which teachers could request but not demand.

These early schedules contained two long-vanished features, one of which disappeared early, the other more recently. The first was a sex differential; the second a distinction according to whether the teacher taught in the elementary or secondary grades. As a rule, women teachers or elementary teachers or both (the two were almost synonymous) were covered by their own schedules; secondary or male teachers or both by others. It also occasionally happened in the few urban systems of the era that although women teachers would be covered by a schedule, the men and the high school teachers would have to negotiate their salaries individually. Medicine Hat had adopted a schedule applicable to all teachers except the principal as early as 1901, but the following year the school board made it apply to women only as of January 1, 1903, and established a different schedule for men. In 1906 the distinction was removed, but in 1908 it was restored. The distinction between men and women for salary purposes, however, was much less important than that which separated elementary and secondary teachers. The school trustees had resolved that "they deem it advisable in the interests of the high school to employ male teachers for high school work."[13] The manoeuvering of other urban school systems during that prewar period in an effort to establish satisfactory schedules was similar to that of Medicine Hat's.

Alberta appears to have adopted from Ontario the practice of paying female teachers less than their male counterparts. But, as Hall notes:

> . . . because of the scarcity of teachers the differences in payment for men and women were never as large as in the eastern provinces. Traditional attitudes existent there did not exercise the same influence in Alberta and the women who came west to take the advertised positions were reasonably independent and were far removed from the local arguments of their home areas for small remuneration. Though salaries offered in Alberta to women were often a little lower than those accorded to men, the differences did not last long.[14]

Besides sex and grade level taught, other factors affected a teacher's remuneration on these first salary schedules. One was qualification, that is, type of teaching certificate held by the teacher. A university degree as such was not recognized directly, but occasionally a school board might specify that the principal had to be a university graduate, in which case he would receive additional compensation by virtue of his administrative duties. Virtually all other graduates were employed at the high school level, which had its own schedule,

[13]L. G. Hall, "A Historical Study of Salary Payments to Teachers and of the Emergence of Principles of Salary Scheduling in Alberta," unpublished doctoral dissertation, University of Toronto, 1967, p. 34.

[14]*Ibid.*, p. 21.

with levels higher than applied for elementary school teachers. Additional remuneration for graduate work was apparently never even contemplated.

The other principal factor governing salary rates usually but not always operated after the teacher was appointed. This was classroom experience. Credit for experience previous to appointment with a particular system generally did not place a teacher on the schedule above the lowest step, and when it did, the advantage was limited. This type of limited placement is still not uncommon in Alberta's urban systems. For the cities, such experience was in effect a prerequisite for appointment. Since urban schools were inherently more attractive than those in the country or small centres, the cities had no difficulty in securing experienced teachers without paying for that experience.

A third and minor factor was specialist employment. Thus in Lethbridge in 1913 the female commercial teacher received an extra $100 per year above her scheduled salary.

Since salary schedules were unilaterally determined, school boards had no hesitation in disregarding them whenever they deemed it advisable so to do. One scheme was to grant a bonus to the most satisfactory (or importunate?) teachers. In 1917, for example, Lethbridge gave $50 raises to seventeen and $100 increases to four teachers. As late as 1938 the Raymond school board exercised its perogative to grant bonuses to certain selected staff members.

The other method of altering salary schedules previously adopted was to cut them, a common practice during World War I. Such cuts took one or both of two forms, a suspension of annual increments or a percentage reduction of salary. Again, they were determined by school board action alone and not by negotiation with the teachers.

Rural school systems, usually employing but a single teacher, had no schedules, unless the advertising of a position at a specified rate of pay could be called one. However, under the blows of economic adversity, even this rudimentary arrangement was subject to breakdown. Note was taken at the third AGM of the Alliance that one school board was advertising for a teacher, "state salary expected."[15] By 1934, in the midst of the Hungry Thirties, the general secretary of the Alliance was flailing school boards for their Dutch auction of teaching positions.

In 1917 and 1918 Alberta teachers were appointed by means of written

[15]Alberta Teachers' Alliance, *The ATA Magazine*, I, 1 (June 1920), 26.

contracts in a form specified by the minister of education, which form, however, could be amended by mutual agreement as long as changes were consistent with the School Ordinance and regulations thereto. A simple offer and acceptance did not constitute a contract, as many teachers learned to their sorrow. Contracts were of two types, term and continuous. The former lapsed at the end of the school year. Neither school board nor teacher was under any obligation to give notice to the other of intention not to renew. Naturally, such contracts provided no security of tenure whatsoever. Continuous contracts were a little better, but not much. At the end of the school year, if either party wanted to terminate the arrangement, he had to give notice to the other.

With respect to security of tenure, the first demands of the newly established Alberta Teachers' Alliance were relatively modest. In July 1918 the ATA executive council requested a form of contract which would automatically be self-renewing, that is, be a continuing contract. For a whole year, beginning in April 1918, the Alliance attempted to arrange for a meeting with the minister regarding the form of salary agreement. Had Boyle continued in office, possibly such a meeting might have been arranged, but the Hon. G. P. Smith seemed quite indifferent to the teachers' representations. In the end, the Alliance prepared its own contract form and distributed it to its members. At that time the School Ordinance made two stipulations respecting teacher–school board contracts. These were that: (a) they had to be signed by both the teacher and the chairman of the school board; (b) they had to be in a form approved by the minister with only such amendments as were not inconsistent with the School Ordinance and the regulations of the department of education.

The teachers' tactics brought the department to the conference table in a hurry and agreement in principle was rapidly reached on a number of matters, specifically: (*a*) continuous contracts; (*b*) adoption of salary schedules; (*c*) cumulative sick pay; (*d*) an amendment to the School Ordinance to make 200 rather than 210 days the length of the school year; (*e*) some form of investigation to be mandatory previous to the dismissal of a teacher.

However, apparently no sooner had the conference adjourned than the minister (or his minions) struck a low blow indeed, as the department of education issued a letter to all school boards pointing out that contracts had to be in a form approved by the minister, and that he had approved only one form. No mention was made about the legality of amendments to the contract. Thus the impression was tacitly created that the addition of such alterations would mean that the contract had been changed so that it was no longer valid.

Further sessions with the minister of education, Smith, resulted in agreement on the principles of continuous contracts, salary schedules, and security of tenure. The Department refused sick pay cumulative to 200 days. The biggest issue remained the matter of investigation into reasons for teachers' dismissals. In the first issue of *The ATA Magazine,* H. C. Newland with typical perspicuity cut to the heart of the matter, saying, ". . . publicity is a protection to the teacher."[16]

Finally, in November 1920, the minister announced a contract with a new tenure clause. The new form would require thirty days' notice of termination and give the teacher, under clause 5, the right to a hearing before the school board. Following such a hearing, notice of termination could be confirmed, becoming effective thirty days later. However, the hearing was before the very body which had given the dismissal notice in the first place, and which therefore was hardly a disinterested body. Such a procedure held little promise for the dismissed teacher. The notice required for the hearing gave little time for the teacher to prepare his case. By this notorious clause 5, the teacher was limited in his choice of an advocate. He could choose a member of his immediate family, an inoperative provision if the teacher came from a distant part of Alberta or from another province or another country. Or he could call on a taxpayer of the district, who was bound to be a friend or neighbour of at least one of the three trustees who were party to a controversy with the school teacher.

Another reason why the ATA was critical of the Hon. Mr. Smith's whole package was that it provided no recognition of the Alliance as the representative of the teacher.

In the fall of 1920, the Alliance was devoting considerable attention to the preparation of a model salary schedule which would allow for schools in different categories, specifically, Edmonton and Calgary schools, other schools of seven or more classrooms, those with four to six rooms, and those with one to three rooms. It also provided for high school teachers, elementary and high school principals, manual training teachers, and others in special categories. Members were urged to apply for salaries in accordance with the ATA model

[16]H. C. Newland in *The ATA Magazine,* I, 1 (June 1920), 19.

schedule and school boards were encouraged to follow it in offering positions. What influence the model schedule had on tenure security and salaries in general it is difficult to say. Even if its direct effect were minimal, it was one more step in education of the ATA membership to demand certain levels of salary and security, and not to be content until they got them, even though such a devoutly wished consummation might be years away.

By February 1921 it was obvious that relationships between the Alliance on the one hand and the trustees and the minister of education on the other were deteriorating. The teachers attacked clause 5 as being illegal. The minister counterattacked by appealing over the heads of the executive council to the members of the Locals; they in turn replied by pledging their support to their organization.

At the same time the Liberal government was fighting on another front, its most serious battle since the province had been created in 1905. This time the opposition was not the traditional opponent, the Conservative party, enemy beloved because is was so predictable, but the socialist-tinged agrarian radicals who called themselves the United Farmers of Alberta. At least as early as January 1920 the Alliance executive in its capacity as the law committee had met the UFA board of directors in an effort to gain some commitments from them with respect to such things as salary schedules, continuous contracts, and the 200-day school year. The two bodies reached general if not complete agreement to the extent that the ATA virtually endorsed the new political movement (its supporters were careful not to call it a political party). The Hon. George Peter Smith, according to Powell, ". . . was so forthright in derision of the A.T.A. that John Barnett took counteraction. In the final days of the 1921 provincial election campaign John spent two days in the U.F.A. Camrose headquarters assisting in the fight to oust George Peter. It may be doubted whether his help was necessary or important. The U.F.A. of course swept the province."[17]

The teachers hailed the election of the UFA government as the dawn of a bright new day. But they soon discovered that they were mistaken. The October 1921 number of *The ATA Magazine* carried a cordial story about the Hon. Perren Baker, new minister of education; the teachers soon discovered that their cordiality was premature. Buoyed with hope, they approached the new

[17]Powell, "The ATA," p. 8.

minister with their tenure and contract requests. In essence, these were for: (*a*) a continuous contract terminable on not less than 30 days' notice; (*b*) a period of notice longer than five days respecting hearings on dismissal notices; (*c*) right of a teacher to be represented at such hearings by an advocate or agent of his own choice; (*d*) establishment of a board of conciliation with a clearly formulated method of acting in cases of teacher–school board disputes.

The minister promised to act on the ATA requests. So he did—by filing them. In 1923 he apparently opened the filing case and granted the dismissed teacher the right to choose his own champion at dismissal hearings—and simultaneously made the change virtually inoperative by reducing the time required for notice from ten days to two. The ATA was indignant about the change for two reasons: the cut in time, and the fact that it had been implemented without previous discussion with the teachers. The minister, however, remained adamant, refusing to reverse or modify his position.

In 1926 the Alliance appeared to be making some progress towards its objectives, for the legislature accepted amendments to the School Act which increased the notice of hearing interval from two to five days and also established a board of reference with power to summon witnesses and make decisions in disputes between teachers and school boards. Once again the gain proved largely illusory, as the board of reference could not enforce its decisions. Nothing prevented a school board from appointing teachers pending publication of the reference board's findings. In 1927, for example, the board heard four cases involving dismissals and recommended reinstatement in two, but the school boards concerned took no action. In May 1929 the general secretary-treasurer reported to the AGM that the ATA had been pressing the minister for a board of reference with power to enforce its decisions. The minister refused on the following grounds: (*a*) School boards should not be limited in their power of dismissal; (*b*) The establishment of large units of school administration would make more powerful boards of reference unnecessary—a typical example of political logic, leaping from an untenable assumption to an unwarranted conclusion; (*c*) In any event, the government had no intention of bringing in amendments to the School Act in 1929.

Perhaps the main action in the fight for security of tenure involved the minister, but skirmishes were occurring on other fronts. Possibly a provincial salary schedule would provide the teachers with the security which they sought.

In January 1927 a strong editorial in *The ATA Magazine* endorsed such a proposal in the following terms: "It is very questionable whether the present haphazard method of obtaining teachers and fixing their salaries will be remedied until there is some democratic machinery to put into operation."[18]

The following year, the editor was having to warn members that a common school board practice was to offer a teacher a position, and then when he arrived to start work present him with an amended contract to sign.

The ATA found even some of the school inspectors to be inimical to their aspirations, perhaps a not unnatural phenomenon since the inspectors have always been a part of the educational establishment. A meeting of the executive council of the Alliance in 1929 recorded the following resolution: "That the Secretary-Treasurer be instructed to write a letter from the Executive to those inspectors who seem to be antipathetic at conventions."[19] The council also determined to send a committee to meet the chief inspector in order to discuss the conduct of school inspectors who mutilate the prescribed form of the teachers' contract. Presumably these inspectors were acting as official trustees of certain rural school districts.

In 1930 the Alliance issued a platform which embodied all its objectives, economic and professional. Many of the planks in this platform had a bearing on the matter of tenure. A summary of the whole platform follows:

1. Official recognition of the ATA as the organization representing the teaching profession in Alberta by the government and the school boards.
2. A provincial salary schedule with increments annually and a proper placing in the schedule according to experience.
3. A form of teachers' agreement which will provide for greater permanency of tenure and afford ample protection against dismissals for other than relevant reasons.
4. The right of the ATA to representation on all boards of inquiry having under consideration the effectiveness and conduct of the teacher.
5. Promotion on the basis of successful service and seniority.
6. Increased government grants.
7. Equalization of educational opportunity; free adult education, extension of high school and university privileges to rural residents.

[18]*The ATA Magazine*, VII, 7 (Jan. 1927), 15.

[19]ATA Ex., Dec. 27-28, 1929.

8. Creation by statute of an advisory board to deal with issuance, cancellation, etc. of certificates of teachers.

9. The creation, by statute, of a permanent consultative committee to give advice and inspiration to the minister of education.

10. Provision for special instruction of talented and sub-normal children.

11. Province-wide medical and dental inspection of schools.

12. Free use of the elective system in framing school curriculums.

13. A tightening of the truancy laws and release of the teacher from the duties of informing.

14. Higher professional training for teachers.

15. Local autonomy in education.

16. The creation of larger units of administration to the extent that the unit shall be sufficiently large to enable it to function with dignity and efficiently, yet without denial of or encroachment upon the principle of local autonomy.[20]

Apparently the manifesto made little or no impression on the minister, for the following year he introduced a form of contract which made the school inspectors less popular than ever with the classroom teachers. The new legislation prevented the school board from giving notice of dismissal (usually 30 days had been required) other than in July, except with permission of a school inspector, or a teacher from resigning, other than in June or July, except with similar permission. The consequences were that the teacher lost the right of appeal against dismissal and the school boards the right to effect a dismissal on their own authority. The minister claimed that the changes which he had initiated were those that the ATA had requested. This was news to the teachers. Their particular objection was that the inspector was an interested party in any dispute between teacher and school board—and he certainly was when, in his capacity of official trustee, he *was* the school board. The teachers did win one small concession. As Kratzmann notes, "The written acceptance of a school board henceforth was to be legally binding until such time as the prescribed form of contract could conveniently be signed."[21]

As it developed, the new legislation requiring inspectoral approval was applicable only to "new" or term contracts but not to the "old" or continuing agreements. The department therefore advised school boards and inspectors to

[20]*The ATA Magazine*, X, 9 (May 1930), 9.

[21]Kratzmann, *op. cit.*, p. 166.

have all old contracts replaced with new ones by July 1, another manoeuvre guaranteed not to endear inspectors to the ATA. However, the Alliance's legal counsel advised that such substitution was not legally necessary, that the "old" contracts could be terminated only by the customary notice and hearing if the latter should be requested. Apparently in those depression days the ATA feared that the new agreements would call for lower salaries than did the old ones.

With the deepening of that Great American Depression, trustees and others attacked the $840 minimum teachers' salary which had stood from 1918. The proposal was that the figure be changed to $600. Rather to the teachers' surprise, with the aid of the public press the suggestion was defeated or at least withdrawn. At this point not the minister of education but Premier Brownlee himself met representatives of the Alliance. At this meeting the two parties reached agreement on a number of points, as recorded in *The ATA Magazine*[22]:

"1. The Premier undertook to take charge of a conference of trustees and teachers on the question of appointment, dismissal and appeal against dismissal of teachers and endeavour to arrive at a mutual agreement, and in the event of its being necessary, in person to carry the question before the Trustees' convention."

"2. The Alliance undertook to have withdrawn the suit against an Inspector whom [*sic*], it was alleged, had approved the termination of a teacher's agreement without enabling the teacher to be present at any enquiry or even to be informed of the parties making the accusation against her either to read or hear the actual complaint."

"3. The Government would withdraw the section in the Bill providing for Inspectoral approval in termination cases . . . to be final. . . . The Minister would issue instructions to Inspectors with respect to procedure to be followed precedent to 'approving termination' of agreements: that the Inspectors be instructed to make reasonable inquiry into the grounds of application for approval of termination and that both parties should be given a reasonable opportunity either personally or by agent to state to the Inspector such answer or defence as they may see fit."

4. The ATA suggested that the $840 minimum not be touched and recommended a number of alternatives, of which the government and the legislature accepted one which became the following amendment to the School Act:

[22]*The ATA Magazine*, XIII, 8 (April 1933), pp. 18-19.

"Provided that upon request of a Board the Minister may authorize engagement at a smaller salary." No investigation by a school inspector would thereafter be required before such permission would be given, a change which those worthy gentlemen no doubt welcomed with a sigh of relief.

If the conference with the premier indicated a warming of the psychological climate in the neighbourhood of the legislative buildings, that near the different school board offices was becoming more gelid. In 1934 the ATA general secretary-treasurer reported to the AGM on evasions of the spirit of the School Act by school boards. These included:

1. Teachers had the choice of paying exorbitant board bills (to $30 a month) or being fired.
2. School boards were paying less than $840 per year even though they had cash on hand.
3. School boards were paying less than than the government grant as salary.
4. Kickbacks were being extorted from the teacher by means of supplementary contracts.
5. Teachers were being charged exorbitant rentals for teacherages that were mere shacks (up to $29 per month).
6. Appointments were being made by Dutch auctions, that is, to the lowest bidder.
7. School boards were terrorizing teachers with verbal threats.
8. Boards were advertising for applications in order to beat down salaries of incumbent teachers.
9. Boards were firing newly appointed teachers in order to be free to hire cheaper talent.[23]

But despite the harrassment by individual school boards, despite the repeated disappointments caused by the Depression, the ATA had reason in 1934 to feel that real progress had at last been made towards tenure security. In that year the government: (*a*) gave the board of reference the power to enforce its decisions; (*b*) changed the board's composition to consist of district court judges; (*c*) precluded school boards from filling disputed positions until the board of reference's finding had been transmitted to the parties in a dispute.[24] However,

[23]J. W. Barnett, "Annual Report of the General Secretary-Treasurer," *The ATA Magazine*, XIV, 8 (April 1934), 10.

[24]Kratzmann, *op. cit.*, p. 166.

the teachers had not yet won the right to a continuous contract. Boards were free to make term contracts, although continuing agreements apparently were also acceptable.

But the following year the government reversed its field. By abolishing appeals to a board of reference, the government swept away most of the teachers' hard-won gains, as is evidenced by the action of the Calgary public school board in dismissing all its teachers and obligating them to re-apply in writing for a position under a board-determined salary schedule at lower rates. In this way the Calgary trustees demonstrated how, when they possessed the power to deal with teachers individually, they could reward merit with salaries commensurate with the services performed.

The Doleful Tale of the Bureau of Education

FLUSHED with the success of its efforts in building a viable organization which counted among its membership two-thirds of the practising teachers in the province, the leaders of the youthful ATA seized every opportunity to serve the membership. One scheme was launched with a cargo of radiant hope and glowing expectation; in the end the craft foundered, to the embarrassment, distress, and financial loss to the Alliance and at the cost of strained and tense relations between two of the founding fathers of the Alliance.

It began innocently enough with a decision of the executive council in December 1922 to establish a Bureau of Education which, for reasonable charges and on easy payments, would provide correspondence courses at the Grades XI and XII levels, where standing was earned on the basis of departmental examinations, as well as professional courses. Other activities anticipated for the new bureau included: (1) preparation of examination papers; (2) preparation and calibration of tests; (3) distribution of test materials; (4) preparation and distribution of stencils for maps, charts, etc.; (5) provision of professional advice.

The executive made a firm decision to go ahead with the bureau in the spring of 1923. W. C. Richards, a former school inspector and educational entrepreneur of wide talents and limitless energy, was interviewed about his willingness to organize and manage the new company which would operate the Bureau of Education. Negotiations were carried on with Richards with a view to his bringing into the new bureau the correspondence department and spare-time staff of Alberta College. He also suggested that the ATA purchase the bankrupt Crossland Printing and Lithographing Company, but apparently this was not done.

The decision of the ATA executive was that it would control the bureau by the purchase of shares, but whether in the bureau or in the ATA Publishing Company is not clear; the two seem in fact to have been identical. The Alliance undertook to purchase 150 shares at $10 a share: $1,200 worth in settlement of the debt owned by the publishing company to its parent concern, the Alliance, and the balance in cash. Another 150 shares were to be sold to members of the ATA. It is probable that most or all of these were taken up by the teachers who did the actual work of the bureau, and that they paid for them in services rather than in cash. Richards was offered the position of manager of the correspondence department.

In the end, the decision was to operate the bureau by the semi-independent ATA Publishing Company, a concern the financial history of which is almost impossible to unravel. Apparently the majority shareholder was always the Alliance itself, but individual members of the ATA also evidently held shares in the corporation. From time to time the Alliance made financial advances to its progeny to liquidate the bureau's chronic deficits; in compensation it received still further shares in the company. In the beginning, then, it appears that the Alliance held most of the stock in the publishing company, which in turn operated the Bureau of Education and published *The ATA Magazine*. Each stratum had its own bureaucracy. All strata were linked through a common secretary-treasurer or business comptroller; for all three this was John Barnett. If at times he did not appear to know which hat he was wearing, this is not surprising. Manager of the Bureau was ATA past-president H. C. Newland, and W. C. Richards was to be in charge of sales.

Although the minutes of the executive council do not so reveal, apparently Richards did not accept the ATA's offer. At least, his name does not appear in the minutes in connection with the Bureau for several years, and when it eventually did, he was identified as the "Manager of the Alberta College Bureau."

The reason why the Bureau was operated as a division of the ATA Publishing Co. rather than by the Alliance itself was apparently that Barnett, according to the minutes of an executive meeting of April 22, 1923, wished to avoid a great deal of detailed work which presumably would interfere with his duties as general secretary-treasurer of the ATA. Just how this objective would be accomplished in view of his threefold responsibilities to the Alliance, the Publishing Company and the Bureau is not quite clear. Barnett also pointed out that the ATA was a fraternal and not a trading corporation, evidently feeling that the operation of a business was not an appropriate activity of the Alliance itself.

By September 1924 *The ATA Magazine* was able to announce that more than 700 teachers had enrolled for teachers' aids and tutorial courses. However, that pulication did not reveal that tension was developing in the executive council. As early as December 1923 editor Newland and general manager Barnett were quarrelling over responsibility for lateness in meeting the magazine's publication dates, a situation that was becoming chronic. The printer, of course, disclaimed all responsibilty; he was merely the innocent victim of the faults of the other two. Since the publication of the *Magazine* was the responsibility of the publishing company and not of the ATA, this problem should have been adjusted by the directors of the former. But the general secretary was not the only one who did not know what hat he was wearing at any particular time; the executive council members were apparently equally confused. Therefore the executive council felt it had the authority to deal with the problem. Accordingly, it finally resolved: "That a contract be drawn up between the Board Business Manager, Editor and Printers with regard to dates for turning in their work in order to ensure the Magazine being out on time and that the party breaking this agreement be reprimanded."[1]

If such a fantastic contract was in fact ever completed, it must have made legal history.

Another example of the extent to which the affairs of the Alliance, the Bureau, and the Publishing Company were intertwined was provided by the relations of the first and last-named with their agent, apparently resigned or

[1]ATA Ex., Dec. 15, 1923.

dismissed, who had been overpaid on his commission account. The council decided that the losses resulting from such overpayments be prorated between the ATA and the Bureau, and written off.

This was by no means the last time that the ATA was to be in trouble through overpayments to its representatives. As early as the following April the executive council was giving considerable attention to overpayments to the ATA's and the Bureau's new agent, who was over-drawn through the withholding of collections on behalf of the two organizations. The council's decision was that "The Executive, after hearing [his] statements and his replies to questions, came to the conclusion that the Bureau commissions were not sufficient to give a man a living wage, even when including commissions from the ATA which [he] considered sufficiently generous."[2] The final result was that the commission rate was increased.

But the problem with the agent was as nothing compared to the controversy which erupted in the spring of 1924.

There were really not one but two basic problems. The first arose from the clash of two strong and self-willed personalities, Barnett and Newland. Because of it, the former did not scruple to go over Newland's head and appeal to the ATA membership despite the fact that Newland was his superior, at least as far as the operation of the Bureau was concerned. Such a manoeuvre was not uncharacteristic of the General Secretary-Treasurer, as the following quotations from a memoir by a past president of the Alliance indicate:

> On occasion . . . John would be confronted in Annual General Meeting or in Executive session with an instruction or an order which he could not argue down and had to accept. If he did not like it as an A.T.A. policy he would bury it in the files. His attitude, tacit but unmistakeable, was 'I made this organization. I remake it every year. It's mine, and no Johnny-come-lately is going to take over any of it.' That was why, until his final year, he could not be persuaded to take a deputy-secretary into his office.[3]

That Newland could also hit below the belt is indicated by a reference to Barnett's limited academic education, when he suggested that the Office of Director of the Bureau would require qualifications higher than those possessed by the General Secretary-Treasurer. Newland acquired four or five university

[2]*Ibid.*, April 25, 1924.

[3]A. J. H. Powell, "The Alberta Teachers' Alliance," unpublished memoir (1962), 31-2.

degrees, including an LL.B. and a Ph.D., with the seeming ease of a prairie youngster stuffing himself with ripe saskatoon berries; Barnett's only university parchment was for his posthumous honorary LL.D.

Probably the roots of the personal animosity between these two complex individuals were at least as old as the Alliance itself. A letter from Fred Parker, ATA president during the 1925-26 term, refers to an incident which occurred during a predecessor's incumbency in that office: "The early 1920's were difficult years for the ATA. I remember attending a meeting of the Executive in the Calgary Public Library, at which meeting John Barnett and Dr. Newland's [sic] went at it hammer and tongs, almost hitting each other across the table."[4]

The second problem with respect to the operation of the Publishing Company and the Bureau of Education appears to have arisen in the executive council itself. It had set up a separate company to publish its *Magazine* and operate the Bureau, a company in which the Alliance owned part but not all of the shares; then it proceeded to act as if it were the sole shareholder and the members of the executive were the company's board of directors—which they weren't. Understandably, Barnett therefore did not really regard himself as responsible to Newland, editor of *The ATA Magazine* and manager of the Bureau, or even to the directors of the publishing company. In fact, as Powell has indicated, he did not even think that the executive council was really his boss. In the final analysis, he considered himself responsible only to the Annual General Meeting, if to anyone.

The executive council's reaction to the latest crisis was typical. It was, in fact, little more than an exhortation to everyone concerned to try to get along, at least until the AGM, when the whole issue could be dumped into the lap of that august body. Accordingly, in April an annual meeting of the ATA Publishing Co. Ltd. was held with reports from the Bureau Department Manager (Newland) and *The ATA Magazine* Editor (also Newland). The AGM, which heard these reports, adopted them unanimously, then politely handed the baby back to the executive council with this resolution: "That the president of The Alberta Teachers' Alliance, Inc. be chairman of the Board of Directors."[5]

A month later the council began to face up to a hard fact of life: that the publishing company was chronically in debt to the Alliance, which debt was

[4]F. Parker, letter of Dec. 28, 1966, addressed to S. C. T. Clarke.

[5]The ATA Publishing Co., minutes of annual meeting, April 21 and 24, 1924.

liquidated from time to time by the issuance of additional shares to the ATA. The Alliance also met a constant demand for new captial by the same device. A committee had been appointed by direction of the AGM to examine the possibilty and desirability of amalgamating the Alliance, the Publishing Company, and the Bureau of Education. Its recommendation was that ". . . The proposed amalgamation of the Alliance and affiliated activities under one general manager appears at present inadvisable if not *ultra vires* of the powers of the Alliance."[6] The old conundrum: could a fraternal organization legally engage in trade?

So the matter drifted for another year, most of it below the surface of visibility like an iceberg, until March of 1925, when H. R. Leaver wrote in the pages of *The ATA Magazine*. In his view: (1) no writer of courses, synopses, solutions or holder of Bureau stock should hold office on the Executive of the Provincial Alliance; (2) such writers and holders of stock must form a company of their own, separate from the Alliance.[7]

Little further appeared in the *Magazine* to indicate that the cutworms were still in the tomato patch, other than a statement in the May issue of the *Magazine* that the Bureau of Education was becoming a headache to the Alliance through bad debts and conflicts of interest, and what could be done about it?

President W. W. Scott's report to the 1925 AGM devoted considerable space to the vexing problem of the Bureau. Part of his report follows:

> It appears to me that the greatest difficulty with the Bureau is that, "in theory," it is controlled by the Executive, but "in practice" it is not. Last year, at the A.G.M. you will remember, there was a resolution passed, asking that the Alberta Teachers' Alliance, the A.T.A. Magazine, and the A.T.A. Bureau of Education, be all placed under one head, a general manager. But it was felt that the hands of the Executive should not be bound, and that if it were possible to co-ordinate these three factors into one harmonious system, with the dual head, it should be done. Now, I may say that during the year the Executive has exerted every effort to establish this harmony, but the experiment can scarcely be called a success.
>
> Now, this is a question that this A.G.M. must settle. Since it involves two prominent individuals of the Alliance, it is a personal question, and should not be left for any Executive to solve.[8]

[6] *Ibid.*, May 31, 1924.

[7] Alberta Teachers' Alliance, *The ATA Magazine*, V, 10 (March 1925), 12.

[8] W. W. Scott, *President's Report, Eighth Annual General Meeting of the A.T.A., April, 1924* (mimeographed copy), pp. 10-12.

It is interesting to note Scott's admission that the executive council members had not followed the clear AGM directive of the previous year, yet when the exercise of its own initiative had failed to solve the problem, Scott had no compunction about handing a very wet baby back to that body.

Probably most of its readers missed the next bit of evidence in the *Magazine* that there were still serpents in the ATA garden. The clue was simply a change in the publication's masthead for the June issue. The editor was now John W. Barnett; Newland's name had disappeared. Not a word of comment appeared in the magazine itself about the change. When the executive council said "Jump," the board of directors merely asked "On whom?" and out Newland went.

The first and perhaps necessary step had been taken to cut out the tumour which had not only been bleeding the Alliance ever since it first began but had set colleage against colleague, perhaps friend against friend. The executive council finally decided to liquidate the Bureau, although it would continue to operate until Christmas under Barnett's management. However, the Alliance was to find that it was easier to conceive and bear the Bureau than kill it off.

In April, H. D. Ainlay brought in a recommendation of the finance committee concerning the controls which should be operative under the new scheme. They were: (1) that no expenditure be incurred by the General Secretary-Treasurer on the Capital Account without the approval of the Finance Committee; (2) no payment should be made to instructors without the sanction of the Finance Committee; (3) that the Finance Committee be responsible for the distribution of charges to the different departments.[9]

These recommendations were discussed informally but it was decided to leave formal instruction until the July meeting. Reading between the lines, one can infer that although Barnett's associates were completely loyal to him, they were having a hard time keeping this maverick in the corral.

Once again the AGM had to deal with this vexatious problem. Powell has given an account of the way it did so:

> In 1927 the plight of the Bureau of Education became the ground for open revolt in the A.G.M. There were those who felt that Barnett was not equal to the job, and that they should look for another man.
>
> What happened as the hassle drew towards a crunch . . . was pure comedy. To

[9]ATA Ex., April 8, 1926.

explain it, one must tell that in those days there were a dozen or so men-teachers who lived so far in the backwoods that they could not join Locals, but loved to sit in at the A.G.M. and were recognized as members-at-large. They were permitted to group in sixes and to choose one of themselves as delegate. The delegate had full voting rights, the others might take the floor.

On Wednesday evening of Easter week 1927, as we sat in the basement of McDougall Church, Edmonton, the air was electric and we knew that "this was it." The debate closed steadily in on the shortcomings of the general secretary. One of the members-at-large rose to a point of order. It took twenty minutes to clear that away, and the acrimony deepened. Presently another member-at-large rose to a point of privilege. The chairman, who had a foot in the rebel camp, whispered to John:

"What do we do?"

"Here," said John, passing him a huge Bourinot, closed. It was one of the very few unkind acts of Barnett remembered against him.

The meeting floundered on, until at the moment of decision the delegate of the members-at-large rose and spoke briefly. He was Fred J. Bendle from parts unknown:

"What does the Alliance need in its executive officer? Does it need a peddler of courses? It does not. Does it need a foreman for its mimeograph shop? It does not. Does it need a research man? It does not. I'll tell you what it needs; the Alliance needs a Fighter. When I was in a dispute with the Boyle Crossing School Board was it a course peddler or a mimeograph foreman or a research student who got me out of a jam? It was not. It was fighting John Barnett, and he is the man we need to head this organization. Mr. Chairman, as a duly appointed delegate of the members-at-large, I wish to move a vote of confidence in our general secretary, fighting John Barnett."

After thirty-five years one cannot swear to the exact phrases, but that was the sense of Bendle's speech, delivered with the Celtic passion and sharp articulation of a Swansea Welshman. The motion was seconded and carried handsomely. One of the malcontents capped the comedy by growling, as the meeting broke up:

"Some of these members-at-large have no business being at large!"[10]

But the problem still would not go away. A year later, the ATA president announced that the Bureau was continuing in operation with a voluntary reduction in the debt owed the course-writers. They had apparently agreed to scale down their claims by 40 per cent. In July, the executive decided to press for collection of outstanding accounts, as the Bureau had evidently been sold to two Calgary teachers, J. R. Davidson and R. D. Webb. Thereafter, the ATA had nothing to do with the operation of the new company, called Western

[10]Powell, "The ATA," pp. 22-4.

Canada Institute, the advertisements of which began to appear in *The ATA Magazine* with the February 1929 number. However, even in 1931 the Alliance was having to intervene in the operation of the Institute's management by virtue of its ownership of some of the business's shares, and in 1932 Webb was requesting an option to buy the ATA's stock after two years at par value plus accrued dividends. Apparently the stock had passed every dividend from the time of the 1928 sale of the Bureau. Perhaps if a search is made, the ATA will find that it still owns shares in that Calgary business.

The final word on the ATA's Bureau of Education may well be that of past president A. J. H. Powell himself: "The Bureau may serve as a horrible example of the sort of enterprise *not* to be undertaken by a teachers' organization in its early infancy."[11]

[11]*Ibid.*, p. 24.

From Trade to Profession

MOST OF THE TEACHERS who provided the drive for the formation of the Alberta Teachers' Alliance were not the impecunious, inexperienced, and ill-qualified young neophytes who tended the lamp of learning in the tiny temples of education that dotted the plains and foothills and parklands of Alberta in 1917 and 1918. Rather, they were the mature, well-qualified, and relatively well-off principals and high school teachers of the province's few cities, people like C. E. Peasley, G. E. Misener, Fred Parker, A. E. Rosborough, H. C. Clark, George Watson, A. J. Watson, Eric Ansley, R. W. Webb, C. E. Leppard, H. C. Newland, J. G. Niddrie, W. W. Scott, D. L. Sullivan, M. W. Brock, Jennie Elliot, H. D. Ainlay, C. L. Gibbs, M. J. Hilton, C. O. Hicks, T. E. A. Stanley, Mary Crawford, and a host of others, including, in Edmonton, an assistant supervisor of music named John W. Barnett. These people were professionals in every sense of the word, in qualifications, in outlook, in total commitment to their calling. They were bright people, versatile in their interests, public-spirited, serving on city councils, hospital boards, library boards. They were esteemed by their fellow-citizens and secure in their positions. If not as well paid as lawyers, dentists, architects, physicians, and some others with comparable backgrounds, they enjoyed certain compensatory advantages. They were on duty only 200-210 days a year in an era when other professionals customarily spent about 270 in their places of work, and they could be ill for a month or more without their income suffering. Even financially they were well off compared with most Protestant clergymen, for instance. One may hazard that what they wanted from the new organization was not so much more money, although they were not completely unworldly in this respect, as the status and recognition of their calling as a profession. It is therefore no accident that the first strike action of the Alberta Teachers' Alliance in 1921 involved Edmonton's high school and not the elementary teachers, and that two of the principal issues were the recognition of their organization by the school board, and the right to be consulted on all aspects of education which concerned them—which meant, directly or indirectly, almost every phase of the school board's business.

Thus from the very first the Alliance had shown a concern about far more than the economic aspects of teaching. It has expressed interest in such matters as departmental examinations, curricula, convention programmes, preparation and certification of teachers, and educational research. With respect to this last, Powell mentions the practical problems which it encountered:

> From the beginning, there were enthusiasts who wanted a vigorous programme of educational research, and before long provincial committees were set up for this purpose. As far back as 1926 Arthur Rosborough's Edmonton committee did a competent research job on high school examination results, and presented it before the 1927 Annual General Meeting. Very few of the delegates understood the report. There was no college or faculty of education in Alberta to which it could be submitted. Its fate was predictable; the executive delegation which took the A.G.M. resolutions to the Minister presented along with them the Rosborough research job. He said, "Thank you, gentlemen," and passed it along to the Deputy who said nothing but filed it away.
>
> In 1929 an indignant Research Committee from Calgary appeared before the provincial Executive and complained that it had been given no assignment. Why not? The harassed executive men, knee-deep in law cases, exiguous finances, proposed tenure clauses and what not, could only say they had had no time, and beg the committee to find itself an assignment.
>
> Research committees always wanted money for statistical reports from Ottawa, for stationery and postage, while the Alliance was barely making ends meet and had none to spare.[1]

[1]A. J. H. Powell, "The Alberta Teachers' Alliance," unpublished memoir (1962), p. 20.

Actually, the matter of educational research did not receive quite as short shrift as Powell seems to imply. In 1920 the AGM had approved the establishment of a bureau of research, and the creation, that year, of *The ATA Magazine* provided a medium for the dissemination of research findings. In its early days the ATA had a number of members or friends who had had rigourous graduate training in educational psychology and related fields, including testing and measurement. Among these were C. Sansom, M. E. LaZerte, and H. E. Smith, all of whom eventually held the presidency of the ATA. Sansom became principal of the Calgary Normal School; the other two were first and second deans respectively of the University's faculty of education. Still other such scholars were G. F. Hollinshead, eventually to become a school inspector, and C. B. Willis, another of the number who found J. W. Barnett somewhat less than wholly endearing.

Although the ATA paid more than lip service to the ideal of research, lack of funds and personnel severely limited its efforts. Research tended to be the spare-time activity of educators who had full-time responsibilities as teachers or administrators. With the establishment of the University of Alberta's school of education, which began operation in 1929, educational research at last found a home. Even then, however, until after World War II most published research in the province emanated from individual projects of candidates who were writing theses in preparation for graduate degrees in education.

The publication of *The ATA Magazine,* which in 1968 is completing its forty-eighth year without interruption, itself represents a professional project of no small magnitude. If a single objective can describe the viewpoint of the successive editors of the periodical, that word is eclectic. Everything of possible significance to Alberta teachers has appeared in its columns: editorials exhorting the members to action of one kind or another, or warning them of professional hazards, or criticizing opponents such as the press, the trustees, or the government; blacklists; news of and tributes to individual teachers; letters to the editor; accounts of Local activities (eventually dropped through lack of space); the department of education's official bulletin; articles on educational topics, often taken from other publications in Canada and elsewhere; news about ATA projects and activities; for a short time a bureau of employment announcements. From time to time, teachers in specialized subjects also had their own columns, for example, industrial arts and guidance. Personal opinions, reminiscences and travelogues, and even short poems sentimental or humorous or satirical, have graced its pages, as have book reviews, which still appear. Almost from the earliest issue the *Magazine* stressed a teachers' helps department consisting of "how to" articles, probably very welcome to poorly prepared teachers isolated in one-room country schools. The feature continued for almost a score of years, last appearing in June 1939. Lists of teachers entitled to vote for members of the executive council for some years occupied many pages each spring. The publication carried accounts of each AGM (now ARA), including resolutions dealt with and action taken following their adoption. Each year there is a story about the Banff conference and other gatherings such as those of the Canadian Teachers' Federation, the Canadian Education Association, the annual western conference on teacher education, and many others. For several years following John W. Barnett's death in 1947 the March issue paid special tribute to his memory, carrying a picture of the late executive secretary-treasurer on the cover.

In its forty-eight year history, two special issues of the *Magazine* have appeared. In March 1960 there was published *The Cameron Report: A Condensation of the Report of the Royal Commission on Education in Alberta.* The October 1964 number was entitled *Submissions of the Alberta Teachers' Association to the Special Committee of the Legislative Assembly on Collective Bargaining between School Trustees and Teachers,* a designation which led one irreverent member of the ATA to remark that he had perused the issue but had not yet had time to read the title.

Format of the *Magazine* has changed with the times. Copies of the issues from the 1920's look almost Victorian in the heavy dignity of two-column composition, staid typeface, and cuts of solemn pedagogues wearing high shoes, heavy vests, and stiff collars, if male; or with their long hair piled high on top of their heads if they belonged to the distaff side of the profession. Gradually the pictures became more numerous and more informal—candid camera shots—and the dimensions of the *Magazine* shrank to a single-column, pocket-sized format. Cartoons, sometimes humorous, at other times mordant, have appeared in its pages from time to time. Eventually pictures began to appear on the covers. At first these were black-and-white photographs of literal or symbolic significance. More recently there have been beautiful colour shots depicting Alberta's wild life, Indian chiefs, industry, and scenery. And of course during the jubilee of the Association the covers have been splendid wrap-around coloured prints illustrating crucial episodes in Canada's history. In this year also the *Magazine* returned to its former 8½" x 11" format.

One interesting phase in the *Magazine's* history lasted from 1930 to 1932. During this period the newly established *ASTA Magazine* was published as an integral part of the teachers' organ. An intriguing situation occurred within the covers of the same publication in which the trustees were taking swipes at the teachers, and the latter were replying in kind. The arrangement was terminated not because of any mutual antipathy, but because the Alberta School Trustees' Association could no longer carry the financial responsibility to which such an arrangement committed it.

The ATA Magazine was one medium of communication between the Alliance and its members; the annual general meeting (AGM) was another. The first one was held in 1918 as a special evening session of the Alberta Educational Association. As long as that organization remained in existence the two groups continued in an almost symbiotic relationship. The AEA furnished a programme of professional and inspirational talks and discussions; the AGM provided the ATA with an opportunity to present reports of its committees and officers, to formulate Alliance policies, to present its budgets and deal with its on-going business. Since about 20 per cent—several hundred—of the teachers attended the Easter gathering, it was widely representative of the teaching profession.

After 1918 the executive officers of the AEA were regularly prominent members of the ATA; the day when the former body was controlled by professors, school trustees, school inspectors, and the like was gone forever. Thus in 1921-1922, Edmonton high school teacher Mary Crawford was its president. She was succeeded by De Voe Woolf, LL.B., a Raymond barrister, but in 1923-24 the position was held by C. E. Peasley, a past president of the ATA. Other teacher presidents included G. R. Woolf, principal of Magrath school and a member of the ATA executive council, for example, and George Clayton, an Edmonton principal.

As the need of the ATA for more and more time at the annual convention grew, the Alliance became more and more involved in its planning and operation. In December 1921 the executive council paid considerable attention to these matters. A year later it was apparent that the structure of the AGM was becoming more rigid and formal when the council decided to invite fraternal delegates from the Edmonton public school board, the Alberta School Inspectors' Association, the United Farm Women of Alberta and others.

The occupational groups with whom the ATA was establishing fraternal relations at that time are interesting, including as they do farming, labour, and the provincial civil service. Despite the ATA's claim to professional status, not one of the learned professions was invited to participate in the gathering. Their verbal pretensions notwithstanding, the teachers appeared to identify themselves with the farming–labouring–low salaried segment of society, in other words, the level which sociologists identify as lower middle class.

When the ATA, some years later, began to establish lines of communication with other professional organizations, it is significant that the first was the Alberta Association of Registered Nurses, a group, like the ATA, made up predominantly of women with less than a university degree by way of professional preparation, not self-employed but occupying relatively low-salaried positions. But in the end the ATA was instrumental in establishing a forum where all the learned professions—law, medicine, dentistry, teaching, accounting, etc. —could meet to discuss common problems.

With respect to the AEA-ATA annual convention, the Alliance found itself more and more involved in its organization. In January 1926 the executive council passed the following resolutions:

"That we accede to the request of the Alberta Educational Association to take charge of the banquet during Education week."

"That we request the Calgary Locals to organize the banquet for the Provincial Alliance." (Apparently this was not the same function as mentioned just above.)

"That we accede to the request of the Alberta Educational Asociation that the Alberta Teachers' Alliance bear one-third share of the rent for the church for the Convention.

"That the ATA accepts the offer of the AEA to print the proceedings of the Annual Convention in *The ATA Magazine,* if the AEA resolves to print the proceedings."[2]

Later the same year a proposal appeared in *The ATA Magazine* to dissolve the AEA, which apparently was "riding on the ATA's coat-tails—a switch from

[2]ATA Ex., Jan. 2, 1926.

1917 and 1918, when the AEA had provided funds to establish the younger organization. However, the dissolution did not happen at that time, perhaps because, although the teachers were now firmly in control, the Educational Association still included among its supporters such people as normal school instructors and school inspectors. The next mention of the continued existence of the AEA appears in the 1932 AEA executive council records as follows: "Resolved: That a formal comunication be sent to the President and Secretary of the AEA requesting that a committee to study the matter of amalgamation of the two organizations, meet during the time when papers are being examined in July."[3] At the July meeting the suggestion was advanced that the AEA executive be appointed as usual, except for the president and the secretary, allowing the corresponding officers of the ATA to act in these capacities. "This was suggested as a basis for amalgamation of the two bodies."[4] Just how the ATA could appoint officers for the other association is not clear. In any event, a joint meeting of the officers of the two organizations was held a few days later, when it defeated a resolution for the amalgamation by a 4-5 vote.

In September another joint conference under George Clayton, AEA president, met to study the situation again. Their proposal was that a federation be formed, consisting of the organizations of the teachers, the normal school instructors, and the school inspectors, each of which would appoint two members to an executive. Members of the federation would include members of the constituent bodies and associate members who paid the convention fee. This scheme, or something like it, was adopted, for in 1933 the Easter convention was held under the name of the Alberta Educational Federation. At that time, ATA president M. W. Brock reported to the AGM on progress to date:

> Some of the business transacted during the 1932-33 period includes the following:
>
> 1. The more definite planning by your provincial executive to close the ranks between the Alberta Educational Association and our own Alberta Teachers' Association [sic]. Immediate amalgamation of these two honourable bodies was practically assured when a liaison committee was set up. The ATA was represented in this important undertaking by your president, Mr. Hicks, Mr. Shortliffe, Mr. Kostash, and Mr. Barnett. As usual it was the particular driving force of our general secretary that affected the result of the final union.[5]

[3] *Ibid.*, March 31, 1932.
[4] *Ibid.*, July 1, 1932.
[5] M. W. Brock, *President's Report to the 1933 AGM of the ATA* (mimeographed copy), pp. 1, 2.

However, if the AEA (or AEF) was dead, it would not lie down. In 1934 the ATA general secretary served as secretary-treasurer of the AEF, which also requested the ATA to guarantee preliminary expenses. Evidently the Federation was not always a smoothly functioning machine, as the following decision of the ATA executive council indicates: "... that no item appear on the programme of the Easter Convention in the event of any of the opposed affiliated bodies taking the stand that the discussion of the subject or item (*per se*) is inimical to the interests of such affiliated body."[6] Apparently this matter arose from some objection which the school inspectors had to the proposed programme.

Convention-goers of a later age might be interested in the 1934 cost of accommodation in Edmonton's Macdonald Hotel. Prices ranged from $3 per day for a single room down to $1 per day per person for four persons sharing two double beds in the same room. No charge was made for meeting rooms if 100 or more delegates registered for the convention. The price of the convention banquet was $1.

As the ATA grew in membership and in the complexity of its projects and programmes, it required more and more time at the Easter conventions, leaving progressively less for the purely professional features which were the primary responsibility of the AEF. As the business activities grew, a convention of perhaps 20 per cent of the province's teachers proved too unwieldy to handle them efficiently. Therefore, others than accredited representatives of the Locals were subtly discouraged from attending. Since 1946 the AGM, which in 1918 had occupied one evening of the Easter gathering, has been the whole convention and the AEF, née AEA, no longer having a function, has disappeared from the educational landscape.

But there is a second type of annual teachers' convention that the ATA has come to dominate completely. This is the local gathering, organized originally by the department of education to provide opportunities for school inspectors to meet their teachers and discuss their work. Traditionally it was held in the fall months of October and November, sometimes earlier. As indicated in an earlier chapter, it is, at least in terms of the foothill province's history, of venerable antiquity, going back to the 1890's if not earlier. As Kratzmann mentions, "The Fall convention has grown in professional stature, passing from the institute for the discussion of Departmental directives to meetings which provide

[6]ATA Ex., April 5, 1934.

for the addresses of prominent educators and exchange of ideas, discussion of current problems, and opportunities for teachers to present and have evaluated study and research projects which they have conducted."[7]

The proprietorial interest which the minister and department of education have shown in these autumn gatherings has been manifested in a variety of ways. In the first place, it is only by the grace of the provincial authorities that teachers have been able to use school days for them and receive their pay. The rule has always been that the teacher must be either in the convention hall or in the classroom during the days designated for the convention, or suffer the economic consequences. Secondly, more than one minister of education has not hesitated to attend such conventions in order to criticize the ATA to its very members, and has not felt the slightest compunction in so doing. Regulations of the department of education have always explicitly stated that the school inspector shall be *ex officio* a member of each convention committee. Originally no doubt he organized the convention; today his function is more that of a consultant or resource person.

The most arbitrary act on the part of a departmental officer occurred in 1931 when the minister of education as an economy measure cancelled all fall conventions on his own volition. This action the editor of *The ATA Magazine* hinted to be illegal, as it was not in conformity with either the School Act or the department's own regulations.

The only other time since the ATA was established when fall conventions were cancelled occurred in 1918. The occasion was the influenza epidemic in late October and November, when all public meetings were cancelled to prevent spread of the disease. Even if this measure had not been taken, in most places there would have been too few teachers still on their feet to mount more than token assemblies, and those few were too busy caring for the stricken to be concerned with less vital matters.

Over the years, the conventions have changed in a number of respects. At first, there was one to each inspectorate, each of which covered a large and sparsely settled area, for example, in 1903 one for Northern Alberta—the territory, not the province. With increasing settlement the number of inspec-

[7]A. Kratzmann, "The Alberta Teachers' Association: A Documentary Analysis of the Dynamics of a Professional Organization," unpublished doctoral dissertation, University of Chicago, 1963, p. 209.

torates grew and the area of each diminished. Then, with better roads and other improvements in transportation facilities, a number of inspectorates would combine to hold one larger and better convention, attended by several hundred instead of several dozen teachers. Now the pendulum seems ready to swing in the opposite direction as some teachers fear that these gatherings are becoming too large for group discussions and workshops. In 1966 the number of such local conventions, aside from the large, wholly urban ones in Calgary and Edmonton, had shrunk to about a dozen.

With the growth and development of the ATA, the influence of that organization has increased proportionately. At first, ATA Local meetings were held on the same days as the conventions after the regular sessions; later they were incorporated into total programmes. After the metamorphosis resulting from passage of the Teaching Profession Act, the ATA undertook to provide "big-name" speakers for each convention at the expense of the provincial budget, if the various conventions so wished. This move meeting general acceptance, the provincial administration of the ATA then began to have a considerable voice in the planning and scheduling of the local gatherings, for each such speaker usually visited a number of conventions at the rate of two per week. However, there has been no tendency to transform the local conventions into wholly ATA meetings as has happened with the large Easter gatherings. These local affairs continue to be, as they always have been, concerned primarily with the professional development of the teachers.

In addition to the local conventions intended primarily for elementary school teachers, for a number of years the high school instructors held their own gatherings in Edmonton and Calgary. A number of factors finally led to the demise of these institutions during World War II. One was the introduction during the middle 1930's of the junior high school organization which took one grade from the secondary and two from the elementary level, blurring the sharp distinctions which had hitherto existed between the high school and the other teachers. Another was that with the organization of school divisions and inclusion therein of towns and villages where the high schools were located after 1937, the high school teachers and principals found themselves increasingly involved in ATA Locals and pressed to fill leadership rôles for which less qualified and less experienced teachers in rural schools felt themselves inadequate. As local conventions grew and high schools became larger and more numerous, the secondary school people found that they did not need to go to the large cities to get whatever they did expect from conventions. Probably the *coup de grâce* to the high school convention came with the imposition of gasoline rationing in World War II, which discouraged long and avoidable sorties.

To speak of fall conventions today is to use a misnomer; in 1966 only three such gatherings were held in October as compared with one in January and eleven in February. The change became feasible when the ATA gradually abandoned the practice of bringing in outside educators and others to ride the convention circuit and undertook to sponsor local choices, often Alberta people, for each individual convention. No doubt another reason for the change was that improved roads and snowplowing, together with better heated, safer, all-weather cars robbed winter safaris of their terror. The big independent-minded Locals in Edmonton and Calgary had never warmed to the peripatetic pedagogues from far places, and held their affairs during the winter months long before their rural confrères adopted the practice.

First rural winter convention was that of the infant Northland Local of the ATA. This assembly first met in January 1962 in the week immediately following the Christmas vacation. The date was chosen because most teachers left their isolated schools anyway at that time, and to expect them to make another journey of up to 400 miles or more each way seemed unreasonable.

In 1963 this convention became a precedent-setter in another way. ATA members for many years have been particularly fussy about not meeting in teachers' conventions with non-teachers; during the 1940's and 1950's they made the correspondence school supervisors, or sitters as they were disparagingly called, quite unwelcome. But the Northland Local did arrange a joint convention with the Alberta Indian Education Association, most of whose members are employed by the federal government in Indian schools, and few of whom hold Alberta teaching certificates despite the fact that their schools follow the Alberta curricula. Not only are they not necessarily members of the ATA; that Association's by-laws do not at present permit them to become members even if they are certificated in this province.

However, the joint convention was a success. Each group met by itself for the equivalent of about half a day to deal with its own association business. The rest of the time was spent in joint sessions to the mutual benefit of the two groups. The Northland ATA Local and the AIEA have held similar conventions ever since, although currently it appears likely that the teachers from Indian schools may be found in several conventions, not just one.

Teachers' conventions and magazines are aspects of in-service education; the ATA has always been concerned also with the pre-service education of its future members. Its interest has been manifold. With better-qualified teachers, better salaries could be obtained and the financial circumstances of teachers as a group would improve. With more highly qualified teachers, the prestige and status of the craft would rise and more nearly approximate that of a profession. For the leaders of the Alliance felt in their bones what psychologists have long known but what business and industry is only beginning to realize: that the prize which the majority of people value most highly is not wealth but prestige. Even wealth is often only a means to this end, as is evidenced by the willingness with which affluent members of society expend their material resources to gain status in the eyes of their fellow men.

There was another profound reason for the teachers' unremitting push to improve the qualifications of classroom practitioners: a deep desire to better Alberta's educational system. Today it is the fashion to regard with a high degree of scepticism any professed motivation other than that of self-interest. But teachers would never remain in teaching (although they might enter the calling) without a high degree of altruism in their character and personality.

Occasionally cynics have accused teachers of pressing for higher qualifications in order to limit the number of those in the classrooms and so push up salaries and obviate teacher unemployment. The rebuttal to this canard is obvious; even when Alberta was short hundreds of teachers and there was no unemployment among qualified personnel the ATA still urged improvement in the selection and preparation of candidates for teaching.

Certainly when the ATA was chartered in 1918, there was no other way for the occupation to go but up. As Powell vividly notes, "Children of grade ten standing were teaching in rural schools by letter of authority. . . ."[8] In comparison, even a third class certificate looked impressive. It had been established originally for student-teachers with Grade X standing, to which was added a few weeks or months of professional training. By 1918 the third class certificate programme was no longer being offered in Alberta, but the credential was granted to candidates who were unsuccessful at the second or first class level.

[8]Powell, "The ATA," p. 3.

By the third AGM the ATA was protesting the issuance of third class certificates and letters of authority; their protests went unheeded. As late as 1924 *The ATA Magazine* noted that of 1,040 students at normal school, 890, or 85.5 per cent, were granted the certificate for the programme in which they were registered (mostly second class), another 120 were awarded third class certificates, and the remaining 30 were issued letters of authority. Not a single candidate was denied some kind of teaching authority; every one was given some credential. Obviously neither the Liberal nor the UFA government paid the slightest attention to the ATA's recommendations.

Such neglect, however, did not discourage the Alliance from making others from time to time. During the 1920's the suggestions it offered on different occasions included the following:

1. Grade XII to be the minimum standing for normal school entrance, and/or

2. Two years of preparation beyond Grade XI to be required for teacher certification.

3. Admission standards to normal school should not only be raised but also tightened.

4. The ATA should be granted representation on all boards and committees concerned with teacher training and certification. In the late 1920's the Alliance recommended an advisory council with ATA representation to deal with certification, qualification, and training of teachers.

5. Minimum age of certification to be the same for women as for men, *viz.*, 18 years. Commonly girls were eligible for certification at 17 years.

6. The practice of renewing teachers' certificates rather than making them permanent should be discontinued.

7. More exacting medical examinations should be required of normal school students.

8. Teachers' certificates should be suspended if not used for five years.

9. Normal school admissions should be limited to the number of teaching positions anticipated to be available. If necessary, one of the three normal schools should be closed (1930).

10. Loans to normal school students should be discontinued.

Throughout the 1920's the minister of education seemed deaf to the ATA's entreaties. In good times or bad it seemed impossible to raise the standards for admission to or graduation from the normal schools. In the days of prosperity there was a shortage of qualified teachers. To raise the prerequisites by one year of general or professional preparation would mean that for a year the supply of new teachers would be drastically curtailed and many schools would be unable to operate.

When the depression of the thirties came and there were an estimated thousand unemployed teachers in Alberta, the argument changed. Then it was urged that to impose an additional year of preparation on neophyte teachers would raise the cost of entering the profession to prohibitive levels, beyond the reach of the sons and daughters of hard-pressed farmers. Accordingly, in 1932 the trustees' association defeated a resolution calling for raising the normal school entrance requirements. Kratzmann reports that the trustees' concern allegedly was "to keep entrance requirements low, to create an over-supply of teachers, and to profit from opportunities to keep salaries low when supply exceeded demand."[9] This appears to be the embittered reaction of an underpaid (and probably unpaid) teacher rather than the documented conclusion of an objective observer of the situation.

The last two recommendations of the ATA listed above appear to be rather desperate expedients not so much to increase salaries as to protect the teachers' positions, a somewhat different type of proposal. Whether in response to teachers' pleas or for other reasons, as the Depression deepened, the UFA government began to act. In 1931 it imposed quotas on normal school admissions, 700 for the whole province, with preference to be given to the best qualified applicants. When only 640 presented themselves, the ATA intimated that admission standards were being lowered to recruit another 60. In 1934 the quota was lowered to 550; two years later it was decreased by another 50. Despite the fact that Edmonton's was the newest and best normal school, it was closed in 1933 and remained so for two years. The Camrose institution might have appeared to be a more likely candidate for closure, as in many ways it was the least satisfactory programme of any, but presumably there were more UFA supporters in the rural Camrose constituency than in urban Edmonton.

The government took other measures to limit normal school registrations. Fees, which had stood at a nominal $25 per year from 1928 to 1932, were

[9]Kratzmann, *op. cit., p. 54.*

doubled in the latter year, doubled again in 1934. Normal school loans, previously with a maximum of $400, were limited to $250 in 1931, abolished completely a year later. In 1935, when it reopened, the Edmonton Normal School limited admissions to those with full Grade XII standing. All applicants, not just the men, had to be the full age of 18 years when they began teaching. From 1935, certification was limited to British subjects—no Yankees need apply. Thus in half a decade most of the improvements which the ATA had long advocated in normal school training—and some they hadn't—were effected, but for economic, not educational reasons.

From 1924 at the latest, the Alliance did not regard the normal school as the ultimate institution for the preparation of teachers. In that year it pressed for the establishment of a school or faculty of education at the provincial university, with a four-year programme leading to a degree in education and, of course, a teaching certificate. Three years later, the Edmonton High School Local raised the matter again, and the Alliance wrote to the minister to advocate a six-year combined programme in arts and education, a programme that is possible today at the Universities of Alberta and Calgary. In 1928 the senate of the former institution announced plans for a school of education to train high school teachers. This school was established in 1928, but did not enrol its first class until the following year. With its advent the Alberta normal schools ceased their programme for university graduates planning to enter high school teaching. This four-to-five month course had led to the academic certificate.

Although the ATA had envisaged a four-year programme in which the student would be registered in the education faculty throughout, the original project at the University was much less ambitious. Its course, limited to one year, required a university degree for admission and led to certification at the secondary school level (Grades VII to XII). The first staff was built around M. E. LaZerte, H. E. Smith, and John Macdonald, all three to become deans at the university. Macdonald was to win this honour in the faculty of arts and science; LaZerte and Smith were respectively first and second deans of education when the pupa of the school passed through the chrysalis stage of a college to metamorphose into a faculty. Both were also to occupy the presidency of the ATA.

Throughout the Thirties, the school was quite small. In 1930, the ATA boasted that all students in the school of education had joined the Alliance, an achievement that loses some of its lustre when it is remembered that that first class graduated only seven teachers. Thereafter for several years the school's annual enrolment ran between 20 and 30.

The ATA was not content simply to have the preparation of teachers accepted as an appropriate function of the provincial university. It also pressed for representation on the liaison committee of the school and the department of education, a necessary channel of communication as, although the school provided the professional preparation, the minister of education issued his certificate to the teacher. However, this request was not immediately granted. Minutes of the ATA executive council indicate that in 1931 LaZerte, director of the school, met the council to discuss this request.[10]

In 1934, the Alliance had gained representation on a committee of the university's senate dealing with the school. With the camel's nose in the tent, the Alliance made every attempt to get the rest of the beast under cover. In April 1934 the executive council moved "That the ATA put forth strenuous efforts to obtain representation on the Senate itself,"[11] and in 1937 the organization succeeded.

Another professional field where the Alliance was early concerned with its function and that of its individual members was that of examinations and curricula. These are closely intertwined, for where there are external examinations, as in all Canadian educational systems, control of them implies control of the curricula—not what is formally set forth in courses of study, but what actually happens in the classrooms. Teachers know that such examinations are but imperfect tools for the measurement of classroom learning—how can one assess the mastery of oral French or even spoken English by a written test, or creativity in art, or growth in social attitudes?—but they realize that they ignore examination results at their peril, that they themselves will be measured by parents, students, administrators, trustees in accordance with the success or failure of their classes in examinations over which they have no control.

In Alberta, the departmental examination system is older than the province, having been established at the secondary school levels by the educational authorities of the North-West Territories. It applied to standards V to VIII, corresponding approximately to Grades VIII to XIII, that is, high school entrance to graduation. Since 1912 when the 'grade' system replaced the older

[10]ATA Ex., April 10, 1931.
[11]*Ibid.*, April 5, 1934.

'standard' classification, provincial examinations have been administered at different times upon completion of every grade from VIII to XII, although for some thirty years they have been limited to high school entrance, now Grade IX, and the high school graduation level, Grade XII.

Originally, and for many years, departmental examinations were set by scholars who were masters of their disciplines but who had either never taught in the high school classrooms, such as university professors, or who were many years away from direct experience therein, such as school inspectors. They were chosen to set the examinations because they had drafted the courses of study on which the examinations were based. The professors were also included not alone for measuring a candidate's qualifications for high school graduation and entrance to normal school but also for matriculation to university. Even today, the body in charge of the examinations is known as the High School and University Matriculation Examinations Board.

In the province's salad days, it apparently simply did not occur to department of education officials to include high school teachers among the pundits who set the examinations, or if it did, they were excluded because they were not trusted—consciously or sub-consciously they would reveal the content of examinations to their own students.

In general, the teachers were not opposed to the principle of external examinations, which were common all across Canada and had been since the days of Upper Canada's Egerton Ryerson in the 1840's. It was felt that any system must possess a great deal of merit to have endured for so long. Furthermore, the system did in some measure protect the teacher from local pressure to promote obviously unqualified candidates, even though it might expose him to severe criticism for not teaching well enough to get the unwilling student over the jumps. But many aspects of the system the teachers did not like. Percentage of successful candidates from year to year or from subject to subject tended to swing through a wide range of unacceptable extremes. Because the whole system of Alberta departmental examinations has been discussed in another context,[12] it is unnecessary to detail its inadequacies here. But not only did the system have inherent defects; the fact that it was being administered by people not actually involved in the instruction of the subjects being tested occasionally resulted in quite fantastic developments. For example, the June

[12] J. W. Chalmers, *Schools of the Foothills Province* (Toronto, 1967), pp. 220 *et seq.*

1920 issue of *The ATA Magazine* carried a criticism of the department of education for setting the Grade XII composition examination on a programme which was not even to become effective until September of the same year, a blunder which the editor felt would have been avoided if teachers had been included among the examiners. In 1921 the ATA published a "Manifesto" which included an item containing the claim that the Alliance should be represented on the examination board. In August 1924 the *Magazine* listed ATA proposals on examinations sent to the minister of education. These included:

1. Only qualified teachers should supervise the writing of examinations.
2. The Alliance was opposed to single examinations which tested more than one subject.
3. It favoured departmental examinations for all grade VIII students, not just those in certain types of schools.
4. It opposed departmental examinations in July.
5. Standards in all departmental examinations should be raised.
6. Results on high school examinations should be sent to the principals involved.
7. The department of education should publish an honours list.

No doubt reluctantly, in view of his lack of enthusiasm for recognition of the ATA, the minister of education by 1928 had appointed a teacher representative to the examinations board which established policy but did not actually set the tests. Minutes of the ATA executive council indicate that in 1934 the Alliance was pressing for a second representative on the High School and University Matriculation Examinations Board.[13]

Even representation on the board of examinations did not silence the Alliance. In 1931, as an economy measure, the department discontinued Grade VIII examinations and some of those in Grade IX. The move was not well received by the executive council of the ATA, at least at the Grade IX level, as they felt that teachers would be exposed to undue pressure to promote unqualified pupils. However, they did not adopt a hard line on this matter, but approved this resolution: "That promotion by recommendation shall be permitted in accredited schools in which there are four or more teachers employed."[14]

As the depression of the thirties deepened, the government was driven to

[13]ATA Ex., June 30 and July 1, 2, 1934.

[14]*Ibid.*, May 15, 1931.

ever more desperate measures of economy. In 1933 the department of education budgeted for only ten months' salaries for its school inspectors and normal school instructors, but placed them on the staff of examination markers (sub-examiners) for the summer, stretching the marking period to the very limit, short of school re-opening in September, to provide them with employment and income. The following year they were returned to twelve-month employment but again had to mark examination papers during the summer to earn their pay. In this way the department avoided hiring as many classroom teachers as it could for this vital function. In June 1934, *The ATA Magazine* listed the objections of the teachers to the government's cheese-paring policy:

1. Some markers have not taught for a long time, if ever, the subjects for which they were marking the examinations, a practice in direct contravention to the department's own avowed policy.

2. Since the candidates pay the costs of marking the examinations they have the right to expect competence on the part of sub-examiners.

3. Salaries of teachers have been cut and they need the additional remuneration.

4. Alberta is the only province with no pension plan.[15]

(This last item seems to suggest that government officials were not the only ones guilty of an occasional *non sequitur.*)

More fundamental even than the Alliance's concern over departmental examinations was its interest in curricula. The former affected only the high school grades (and admissions to high school); the latter were vital at every grade level. As Kratzmann notes, "From the outset, the ATA claimed that the teachers as a body were best qualified to determine the subject matter for curricula."[16] The leaders of the Alliance were concerned over the lack of involvement in curriculum on the part of most Alberta teachers and the paternalistic operation of departmental curriculum committees, which usually consisted largely or wholly of normal school instructors and school inspectors. Teachers who had received their training and done their teaching in Alberta or other Canadian provinces found nothing in the situation to alarm them, since they had known no other; they were wholly willing to let the department of education prepare the courses of study as long as they were left with a reason-

[15]*The ATA Magazine,* XIV, 10 (June 1934), 1-2.

[16]Kratzmann, *op. cit.,* p. 225.

able degree of freedom to teach them to the best of their ability. But those who had come from the United Kingdom, such as J. W. Barnett and H. C. Clark, or from the United States, in both of which countries the programmes of study are determined at the local level, or even by the individual teacher, found the Alberta (and Canadian) situation quite frustrating. They wanted teachers on curriculum committees—and they wanted them there as representatives of the Alliance.

The first was easier to obtain than was the second. In 1921, 1929, 1933, and 1934 the Hon. Perren Baker, minister of education, called on teachers to assist in curriculum revision, but in the eyes of the ATA, appointment of its members did not mean appointment of its representatives. Unless the Alliance could choose those who sat on the committees that drafted the courses of study, it—and the teaching profession—was not represented. Teachers serving on such committees were serving simply as individuals, not chosen representatives of their own organization. In 1921, while the UFA government and the ATA were still enjoying their honeymoon, the department of education did seek the active co-operation of the Alliance, and that year its executive gave a great deal of time to the proposed revision of the high school programme and the appointment of teachers to assist in it. *The ATA Magazine* in 1923 announced that the Alliance was represented and active on both the public (that is, elementary) and high school curriculum committees.[17] In 1929 the department revised the high school curriculum with the assistance of individual teachers. However, the much-touted new model turned out to be the same old Model A with a few superficial improvements—hydraulic instead of mechanical brakes, and power rather than manual windshield wipers. A few years later a complete retooling took place. In 1933 the executive council of the Alliance received a visit from that educational master diplomat, G. F. McNally, who as supervisor of schools had the responsibility for the engineering of the new model.[18] He was so successful in enlisting official ATA co-operation that the Alliance nominated fifteen members to his committee, as well as alternates. The high school course of studies which resulted from deliberations during the 1930's was so successful that it has continued without alteration in its basic principles to the present day.

Despite its cordial welcome to the new minister of education in 1921, the ATA

[17]*The ATA Magazine*, III, 2 (April 1923), 7 *et seq.*

[18]ATA Ex., Dec. 28-29, 1933.

seldom saw eye to eye with the Hon. Perren Baker. However, on one subject they never disagreed, the desirability of a large unit system of school administration, which the Alliance supported without reservation from 1922. Anticipated advantages of replacing the "4 x 4" (that is, four miles square) school district with a large unit which would encompass not just a single one-room school but dozens of them were manifold. For the teacher it would provide greater stability in employment; if by any reason one school were closed, others would remain open. It would remove him from local pressures and criticisms that many teachers found intolerable. By providing a wide base for taxation, school finances would be stabilized so that Buffalo Jump school district with a large assessment would no longer bask in comparative affluence while near-by Gopher Creek remained in chronic poverty, unable to offer adequate salaries to its teachers or pay those which it did offer. A single large system with its greater buying and bargaining power would be able to operate more economically and more efficiently than many tiny ones, and have more money left to pay better salaries to its instructional staff. A large system would have enough pupils to operate a graded school, providing better service than one-room institutions, and would also have the resources to transport the pupils to schools.

As early as 1922, the ATA was pressing for the enlarged units. In 1926, articles appeared in the September and October numbers of its *Magazine* advocating a municipal system of school organization. The rural municipalities, commonly much larger than rural school districts, could provide the desired advantages. In November, the *Magazine*'s lead article, by H. C. Sweet, was entitled "The Larger Administrative Unit."[19] A year later, another article on the same topic, by A. J. Watson, appeared in the same publication[20] and in December 1927 the executive council of the Alliance endorsed the idea of municipal school boards.

During the same period, beginning actually in 1926, Baker was stumping the province in an effort to sell the concept of school divisions, as he called them. For five years he preached the new gospel, but outside the teaching profession his converts were few. Rural trustees rightly saw the proposal as one which would drastically diminish if not eliminate their functions and influence. In 1928 the minister introduced the famous Baker Bill to establish the school

[19]*The ATA Magazine,* VII, 5 (Nov. 1926).

[20]*Ibid.,* VIII, 4 (Nov. 1927).

divisions; because of lack of support even from government benches it was withdrawn. From 1928 to 1930 he proposed modifications of his scheme to the Alberta School Trustees' Association; never did he enlist any but the most equivocal support. For example, the Association regularly resolved that the divisions should be introduced only after favourable local plebiscites. In September 1928 Premier Brownlee announced the possibility of a county system for Alberta, in which school and municipal business would be handled by the same board. Perhaps he was flying a political kite, for no more was heard about that scheme for the next twenty years.

In December 1929 the executive council of the Alliance met with C. L. Gibbs, Edmonton teacher and Labour M.L.A., to discuss Baker's revised proposal, due for presentation at the 1930 session of the provincial legislature. As an alternative, it suggested school districts based on enlarged municipal districts, each of which would be under a municipal school principal (read "superintendent") who would provide closer supervision than the school inspectors were able to do. Essentially this was Brownlee's proposal, a remarkably prescient forecast of the counties first erected in 1951.

Baker addressed the ASTA in February 1930 in one last effort to sell the school division idea. The results of his exhortation, as noted in another context, were discouraging:

> Those [resolutions] proposing various alternatives were systematically tabled; those unequivocally opposed were defeated, perhaps from respect for the courage and determination of the minister in bringing his proposal forward time after time. But no resolution endorsing the scheme was submitted, as had been the case in 1929, let alone approved.[21]

Despite the opposition of the trustees, Baker again introduced his bill. The results were predictable; it survived the second reading but did not come up for the third. Baker never tried again, perhaps because of the economic and political problems which beset the UFA government during the remaining five years of its existence.

But the Alliance never stopped advocating the divisional concept. In May 1930 a published statement of its aims included creation of larger units of administration to the extent that each unit would be sufficiently large to enable it to function with dignity and efficiency, yet without denial of or encroaching

[21]Chalmers, *Schools of the Foothills Province*, p. 387.

upon the principle of local autonomy[22]—a neat trick, forsooth. The same idea, slightly modified, reappears in a statement of ATA aims in the *Magazine* a year later; specifically, the aim was for an overhaul of the School Act to provide for large units, supervision rather than inspection, and freedom of teachers from rural school board control.[23]

If Baker was unsuccessful in implementing the large unit in Alberta, at least two things connected with the proposal must be remembered to his credit. One was that he was responsible for two large-unit pilot projects. The first occurred in the southern part of the province:

> This project was the Turner Valley School District, formed by the amalgamation of five districts embracing four hamlets and the village of Turner Valley. Originally a quiet, pastoral region, the Valley had become an industrial area with the discovery of oil in 1928 and the influx of oil drillers and refinery workers. Throughout the whole region the relation between assessment and students was disturbed, since workers lived in one district but refineries were built in another. Within a year the 80 square miles in the five districts had been welded into a single system. The underground oil weath assured the success of the project, and school services improved forthwith.[24]

The other example occurred in a depressed agricultural area:

> By 1933, in the drought-stricken Berry Creek area east of Drumheller, school services had collapsed because of the exodus of hundreds of drought-stricken farmers. Sometimes not even locking the doors behind them, they climbed into their dilapidated trucks and abondoned their dessicated acres to the Russian thistle and the gophers. Where a short twenty years before there had been a school every four or five miles, one might travel twice that distance without seeing even an occupied dwelling.
>
> Yet, here and there a family remained, too stubborn or too poor even to pull out. To provide their education the government merged 67 rural districts into the Berry Creek School District. As a result, the school tax was equalized over the whole area, the school services improved, and the Department gained valuable experience in the administration of a large system operating a number of rural schools.[25]

Perren Baker's second achievement was to draft the blueprint for the divisional

[22]*The ATA Magazine*, X, 9 (May 1930), 9.
[23]*Ibid.*, XI, 5 (Jan. 1931), 19.
[24]Chalmers, *Schools of the Foothills Province*, p. 284.
[25]*Ibid.*, p. 285.

system, or have his department do so, and to acquaint the trustees and the public of Alberta with the plan. But, like Moses, although he led the way to the frontier of the Promised Land, it remained for another Joshua to lead the march across the Jordan. His name was William Aberhart. Premier and minister of education, in 1936 he introduced the legislation which in the following three years blanketed most of the province with the school divisions that the ATA had recommended for so long. This achievement has been held, and rightly, greatly to Aberhart's credit, yet the contributions of his predecessor should not be forgotten. The voice was the voice of Jacob, but the hands were those of Esau.

In at least one other area of professionalism the UFA years were significant to the ATA. At the very first session in 1918 a "Code of Honour" had been studied and accepted to establish teachers' standards of ethical conduct. In 1932 the AGM adopted a declaration of principles further to buttress such standards. As Kratzmann notes:

> This 1932 declaration set forth three basic principles underlying the professional ethics of the members of the Alliance—that non-membership is unethical, there being no standard of morality apart from the group, that the function of the teacher was the whole function as laid down in school statutes, and that no certificated teacher could be deprived of any part of this function, and that it was the duty of members to instruct persons seeking entrance to the profession in the ethical code.[26]

At the time of its adoption it was difficult to realize the importance of the declaration. The ATA could not enforce its principles on either ATA members or other teachers, and could not punish violations except by censure or, if the culprits were members, by expulsion from membership. But the declaration may have had a different kind of effect, in convincing legislators and others that the ATA was a responsible organization under the leadership of professional teachers and therefore could be trusted with the responsibilities with which the organization was changed in the Teaching Profession Act of 1935 and the amendments of the following year. The principles also provided a ready-prepared recipe which served as a basis for ATA by-laws when it was given authority to enact and enforce disciplinary powers over its members, who from 1936 included all the teachers in the foothills province.

[26]Kratzmann, "The ATA," p. 62.

Eyeball to Eyeball

WITH INCREASING MEMBERSHIP during the early 1920's (2,204 by 1923), the ATA became ever more militant in resenting injustice to and exploitation of its members. An example of such exploitation was a decision on the part of some school boards not to hire caretakers but to expect the parents to take turns in providing the service. Although some families were perhaps conscientious in meeting their obligations, others were not, so that soon none would put themselves to the trouble, and the unpaid chore was left to the teacher.

Provision of janitor services in one-room schools, incidentally, was never satisfactory as long as this venerable institution graced the Alberta countryside. Most people could not be bothered with the job, especially when, as was usually the case, the school was located some distance from the nearest residence. Often an older pupil, usually a boy, took it on, although the $5 to $15 a month, even in the late forties, was not enough to inspire any excess expenditure of energy, nor were farm boys celebrated as housekeepers. Their particular talents, those which gave them preference over their sisters, had to do with splitting wood and building fires, but with respect to sweeping, dusting, and such housewifely tasks, they usually belonged to the "lick-and-promise" school. In some districts, teachers were coerced into taking on the janitorial duties for, say, $10 a month. But they were less than enthusiastic about this arrangement, for a number of reasons. They didn't like the job itself; in fact, it is conceivable that many of them had entered teaching mainly to escape from such uninspiring work,

They suspected that when they were offered a package deal, teaching-cum-caretaking, the total remuneration was no higher than if they had been appointed only to teach. Finally, they probably felt that the combination of caretaking with teaching did not present a very good picture—today we should say "project a favourable image"—of their profession. The solution of the problem of providing satisfactory janitor services for the rural ungraded school was never really solved, but disappeared when that institution itself vanished.

Other dilemmas were more amenable to resolution. By 1924 the Alliance was able to announce that it had been quite successful in collecting salary arrears in a number of cases. In one at least it felt that it had to intervene with the department of education itself on behalf of a teacher who was being pressured to repay a normal school loan despite the fact that his salary was in arrears. In May of 1924 the AGM was told that during the previous twelve months, legal action on behalf of teachers had been threatened in no fewer than 76 cases, only three of which actually went to court. By no means all litigation (or threat thereof) was undertaken simply to collect salary arrears, admitted but not paid by the school boards. In fact, such simple cases seldom led to court action. Other cases did, although some were settled outside the courtroom door.

One such involved deliberate deception, in which a school board appointed three teachers to the same position, then informed two of them that a mistake had been made and refused them formal contracts. This scheme had been adopted to ensure that at least one teacher would be on hand when school started in September; unfortunately, all three were. In another case, the board refused to keep the school open for the full 210 days which constituted a school year and would not pay its teacher a full year's salary, even though the teacher was willing and able to teach the required number of days. In all these cases and others the names of the school districts and teachers appeared in *The ATA Magazine*.

Nor did the Alliance hesitate to take equally harsh action against teachers whose actions were detrimental to the profession as a whole. For example, in January 1925 it was decided that the names of two teachers proven guilty of unprofessional conduct in assisting a school board to commit an injustice to a fellow teacher should be "officially kept on record in the Executive office."[1]

[1]ATA Ex., Jan. 1925.

Nor did the association hesitate to publish the names of teachers who accepted positions in blacklisted schools.

One interesting dispute over the exercise of professional judgment arose in Castor, where a principal and a teacher were both sued for damages as a result of suspending two boys from school for repeated truancy. The claim was for $50 for each boy against each teacher, a total of $200, and in the District Court a judgment was given in favour of the parents. The minister of education undertook to have an amendment enacted to the School Act to make truancy punishable by suspension, and the attorney-general apparently gave some undertaking to appeal the verdict. The appeal was launched, but by the Alliance and not by the attorney-general. The appeal court reversed the decision, with costs to the teachers. One of them was A. J. H. Powell, later a president of the ATA.

In May 1926, G. H. Van Allen, the Alliance solicitor, reported on the value of a legal department for the Alliance in these words: (1) the successful termination of a number of important law suits has had the effect of greatly augmenting the prestige of the Alliance before public opinion; (2) school boards now know that the Alliance is a power to be reckoned with and they are less likely to offend against the law; (3) in some cases important amendments to the School Act have been brought about; (4) we are establishing precedents in settling various questions between school boards and teachers which should have been settled 25 years ago.[2]

But the Alliance couldn't win them all. One place where it suffered what amounted to practically total defeat was in Blairmore, a set-back particularly disappointing because the labour-dominated Crow's Nest Pass had always been more sympathetic to teachers' aspirations than had most areas. In fact, this district had an agreement as a result of collective bargaining with its staff long before most districts had got beyond the hiring and firing of teachers as individuals. Nevertheless, in 1926 the school board cancelled the agreement and imposed cuts instead of the promised increments. Apparently the reason for the cuts was that the school board had decided that a new classroom should be added to the school, at an estimated cost of some $10,000. Instead of charging this sum to the taxpayers, the school board decided to recover the amount over a short span of years by reducing the teachers' salaries. Teachers' objections

[2]G. H. Van Allen, *The ATA Magazine,* VI, 12 (May 1926), 36.

were met with dismissals of the whole staff—in effect, a lock-out. Appeals to the department of education resulted in conflicting opinions as the legality of the school board's action. The deputy minister believed that the dismissal was illegal; the minister—politically motivated—thought otherwise. The trustees, two of whom were senior officers of Western Canadian Collieries, largest taxpayer in the district, started to recruit a new staff. By the middle of September they were able to open school, but it was three months before they had engaged the full staff of thirteen which they needed. So much difficulty did they encounter that they refused to give the electors an opportunity to talk to their appointees, or even to learn their names. And for good reason, it appeared, when *The ATA Magazine* published the names and qualifications of the replacements in its December 1926 number. The principal had a Montana second class certificate, and two other teachers' qualifications were even lower.

The thirteen locked-out teachers, refusing to accept their dismissal as legal, continued to reside in Blairmore as late as January 1927 and to make themselves available for duty. They were supported by their colleagues, the ATA having established the Blairmore fund in the previous fall, with Alfred Waite of Edmonton as its treasurer. The teachers received considerable moral support from the public and at least one Blairmore trustee espoused their cause. An inspector's report on the school was rumoured to be unsatisfactory, but the school board declined to release it to the electors and demanded a new inspection. This demand was granted at the end of January. When the second report was made available to the public, after considerable delay, it was found to be most unfavourable.

At the March election, despite the objections of the parents, the trustees opposing the teachers were returned to office. In those days, only taxpayers could vote, but many parents, if not most, were tenants in company-owned houses. Despite considerable union support, the teachers' champions went down to defeat, largely because of the votes of 64 sawmill workers who lived in the district but not in the town. Nevertheless, they all paid their poll taxes—or somebody did—thus becoming voters, and they did their duty as their bosses saw it. All the officials and the office staff (presumably non-union) also cast their ballots. These white-collar types also provided cars to transport voters—the right ones—to the polls.

Convinced of the rightness of their cause, the former Blairmore teachers, with

Alliance support, sued the district for unlawful termination of their appointments. When their suit was dismissed, at a cost to the ATA of about $900, the Alliance had suffered the worst legal defeat in its history. The teachers concerned ultimately moved away to other positions or other careers, but for many years the Blairmore school district was blacklisted in *The ATA Magazine.* In fact, it wasn't until 1932 that the breach between the Alliance and the district was finally healed, with the concurrence of the local staff, by action of the school board in seeking to co-operate with the Alliance.

The Blairmore case was not the first, of course, in which the ATA and its members came to the assistance of beleagured colleagues. When the Edmonton high school teachers went on strike for two weeks in 1921, a strike fund was established which the naive pedagogues, inexperienced in such projects, managed to make so complicated that it took almost four years to straighten it out. The teachers concerned lost $8,890 in salary, which the infant Canadian Teachers' Federation undertook to raise if given sufficient time. But to provide immediate relief, 19 Locals and 18 individuals contributed (or loaned) $6,312.28, which was administered by trustees of the Edmonton strike fund. The difference plus expenses of $592.60, or a total of $3,130.32, was advanced by the Alliance, which in turn sought reimbursement from the CTF. The national body had undertaken to find the total amount of all the expenditures, amounting to $9,442.60, raising this sum through requisitions on its constituent associations. It discovered, however, that it simply could not make commitments on behalf of its provincial affiliates. It could not find $9,442.60 or even $3,130.32 but apparently did raise between $1,300 and $1,400, although one ATA president recalls that the amount was in the neighbourhood of $2,000. Individual contributors in the meantime had their contributions credited towards their ATA fees; in effect, these sums were a contribution or a loan on the part of the ATA to the fund. To complicate the picture still further, the fund trustees advanced the ATA $1,000, presumably temporarily to offset the loss of revenue through crediting ATA members' individual contributions against Alliance fees.

The high school teachers who had been on strike, were, after they had been compensated for their loss of pay by the money at the disposal of the fund trustees (presumably except for the $1,000 which had been advanced to the ATA), out of pocket an average of $49 each, with the CTF contribution still to come. Virtually all of this would go to the striking teachers, but as the strike was long past, the ex-strikers themselves suggested it become the nucleus of a contingency fund, to be administered by a committee of the ATA. In July 1925, four years after the strike which precipitated the whole labyrinthine proceedings, the ATA executive council, the trustees of the fund, and the officers of the high school local agreed: "That a separate bank account be opened in the name of the Provincial Alliance Reserve Fund and that deposits be made from the Provincial Alliance Funds of not less than $500 per year, same to be paid into the above-mentioned Bank account not later than March 1st of each calendar year."[3] At the same meeting, regulations for the administration of the fund were adopted.

The four-year experience with respect to the Edmonton strike fund did have one very important result; it demonstrated the necessity of the Alliance's having a "war chest" if it were to embark on any kind of strike action with any hope of success, a lesson which industrial and craft unions had also had to learn. It also led to the establishment of a strike fund, even though it might euphemistically be called a general or emergency reserve.

As the ATA enters its second half-century, it is hard for high school teachers today to realize that even into the 1940's the typical Alberta high school instructor was not teaching one or two subjects in a large institution with a staff ranging from 15 to 20 to well over 100 teachers. More usually he (or sometimes she) was entirely responsible for a complete matriculation–normal entrance program in Grades IX to XI, or after normal entrance was raised in the late 1930's, in Grades X to XII. Furthermore, the pupils were expected to pass all the departmental examinations, which until about the mid-thirties began in Grade IX, and if they did not, the teacher was automatically to blame, no matter how poorly prepared the boys and girls had been in the one-room schools from which many of them came to high school. In 1930, Thomas Richards, principal and sole high school teacher at Athabasca, received a dismissal notice because his pupils' examination results had proved disappointing to his employers. As Richards had good professional qualifications for those times and had satisfactory inspectors' reports behind him, he decided not to accept this action without a fight, and accordingly sued for damages for wrongful dismissal. His action was dismissed on the technicality that he had not first appealed to the minister of education for re-instatement. With Alliance support, Richards'

[3]ATA Ex., July 16, 1925.

appeal to the appellate division of the Alberta Supreme Court on the grounds that the reasons for dismissal were inadequate and the procedure followed was irregular. The appeal was dismissed for the same reason as the district court had advanced. At first the Alberta Supreme Court refused leave to appeal to the Supreme Court of Canada, but later granted such leave. The Alliance supported Richards' action, and the appeal was granted with damages and costs. The learned justices at Ottawa ruled that an appeal to the minister was required only in cases of summary dismissal or suspension from duty by reason of gross misconduct, neglect of duty, or neglect of or refusal to obey a lawful order of the school board.

This case had wider ramifications than appeared on the surface, as it reversed a decision, previously considered binding, involving the Ponoka school district. The defence that a teacher had not applied for re-instatement was no longer valid, except in special circumstances.

Sometimes a legal action went no further than a magistrate's court. Powell tells of one where John Barnet himself acted as counsel for the defence:

> Somewhere west of Edson a male teacher was hauled into court for brutality to a boy pupil. John was there to defend the teacher. (He often did minor court jobs to keep legal costs down.) The victim was in the witness box, and showed great blue bruises on his arms. Rising to cross-examine, John kept his left hand in his pocket. "Mr. J—— did that to you?"
>
> "Yes, sir, he did."
>
> "Dear me," in a gentle voice. "Let me see."
>
> Taking a firm hold of one hand, John drew forth a handkerchief, damped it on his tongue, and rubbed it on the child's discoloured arm. Without further word, he showed the blue-stained handkerchief to the magistrate, and that was that.[4]

Not all actions were civil cases, of course. In 1931 a magistrate fined a Wetaskiwin teacher $5 as a result of an assault charge arising out of the strapping of a child. The penalty was nominal; the consequences to the teacher's reputation were much more serious. Therefore the Alliance financed an appeal to the district court, where the charge was dismissed.

The particular significance of this case was that the attorney-general's department had acted for the complainant. There might be some shadow of justification for the government supplying legal aid to school boards, although school districts are corporations in their own right, well able to assume their

[4]A. J. H. Powell, "The Alberta Teachers' Alliance," unpublished memoir (1962), p. 19.

legal responsibilities. In this particular case, however, the school board was in no way a party to the action. The Alliance members were therefore understandably bitter about the government's action in supplying legal counsel to any board or even any individual who found itself or himself in litigation with a teacher. The teacher, of course, was legally responsible for his own legal expenses, but the action of the government in supporting anyone in legal conflict with him seemed to indicate an unremitting hostility to the whole profession. Another burr under the ATA's saddle was the action of the department of education in advising school boards of the technicalities they had to follow in order to make their dismissals of teachers legal.

One such case where the department of education's advice proved a frail reed occurred in 1933 and involved the Acme school district. In this instance, a teacher on an "old" or continuing contract received a dismissal notice after June 30 without inspectoral approval. Teachers on "new" or term contracts did not require such approval as a result of a recent amendment to the School Act, and the school board, acting apparently on departmental advice, assumed that all contracts were so terminable. In this case it was the school board, with legal counsel supplied free by the attorney-general's department, which carried the appeal all the way to the Supreme Court of Canada, losing at every step on the judicial ladder. The government tried every possible device to validate its original position, even to the extent of introducing legislation to have retroactive effect, but without success; the teachers' cause emerged triumphant.

This case led to a complaint by the ATA that often an inspector's approval of a dismissal was sought and given without any knowledge on the part of the teacher concerned.

Sometimes the school boards played rough, as this resolution from the December 1931 minutes of the executive council indicates: "Resolved: That the Executive give instructions to the Solicitors of the Alliance to proceed against the Egremont S. D. on behalf of Miss M. for Breach of Agreement or unjust dismissal also for false imprisonment."[5]

A footnote to legal aid by the ATA appears in the executive council minutes for December 27-28, 1934, when it was stated that some teachers were complaining at having to pay charges for the collection of back salary after success-

[5]ATA Ex., Dec. 1931.

ful litigation. The council decided by resolution that they would continue to expect such teachers to pay "this comparatively insignificant charge."

Not every dispute between teacher and school board was settled in the courtroom; many were resolved—won, lost, or compromised—in the school board's offices or meeting rooms. A number of past presidents have drawn on their own experience to narrate some of these cases. Powell tells of one in which he and Barnett were involved:

> A tenure case with a curious angle was that of a young principal at Smoky Lake who received notice of a board meeting at which his impending dismissal should be discussed. The writer went out there with John Barnett who was as usual to act as the teacher's advocate. They were met en route by the local inspector who said, "John, you know me—I'm an ATA man from away back, and I'm telling you. Don't touch this case, it's dynamite." John asked for further elucidation, but the inspector would say no more, whereupon John summed it up: "Well C——, you can take care of the Departments interest in the matter. The board can take care of the taxpayer's interest. I am here to take care of the teacher's interest, and that is just what I am going to do." And he did, at a well-conducted board meeting which lasted from 8 p.m. until 1 a.m. Sunday morning. No vote was taken at the meeting, but John was informed by phone within a few hours that the dismissal was withdrawn. The nigger emerged from the woodpile a few months later, when the young principal was elected M.L.A. for the riding. Someone else had had political aspirations, and it had seemed a good idea to get the young principal out of the way.[6]

Powell also remembers a couple of cases where he was on his own:

> One concerned an elderly, very dedicated Miss H—— who had come to Canada many years ago, sponsored by an Anglican missionary society. I forget now what the technicality was, but I went out to Kisylew School, met the trustees on the playground (one of them with a hay-fork) and showed them they were at fault. So they called another "meeting for hearing" for two weeks later, and I told them "we" would be there for fair play. Two weeks later John and I drove out again. At the appointed hour no trustee had shown up. We waited an hour, then walked over to the secretary treasurer's place, demanded and received the school house key. This we delivered to Miss H., and she taught school there the next year.
>
> The second case was of interest because the fired teacher was a daughter of [the] member of parliament, and the big man on the school board was M.L.A. for the local riding. I succeeded in getting the dismissal reversed but could not persuade the board from cutting the young lady's salary by $100.[7]

[6]Powell, *op. cit.*, pp. 18-19.
[7]Powell, letter of Jan. 25, 1967 to S. C T. Clarke, p. 5.

H. D. Ainlay draws on his memories for two typical cases that occurred during the Twenties:

A meeting was called by the parents at a school near Cooking Lake to protest against the school board for giving notice to the whole staff. It seemed that members of the board had friends or relatives whom they wished to get into the school. The parents were real hot about it. I remember a tall raw-boned Swede who said that they were good teachers. He told me of his homestead experiences. He said that on one occasion while chopping down a tree a large branch landed on his head. He said, "If I be not a Swede, I be not here today." This was merely one of the hundreds of cases which arose because of the operation of the small local school boards.

I went down to Wetaskiwin about a case where a young lady teacher had been given her notice. I met the school board chairman at his manure pile where he was loading for his field. He said that her main trouble was discipline. I asked him, "Did you ever say anything about her discipline and advise her about it?" He answered that he had not. Then I said, "It seems to me that you are the one who should be fired. What are your duties as a board member?" He thought for awhile and said, "I believe that you are right." Then I asked, "What are you going to do about it?" He replied that he would call another meeting of the board and withdraw the notice.[8]

During the second and third decades of this century, the Alberta's teacher's lot was not a happy one, largely because of insecurity of tenure. With the coming of the Hungry Thirties, all before appeared but as prologue. Hard-won gains respecting tenure, minimal though they might be, were swept away, and salaries plummeted from $1,200, which the Alliance regarded as a minimum, even below the $840 per year which the Alberta legislature had long regarded as the threshold of bare existence. Of course, the minister of education had to give his permission, granted only in some hundreds of cases, for a school board to pay such a sub-survival rate at $700 per year, the most popular figure, at least with the school boards. Some were lower.

For the first and only time in its history, during those hungry years the province of Alberta experienced a surplus of qualified teachers. Jobs were hard to find, and often harder to keep.

At least one school system which earned the displeasure of the ATA was operated not by an elected board but by an official trustee appointed by the minister of education. This was Turner Valley, where the minister's appointee was the local school inspector. In dealing with a dispute involving this district, the executive council of the Alliance showed its willingness to turn to any

[8]H. D. Ainlay, unpublished, untitled, undated memoir, p. 5.

weapon at hand, for "It was agreed that this matter be dealt with by publicity with a view to embarrassing the government, there being no other course open."[9]

In acting to protect the interests of its members, the ATA occasionally found itself in conflict with other teachers, members or otherwise of the association, as the following quotations from the ATA executive council minutes indicate:

> Miss P. was present at the meeting and laid a charge against Mr. N. that he had sought her position and dictated a letter which went to her stating the reasons for her dismissal by the board of Sunland S. D. After considerable discussion it was decided that the charge laid against [him] should be referred to the Executive for investigation.[10]

In these days of security of position, teachers even on contract can still be dismissed for cause, a fact that they forget at their peril. In general, however, acceptable reasons for dismissal are few: gross misconduct, neglect of duty, failure to obey the lawful order of a school board, closing of a school (there being no other position open in the system), proven inefficiency. Forty years ago the situation was far different, as the following list of reasons for dismissal, from a 1928 number of *The ATA Magazine* indicates:

1. Teacher objected to filthy condition of classroom after a midweek dance.
2. Teacher refused to promote board member's child.
3. Teacher went to dance with fiancé and returned late.
4. Teacher allowed her unwell fiancé to remain in the teacherage while she was absent.
5. Teacher's mother quarrelled with female chairman of the school board.
6. Son of the chairman was ready to step into the position.
7. Teacher was a Roman Catholic.
8. Teacher was a Protestant.
9. Teacher changed boarding house and therefore must have contracted tuberculosis.
10. Teacher younger (than 35) was required.
11. Teacher smoked cigarettes in the boarding house.
12. Teacher was absent through illness and the board had tried to avoid paying salary due.

[9]ATA Ex., June 30 1937.
[10]*Ibid.*, July 31, 1931.

13. Teacher refused to forego salary when school was illegally closed.
14. Board wanted a teacher lower on the salary schedule.
15. Teacher disagreed with a board member on politics.
16. Teacher's father was a prohibition crank.
17. Inspector reported lower salaries in near-by schools.
18. Teacher strapped boy.
19. Teacher rejected secretary-treasurer's advances.
20. Drinking fountain was cracked and the teacher was (falsely) blamed.
21. Teacher's English was too "flat."
22. Teacher's father was a suicide.
23. Teacher brought a pupil's delinquency to the board's attention.
24. Teacher pressed for payment of salary arrears.
25. Uninvited, a trustee's dog entered the teacher's kitchen and ate poison.
26. Teacher bought a farm that a trustee wanted.[11]

And of course Sex reared her lovely head, as Powell remembers:

> John's classical example was that of a young teacher who was dismissed to make room for the daughter of Trustee B; an agreement having been reached that Chairman C's herd should have the services of Trustee B's pedigree bull when the appointment was made.[12]

[11]Alberta Teachers' Alliance, *The ATA Magazine,* IX, 1 (Sept. 1928), 19-20.
[12]Powell, "The ATA," p. 15.

Interlude

They Rode with John

Among the baggage which an organization accumulates as it grows rich in years and wisdom are its legends and traditions. In half a century the ATA has amassed an impressive store of folklore, which is still told and retold when those few remaining veterans of the First World War and post-war years foregather, those gallant pioneers who pledged their personal credit to launch the frail frigate called the Alberta Teachers' Alliance, or those almost equally venerable patriarchs (of both sexes) who led the organization through the turbulent twenties and a little later. Sooner or later their talk always comes around to the legendary safaris they made with John Barnett, occasionally to centres far afield, usually to points within the province. A few of the ATA's past presidents have drawn on their stores of memories to tell of their journeys with John. Among the earliest of his fellow-travellers was Fred Parker, who held the Alliance's highest office in 1925-26.

"In 1925 the Canadian Teachers' Federation met in Toronto. The strike was on in the Crow's Nest district, and as President I had to go down and castigate the Ontario group for not giving us more financial support. I pointed out how disgusted and disappointed we were at getting a measly $2,000 (approximately). When I sat down Dr. Hardy got up and lambasted me. (I think all the delegates were sorry for me!) For a few seconds, I was at a loss what to say. Then I got up and said 'Mr. Chairman, in spite of what Dr. Hardy has said, I still contend that any group or organization capable of giving $5,000.00 – $10,000.00, which gives only $2,000.00, has only given a measly amount.' John Barnett burst out laughing, and soon everybody followed suit." (Fred Parker in a letter addressed to S. C. T. Clarke, dated December 28, 1966.)

A. J. H. Powell became president in 1929, but of

course he had been very active in the Alliance for some years before that date, in fact, from the time he came home from the trenches of what was then known as the Great War. Like other ATA stalwarts of the era, he had a first-hand knowledge of the boondocks, and he set much of it down in his unpublished memoir of the Alliance (1962); the following extract begins on page 9:

"Few teachers of the middle Sixties can really remember the Alberta roads of the early Twenties. In the major cities there was a skeleton of hard-top main thoroughfares, though couch grass still flourished between the street-car rails. The main stem from Edmonton to Calgary was prairie soil cambered enough to shed water; so were the busier lateral roads to Saskatchewan. But the first hard-surfacing material outside the city limits was not applied until 1925. It consisted of 19 miles of egg-sized gravel laid to a depth of nine inches between North Edmonton and Fort Saskatchewan. Within a year or two a similar surface reached from Edmonton to Calgary. It was soon rolled down sufficiently to form a useful all-weather highway, provided one looked out for loose gravel patches and for dangerous potholes at the ends of any trestle bridge. And it must be remembered that for many years this highway, or long stretches of it, fell to ruin with every spring thaw.

"Cross-country driving could be heaven or hell, depending on the weather. In a dry summer with the road well dragged, the going was good so long as one kept ahead of the other fellow's dust. One took the right-angled turns slowly, for there were Death Corners of dreadful repute in those days, and one met or passed carefully skirting the soft-shouldered ditch.

"But in the spring thaw or a rainy spell there was nothing to mitigate the sheer misery of driving on the Alberta secondary roads, unless it was a mile or two of sandy road here and there. Put on your chains, grind your way through, stay out of the ditch if you could. This writer recalls riding through with John Barnett and a car-load of Executive men down to Calgary for the annual general meeting of 1928. We left John's home in his ancient Jewitt at 8 a.m., stopped for a leisurely lunch at Red Deer, and after a grim and hazardous trip arrived at the York in Calgary at 7:30 p.m.

"It was on these diverse and unpredictable roads that our first general secretary drove out each year for twenty years to build and rebuild the Alberta Teachers' Alliance.

"Now we can rejoin John Barnett and his Gray Dort. He has veered eastward from Westaskiwin, and after combing the countryside around Meeting Creek and New Norway he drives up to the front door of the Camrose Normal School. This will be one of his happier days. The principal is William A. Stickle who takes his opinions from nobody but thinks it is high time for the teachers to organize themselves. He has had notice of Barnett's visit, and at 3:30 the student body and staff are assembled in the auditorium. The principal introduces John so warmly that not only the students but all the teachers know where he, Stickle, stands. Barnett makes his appeal on sound philosophical grounds, then offers recruit membership at one dollar per student. He expounds the provincial ATA policy of a minimum salary of $1,000 per year, and urges all the students to accept no less. Before closing his address he obtains from the floor the names of five students who are to be the executive of the Camrose Normal School local. A future president of the provincial Alliance is one of the five. When the assembly is dismissed, John meets this executive and gives it a forty-minute briefing.

"After signing in at the Arlington and eating a hearty dinner, John calls upon the high school and practice school principals to set up cordial relations with them, and then drops in to see his old friend John Russell, from whom (after some swapping of yarns) he gets the names and particulars of outlying schools and their teachers. This Barnett is no nine-to-four operator. The writer recalls riding out with him to an evening rally at Radway Centre. As we came back into Edmonton on the north road it was 11:30 p.m. but John did not head for the high level bridge and home. Instead he turned left to the Corona Hotel, in order to catch a few minutes with the MLA from Warner and ensure his support for a clause relating to the Teachers' Reference Board, due to come up in the House the next day. He found his man in the rotunda and worked on him for thirty-five minutes. Then he drove home.

"Barnett's normal school visits were not always as cordial as the one just related. At one normal school his credentials were rejected and he was denied permission to address the students. It was not until he had wrung from a reluctant Minister an order for his admission and proper reception that he was able to deliver his message and set up his ATA Local in that school.

"South from Camrose John would work down through Drumheller towards Calgary, all the way meeting and canvassing teachers — willing, reluctant, hard-up, lonely, indifferent, unpaid, cordial, harassed or stepping-stone teachers. There were hundreds of these last — teachers looking for a bright young farmer to marry; teachers financing themselves through medicine, dentistry or law; teachers who hoped to buy shares in a little store or even a beer parlour; teachers who saw no future in teaching. With few exceptions they were saving (with that dedicated penurious thrift the pioneers knew so well) to get into something else. Barnett or anyone else would have a hard time trying to sell them five dollars' worth of professional solidarity.

"On into Calgary, where he would arrive in time for a regular meeting of the Men's or the Women's Local, or perhaps both. There he would give a comprehensive survey of all ATA work and of the legislative targets set by the provincial Executive for improving salaries, tenure and prestige. If necessary — it was often urgently so — he would appeal for an immediate membership drive in every school, and for prompt payment of dues into the

Head Office. Before leaving town he would renew friendships with the stalwarts, T. E. A. Stanley, W. W. Scott, Fred Parker and others, and perhaps make contacts with other sound fellows who seemed coy about accepting office or leadership.

"The same job had to be done at Lethbridge, with a busy round of calls on A. J. Watson, Harry Sweet, George Watson and others; and at Medicine Hat where the reliables included Charles Peasley, Mary Fowler, David Sullivan and Eric Ansley. Sometimes John would journey as far south as Cardston or Manyberries, but too frequently the pile-up of trouble cases and other crises brought him hurrying by way of Innisfail and Red Deer back home to Edmonton.

"And of course the Fall conventions were covered. Many of them John attended himself, making his appeal and setting up two or three executives to foster Locals in the small towns. He would personally canvass all the teachers in attendance. To other conventions he would send teacher-agents from the Executive – people like Harry Ainlay, Harry Clarke and A. J. H. Powell. These had varying success in collecting dues, but as the years went on they blanketed Alberta with news of the Alliance and what it was doing.

"There was no rest or surcease for John Barnett during those twenty years. If he had once balked at that long, exhausting Fall campaign, the young Alliance would have died. . . . As it was, John nearly died early in the story. After one of those strenuous drives in stormy weather he went to bed with pneumonia. That was before the word antibiotics was heard, and only John's fine constitution and fighting spirit saved his life."

H. D. Ainlay, like many another teacher of the depression years, was a socialist at heart and well known to be. After he had been president of the ATA, he served two terms as mayor of Edmonton. When he assumed the mayoralty, it was to the widespread consternation of members of the local chamber of commerce, but when he left the position, the same people gladly acknowledge that he was one of the best mayors the city had ever had. His interest in people is evident in his own recollections (in an unpublished memoir) of Travels with John.

"John had one fetish. It was that if a teachers' meeting was announced he would attend it if it were physically possible. In those days a gravelled road was a godsend for it would guarantee that outside of a car breakdown it would be possible to reach our destination. Most of the roads were just plain mud and after a rain it took the real pioneer spirit to venture upon them. In spite of advice, John would constantly take a chance. 'We must not disappoint those teachers who will be at the meeting,' he would say. So away we would go. It often meant getting out of a mud-hole behind a farmer's team of horses.

"I recall one such expedition. There was a lady teacher out from Slave Lake who had been given notice. We found out later that the reason was that she resisted the amorous advances of an influential rural storekeeper. We drove to Slave Lake and the storekeeper there said that there had not been a car into that road since spring. John sent a wire to the secretary to meet us the next day with a team and wagon to take us in. We went on to the lake and fished and camped for the night. On returning next morning to Slave Lake town we found no team or wagon. John was determined to get in so we borrowed an axe and shovel from the storekeeper and started in. It was on a part of the old Yukon trail and the ruts were worn down so deep that the rear housing of John's car would ride on the middle. Then we would round up some small logs or brush to put under the wheels.

"However we made it to the home of the secretary and we soon knew why he had not met us. We were on hostile grounds. We sat with the board all afternoon but with little success. We started back and arrived at Athabasca about midnight for our first meal since leaving our camp at the lake. We arrived back in Edmonton in the late morning hours. The aftermath was that the organization got the teacher a better position and later the board secretary was found guilty of using school funds. We were, of course, very sorry for him.

"On another occasion five of us drove south-east to attend two meetings on the same night. We divided forces and covered both. We landed back at the principal of the first school for a midnight snack. I believe that those present were: John, Hicks, Powell, Leaver and I. We started off for Edmonton. We drove through Leduc and on the old trail came to the intersection and a blind road where we were supposed to turn right over the tracks.

"John went straight ahead. We were sure he went to sleep and drove into a shallow ditch and up against a fence. John asked me to see if I could get the car straightened in the ditch. After some manoeuvring I did so. He took a spotlight and waved me to drive up the ditch and over the tracks to get on the road. I tried it but stalled on the bank. He waved me on to try again and this time I made it to the tracks but the rear housing broke on the rails and the fly-wheel sent a shower of sparks flying. So there we were. There was nothing to do but walk back to Leduc. The only place open was the station and it was full of transients trying to keep warm in an unheated room. Later we were able to get a taxi open and get home again in the late morning hours. The car had to be towed to Edmonton later."

Former school inspector Cedric O. Hicks, when he was president, had the experience of accompanying Barnett to the annual Canadian Teachers' Federation meeting at Moncton in 1932. He tells (in unpublished "Reminiscences," p. 7) of one outing he spent in the company of the general secretary-treasurer.

"The first gala event was an afternoon off to visit beautiful Chadiac [*sic*] Bay a short drive from Moncton and be the guests of Mayor La Fleche and Madame La Fleche. We arrived at Chadiac just at full tide after a hot sun had warmed the sands for several hours. Never had we seen a beach like this in Canada, stretching for miles with deep sand and clear water so warm that one could scarcely bathe all afternoon. There was a large anchored diving float quite some distance out so John accompanied me as we swam this considerable distance and after a good sun bath we returned to shore. I thanked John for making me feel so secure and explained to him how I heard he was a long distance swimmer who also had taken life saving lessons. When he replied that he knew nothing of life saving it almost gave me a cramp even on shore."

Hicks was associated with Barnett in less extended Odysseys. He has given us a little information about some of these (pp. 15-16 of his memoir):

"When John had assigned you a task and you had proved able and reliable you became a 'Good Boy.' This was John's highest appelation for teachers rendering distinguished service to the ATA and I am sure he used this term quite unconsciously. We have heard him so often say, "I am going out to Newville today. Jim Doe out there is a 'Good Boy' and he has arranged a meeting for me with the teachers.'

"Often John was called upon to visit more than one scene of trouble on the same date, usually a Friday evening or Saturday. He assigned himself the harder meeting and called upon one of his many 'Good Boys' to attend the other.

"Many Edmonton teachers shared the trips with John in the area within two hundred miles from the city. He would take three teachers if available but would settle for a single companion when no more were free to go. John simply detested driving long distances alone and he appreciated having moral support from Edmonton at his meetings in the country."

One of Barnett's good travelling companions is at this writing approaching his diamond jubilee in the service of public education in Alberta by being a member of the Edmonton public school board of trustees. He has been successively teacher, school inspector, professor, and dean of education. He has served as president of the Canadian Teachers' Federation, the Canadian College of Teachers, and the Canadian Education Association. This paragon is Milton E. LaZerte, elected president of the ATA in 1937. Like others who have adorned that high office, he rode the country trails with Barnett, and has put some of his memories on paper. The following passage begins on page 7 of his unpublished memoir on "The Development of the ATA."

"John was a grand gentleman, a genial companion, well informed, a man of vision. He enjoyed a good argument. We had many rural trips together — with John at the wheel I had not fear of pot-holes or even moderately high speed of travel.

"These trips were memorable. John and I made a tour of all locals in the Grande Prairie-Peace River country. We visited about 80 per cent of all teachers in the region in this series of pre-arranged meetings. The schedule called for business in the evening and gun practice in the afternoon and early evening. We were lucky enough to have the trip coincide with the shooting season. Unfortunately when the geese and ducks heard that John and I were wandering about with shot-guns they staged a sit-down strike on the remote beach and followed this with an early migration to southern grain fields.

"Returning one night from a meeting at Innisfail that delayed our return until about 1:00 a.m., John was pressing on the accelerator a little more than usual. I remarked only once that I wasn't in a hurry and heard John's reply, 'I could drive this with my eyes shut. I've been over this highway hundreds of times.' About ten minutes later I thought that probably he was testing the truth of his statement when the car refused to follow the turn in the road. No harm done. No delay.

"On another occasion when we were returning to Spirit River from Fairview our car developed engine trouble just as we approached the town garage. We stopped for help. The station attendant remarked that the car might operate better if we had a gas tank. The tank had dropped off a little distance down the street but the reserve gas in the carburetor had carried us into town. We retraced our path and recovered the gas tank. What a story we now had! On first telling the gas tank was found a mile down the road. After the story had been told and re-told many times, it appeared that the tank had dropped off near Dunvegan but John's speed sufficed to carry us to Spirit River."

Another story is possibly apocryphal but reveals the character and personality of the old warrior as much as more validly documented tales. Barnett was on one of his safaris to defend a young teacher to whom the ruthless school trustees had done wrong. He discovered at his destination that the nefarious school board chairman was apparently on his death bed and would indeed die if he could not receive a blood transfusion. In those unsophisticated days before blood banks, a live donor was imperatively necessary. Somehow Barnett discovered that his blood was the required type and promtly volunteered for the transfusion which saved the trustee's life. Commended on contributing his heart's blood to an avowed enemy of the profession, Barnett growled that he had done so only to prevent the chairman, whom he intimated had been born on the wrong side of the blanket, from so easily escaping the Barnett wrath.

Dr. LaZerte concludes his memoir (p. 9) with the tribute he paid his old trail-mate on the occasion of the opening of Barnett House in 1962:

"The outstanding figure in the ATA, the dominating personality in the organization from 1917 until his death on June 29th, 1947, was Dr. John W. Barnett, who with industry, patience and fearlessness, worked day and night, in season and out, for both the improvement of the teachers' social and economic status and the general welfare of education in the Province."

II

The Association

The Teaching Profession Act

WITHOUT DOUBT the legislation of greatest significance to the ATA is that embodied in the Teaching Profession Act of 1935 and amendments of 1936 and after. The Alliance had always advocated an organization comprising all certificated teachers in public education at the elementary and secondary levels. Such a situation applies in other professions like pharmacy, law, architecture, medicine, and nursing. Establishment of a similar body for teaching would bring many advantages. For one thing, the tremendous cost in money, time, and effort devoted each year to building and rebuilding the Alliance's membership would be saved, and would be available for more productive projects. For another, if the ATA could speak for all teachers instead of just some of them, its influence would be that much greater with the legislature, the government, the press, the trustees, and the general public. With 100 per cent membership it could establish codes governing professional conduct and put some teeth in them. Finally, legislative endorsement of the ATA would go far, it was felt, to implement recognition of teaching as a profession comparable to those others and endow it with prestige in proportion. Powell has outlined the circumstances which led to the passage of this crucial statute:

The declining years of the U.F.A. administration (1934-35) were years of sheer frustration for the Alliance. The best efforts of their Executives had only partially stemmed the economic debacle for the teachers; one by one their small legal gains in security of tenure were annulled. To the A.T.A. it seemed that every interest of the teachers was being tossed away to appease the U.F.A. caucus, angry and distraught at the loss of its leader and Premier, John E. Brownlee. Then the Hon. Perren Baker came forward with a proposal which rocked us all by its sheer unexpectedness. He would introduce a Teaching Profession Bill, which would establish the A.T.A. as the legal entity of the teachers of Alberta, on a par with the medical, dental and legal professions. Perren Baker was a shrewd, down-to-earth thinker; he had doubtless made up his mind that the A.T.A. was here to stay, and that now was the time to remodel its image before the public. Hitherto it had been disliked as a jumped-up, talkative, interfering busybody. It should now be made sober and respectable, and learn more decorous ways.[1]

Actually, it was not all that simple. Discussions between the ATA and the UFA government were on a proposal that a government bill be introduced to establish a teachers' organization to which all teachers would belong as a condition of employment, provided the Alliance could demonstrate that there was a consensus among all teachers, not merely those who already belonged to the ATA. *The ATA Magazine* for October 1934 announced that a ballot on the question was being distributed to the whole teaching body. In January 1935 *The ATA Magazine* was able to announce the result of the poll: favourable 2,770; adverse, 54; majority, 98.4 per cent of the votes cast.

General Secretary Barnett could not envisage any refusal on the part of the legislature to pass the required professional act, for it did not infringe on the curriculum or departmental policies, it did not add to the cost of education or affect taxpayers where it might hurt, in the pocket-book, it had no prejudicial effect on the rights or interest of the general public. Nevertheless, the proposed bill aroused a storm of opposition, chiefly from rural trustees, who felt that if it were passed, they would find themselves at the mercy of a well-disciplined body of teachers who could close their schools if they did not remain in the good graces of the ATA. The government therefore began to hedge on its commitments to the teachers—as usual. The legislation was introduced not as a government measure but as a private bill, sponsored by C. A. Ronning, a Camrose school teacher who was eventually to become one of Canada's most distinguished diplomats. This tactic, of course, allowed for a free vote on the measure; it could be rejected without the government suffering the ignominy of defeat.

The Alberta School Trustees' Association lobbied diligently against the bill,

[1]A. J. H. Powell, "The Alberta Teachers' Alliance" (unpublished memoir, 1962), p. 26.

the Alberta Teachers' Alliance for it. For a period, MLA teachers were virtually members *ex officio* of the ATA executive council. Among these was Isadore Goresky; he and C. L. Gibbs, Labour, had for some time been as it were unofficial ambassadors between the ATA and the UFA government. With a number of amendments the bill was finally passed by a very narrow margin, the vote being 25 to 23. With one of the changes the ATA was in whole-hearted accord. This altered the proposed name of the new organization from Alberta Teachers' Society to Alberta Teachers' Association, thus preserving the initials by which the Alliance was commonly known, a designation to which many veteran teachers and younger ones too had a deep emotional commitment. But the other amendments cut the heart out of the bill: they removed the requirement for automatic or compulsory membership, and they deleted any sections which would have given the Association power to discipline its members. The non-partisan nature of the support of the bill is indicated by the political affiliations of those who voted for it. Its supporters included four Liberals, one Conservative, all three representatives of Labour, the only political party which to that time had been consistently friendly to teachers, and 15 UFA or government members. This last group included the Hon. Irene Parlby, first cabinet minister of her sex in the British Empire, teachers Ronning and Goresky, and former teacher A. G. Andrews, who was to serve many distinguished years as secretary-treasurer of the Alberta School Trustees' Association.

That the farmer members, many of whom were rural trustees themeselves, should have been opposed to the main principal of the legislation, that of compulsory membership, was understandable to the teachers. What aroused the fury of *The ATA Magazine* (or rather, no doubt, of its editor, J. W. Barnett) was that many legislators who enjoyed the privilge of membership in comparable organizations were in the forefront in attacking the teachers' aspirations for the same benefits. His burning sense of injustice found expression in an editorial which appeared in the May issue of the *Magazine:*

"I AM HOLIER THAN THOU"

As one listened to the debates on *The Teaching Profession Act,* 1935 one could not but be impressed by the members of the Legislature who happened to be members of other professional organizations. Hon. Mr. Lymburn the Attorney-General, the ex-premier, J. E. Brownlee, K.C., and Mr. W. R. Howson, K.C., were notable exceptions. Prominent among those leading the attack were L. A. Giroux, barrister, member for Grouard; Dr. W. A. Atkinson, medical doctor, member for Edmonton;

Normand Hindsley, Chartered Accountant, member for Calgary; F. C. Moyer, K.C., member for Drumheller. Not one of the other "professional" men, members of the House, voted in favour of the main principle of the Bill—that of requiring membership in the professional organization as a condition of practice.[2]

The June issue of *The ATA Magazine* announced that The Alberta Teachers' Alliance, Inc. (the ATA) had officially become The Alberta Teachers' Association (the ATA). What else had been accomplished? On the face of it, not much. The Charter obtained under the Societies Act seventeen years before had given the ATA the right to own real property, to sue in a court of law and to be sued, and all the other rights and privileges attendant on the legal existence of a corporation. The Teaching Profession Act of 1935 did no more. Of course, it now made it legal to refer to teaching as a profession, a courtesy which had been extended to the calling for many years.

Allowing its own supporters to emasculate the Teaching Profession Act was the last disappointment which the UFA government administered to the ATA. In August 1935 the movement which had dominated the political landscape for fourteen years was defeated at the polls so resoundingly that not a single UFA candidate was elected. For the first and only time in history a political organization founded on the economic theories of social credit formed a government. The reasons why this off-beat movement, whose ideology seemed a strange blending of fundamentalism, Christianity, socialism, conservatism, and fiscal radicalism was successful are beyond the scope of this work, and in any event have been ably told elsewhere, notably in J. A. Irving's *The Social Credit Movement in Alberta.* After 1935, the government no longer represented a single segment of Alberta society, the agricultural population, but was widely based, drawing its support from small farmers, little storekeepers, wage-earners—those who are sometimes patronizingly called "little people"—and from school teachers and clergymen, those whose classes and congregations were the worst-hit victims of the Great Depression. Other professionals—physicians, dentists, lawyers, professors—and big business men, with a few notable exceptions, opposed the new movement, but they were too few to stem the wave of the future.

The election of the UFA government in 1921 had meant little to the ATA; the advent of the Social Crediters fourteen years later was to be of the most profound significance to the newly renamed Association. William Aberhart, the

[2]Alberta Teachers' Association, *The ATA Magazine,* XV, 9 (May, 1935), 1.

new premier and minister of education, was a Calgary school principal and teacher who had absolute control of his new cohorts. In effect, he had elected them to their offices, not they him. He chose several school teachers as members of his cabinet, and others were ensconced on the government's back benches.

The new government moved vigorously into the field of educational legislation. Within a few years it had made a beginning on a contributory pension scheme for teachers, provided them with the security of tenure, established an independent tribunal to act in the case of dismissals of teachers, set up collective bargaining procedures, introduced the large unit or divisional system of school administration, and initiated moves which were ultimately to place all teacher education in the hands of the provincial university. But probably none of these measures affected the ATA as intimately and profoundly at the time as did the 1936 amendments to the Teaching Profession Act. The new government granted what its predecessor had not dared to: automatic membership in the Association for all teachers in Alberta's public and separate schools, and power to enact by-laws (subject to ratification by the Lieutenant-Governor in Council) which would enable the ATA to discipline members for unprofessional conduct, even to the point of recommending suspension or cancellation of an erring teachers's certificates, and having the recommendation accepted.

There was one slight and temporary exception to the principle of automatic membership in the ATA for all practising teachers. This exception affected religious orders. Only one member of each order was required to belong to the ATA in order to validate the teaching credentials of all her sisters or his brothers in Christ. However, within a few short years the Act was further amended to include all practising teachers without exception.

From time to time, irate trustees or members of the public have accused the ATA not only of being a labour union, the most powerful in Alberta if not in all Canada, but of insisting on a closed shop as well. The first accusation does not ruffle the mature and experienced teacher, even though he might not agree, for he knows that many of Alberta's best citizens are proud of their labour affiliations. When the critic further charges that teachers are not professional because they (rarely) go on strike, the teacher need only remind said critic that it is not unknown for doctors and nurses to withdraw their services, even though they may not call such action a strike. That the teachers insist on a closed shop, however, is patently untrue.

Where a closed shop exists, an employer may not hire a worker unless he is a member of a union with which the employer has a contract, unless the union certifies that no union member is available. In such cases, the employer may then hire non-union labour as a rule, and the employee is generally given a certain length of time to join the union. Often such membership obligates the initiate not only to pay regular union dues but a high initiation fee as well. Unions in highly skilled trades—and these are ones where closed shop agreements are common—also have a great deal of influence on entrance into the trade, not only in the setting of formal admission requirements and the length and kind of training, but often in covertly applying other criteria as well. The most frequent of these have to do with race, ethnic background, and nepotism—sponsorship by a member of the union. It is notorious that in certain parts of North America it is impossible, even today, for a Negro to become an apprentice in certain trades, and extremely difficult for anyone other than a brother, son, or nephew of a member to do so.

The Teaching Profession Act does not require a person to be a member of the ATA in order to apply for and accept a position. On the contrary, it requires the Association to admit him to membership (without initiation fee) once he is appointed. For this reason, membership in the Association is more correctly termed automatic than compulsory; the latter term suggests that the teacher must be a member of the organization when he applies for a position. The former implies that he becomes a member as soon as he begins to teach.

From time to time the Association has been criticized for not taking some responsibility for the professional short-falls of its members. It surely does insist on adherence to its code of professional conduct and can be quite harsh to teachers who knowingly flout it. But with respect to the professional adequacy of its members, officers of the ATA point out that until the Association is responsible for establishing the standards which those entering the profession must meet, and the kind of professional preparation they receive, the ATA can hardly be held responsible for their deficiencies.

The Teaching Profession Act with the all-important amendments added by the first Social Credit government had tremendous consequences for the ATA, both long-term and immediate. Among the latter was the fact that no longer did the general secretary-treasurer and others have to make colossal expenditures of time, energy, and money to maintain the Association's membership roster and its exchequer; these resources could now be devoted to other projects, both welfare and professional. On the financial side, not only did money not have to be spent on annual membership drives but the Association's income was also increased, since all teachers instead of just two-thirds of them or thereabouts were now contributing to the organization's coffers. The difference in additional fees, of course, was by no means all gravy, for with additional membership came added problems and added costs. In balance, however, the ATA now found itself for the first time with an assured and adequate income for the tasks which it had assigned itself.

One may wonder what would have happened if the vital automatic membership clause had not been incorporated into the Teaching Profession Act. With the growing structurization of Canadian society, in which today even civil servants are being given the right to collective bargaining, the long-term difference would probably have been slight. As more and more teachers joined the ATA—something that rising salaries of the post-war era made more and more feasible—the pressure on the decreasing proportion of non-members to unite with their colleagues would become less and less resistable. Had the automatic membership change never been made in the statute, perhaps only 95 per cent of the province's teachers would today belong to the Alberta Teachers' Association, instead of 100 per cent.

The long-term, non-economic results of automatic and therefore 100 per cent membership in the Association are perhaps not all apparent, even now. For one thing, the change gave the ATA the right to speak for all Alberta teachers, not just for some of them. In time, the Association's voice changed in tenor from shrill assertiveness to quiet self-confidence. Its officers and committeemen could claim that they and no one else spoke for the teachers; all pretensions to the contrary were specious. Whether the forum was a departmental curriculum committee room, an examination board, a session of the board of teacher education and certification, a trustees' or other convention hall, a bargaining session with an obdurate school board, a meeting of the University of Alberta Senate or of its education faculty council, the Association's representatives could claim that just as their medical or legal opposite numbers spoke for all the physicians or lawyers, so did they for all the teachers.

Magistri Neque Servi—at last!

Old Wine in a New Wineskin

DURING THE DECADE which followed the 1935 electoral success of the Social Credit movement the newly renamed Alberta Teachers' Association changed in many ways. At the beginning of the period it consisted of voluntary members, each of whom joined the ATA and remained therein because he believed in the Association. Sometimes it was because of the firmest conviction that a brighter and richer future for themselves was possible only through the efforts of all teachers working together for the common welfare. Sometimes teachers joined because they sincerely believed that the ATA was good for Alberta education. Others no doubt had other motivations: the fellowship that came from meeting regularly with colleagues who had the same problems and the same interests, or the social pressure not to be isolated. No doubt the motives of most were quite mixed, but for many, especially those who quickly or gradually found themselves committed to a lifetime of teaching, membership in their own organization was an integral part of their way of life.

With the 1936 amendments to the Teaching Profession Act which made adherence to the ATA a condition of employment, the character of the membership changed somewhat. Now the Association's ranks included many who were indifferent to it—otherwise they would already have joined—some who were actively hostile, a number who were antipathetic to the general secretary-treasurer personally or to other officers, a few who were opposed in principle, and even those with a foot in the trustees' camp: sons, daughters, and wives of school board members. All of these people the Association had to consider. L. G. Hall tells how it did so:

> Many teachers who had never belonged to the Alliance now found themselves included in an association from which they could not withdraw and to which was given the power to exercise control over the activities of its members. It took some time and patient tolerance to persuade teachers who were forced into membership to identify their interests with the policies and actions of the Association. But newsletters, bulletins, and relationships with others in local organizations facilitated the growth of more common attitudes.[1]

Another legislative change which affected the ATA, this time in its structure, consisted of the amendments to the School Act which established Baker's long-sought school divisions. The legislation was passed in 1936; the first eleven were created in 1937, mostly in the depressed southeast corner of the province. Another eleven followed in 1938; in 1939 most of the remaining populated areas of the province were included in another 22. Although a few more were to follow, by the outbreak of World War II the job was virtually completed.

Originally, each school division consisted only of rural school districts, typically, 50 to 100 or more of them. Urban, town, village, and consolidated districts were not originally included, although subsequently most of the public districts, except urban, entered the divisions on their own volition. A typical division would be 20 to 30 miles in width, 40 to 60 in length. It was controlled by an elected board of trustees, usually numbering three to five, each chosen to represent a specific area, called a sub-division. Chief instructional officer was the superintendent of schools, appointed and paid by the department of education. The school divisions and districts within their boundaries replaced the former inspectorates; in fact, the school inspectors were the ones who became the superintendents.

From its beginning the ATA had been organized in branches known officially as Local Alliances, more commonly as Locals. Each Local had a minimum number of members, perhaps as few as ten, who were employed in the same general geographical area. In some Locals, all members taught for the same school district, as in the cities. In rural areas, each member might theoretically be employed by a different district, as the sole teacher in its one-room school.

[1] L. G. Hall, "A Historical Study of Salary Payments to Teachers and of the Emergence of Principles of Salary Scheduling in Alberta," unpublished doctoral dissertation, University of Toronto (1967), p. 111.

Usually, however, the Local was organized around a nucleus consisting of the staffs of one or more graded schools. With new schools being opened, old ones being closed temporarily or permanently, and with constant change of teachers, who had varying degrees of commitment to the ATA, the Locals tended to have rather amorphous geographic boundaries. To provide greater stability to its grass-roots structure, before 1935 the Alliance had made some progress in organizing the rural Locals into Districts. Usually each of these coincided more or less with the department of education inspectorates, an obvious advantage when it is remembered that the fall teachers' conventions were organized on the same principle.

This District principle served the ATA in good stead when the school divisions were erected. Charters for the previously existing rural Locals were cancelled and new ones were chartered, each of which included in its membership all the teachers employed by a single school division plus those who taught in the town, village, and consolidated districts inside the boundaries of the division. The new organization had a number of advantages. All of the teachers, except those in the high school, were under the supervision of the same school superintendent. Again excepting the high school teachers, and those only temporarily, all attended the same fall conventions, when Local meetings could easily be arranged. But more important, when collective bargaining was introduced, all the teachers employed by any one school board were members of the same Local, which therefore became the proper and logical agency to represent the teachers in salary negotiations.

In most cases outside the cities, the previously existing Locals reverted to sub-local status, and the Sub-Locals received certificates rather than charters. The Locals proved to be much more stable organizations than the Sub-Locals. The former had a continuing economic function of vital importance to the individual teachers. The latter were left to function in the professional rather than in the economic field. Sub-Locals waxed and waned in accordance with the enthusiasm and particular interests of a few individual members. Thus at the AGM the general secretary would report on the numbers of Locals and Sub-Locals. He was always very specific as to the number of the former, but never announced the total of the Sub-Locals except approximately.

There were—and still are—a few anomalies in the organization of Local associations. The norm was for all teachers in the employ of one school district

Former Imperial Bank of Canada building, Jasper Avenue and 100 Street, Edmonton, long the home of the ATA. (Photo by McDermid Studios, Edmonton)

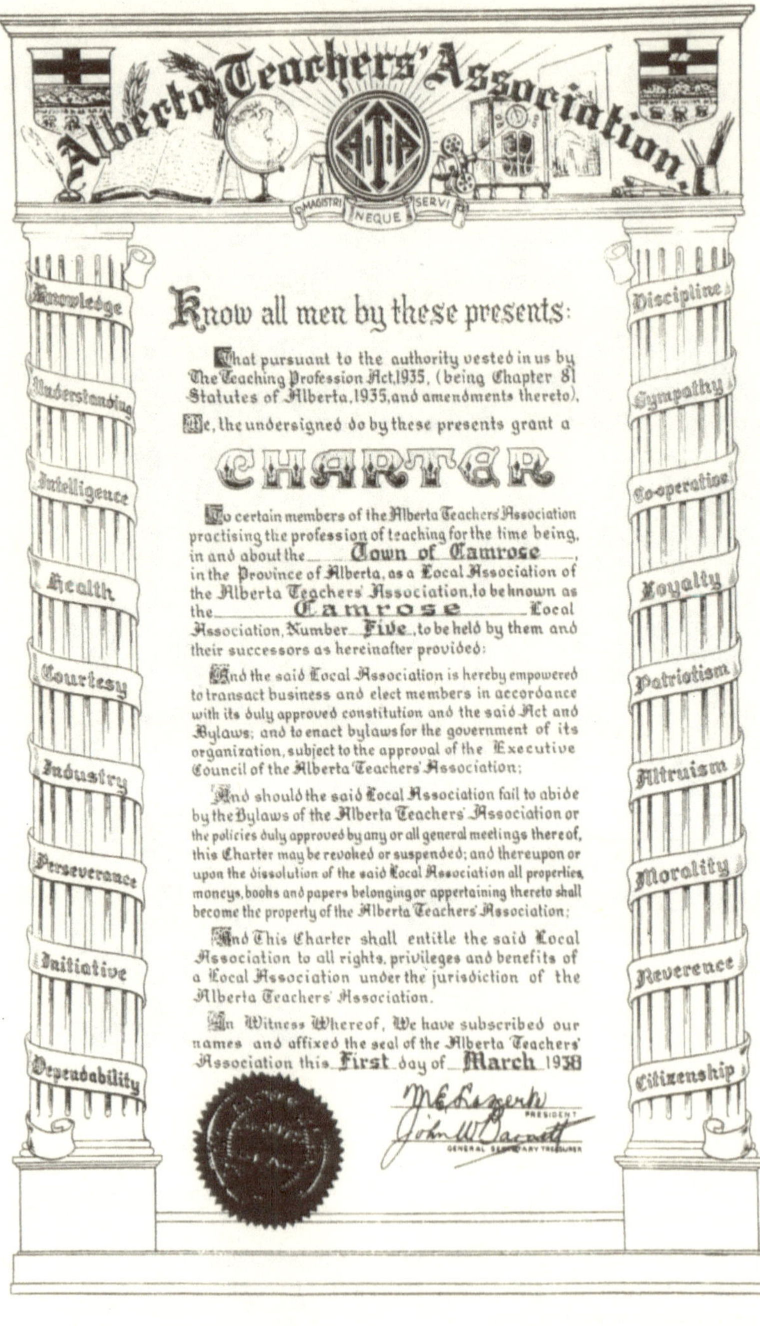
Alberta Teachers' Association.

MAGISTRI NEQUE SERVI

Knowledge · Understanding · Intelligence · Health · Courtesy · Industry · Perseverance · Initiative · Dependability

Discipline · Sympathy · Co-operation · Loyalty · Patriotism · Altruism · Morality · Reverence · Citizenship

Know all men by these presents:

That pursuant to the authority vested in us by The Teaching Profession Act, 1935, (being Chapter 81 Statutes of Alberta, 1935, and amendments thereto),

We, the undersigned do by these presents grant a

CHARTER

To certain members of the Alberta Teachers' Association practising the profession of teaching for the time being, in and about the Town of Camrose, in the Province of Alberta, as a Local Association of the Alberta Teachers' Association, to be known as the Camrose Local Association, Number Five, to be held by them and their successors as hereinafter provided:

And the said Local Association is hereby empowered to transact business and elect members in accordance with its duly approved constitution and the said Act and Bylaws; and to enact bylaws for the government of its organization, subject to the approval of the Executive Council of the Alberta Teachers' Association;

And should the said Local Association fail to abide by the Bylaws of the Alberta Teachers' Association or the policies duly approved by any or all general meetings thereof, this Charter may be revoked or suspended; and thereupon or upon the dissolution of the said Local Association all properties, moneys, books and papers belonging or appertaining thereto shall become the property of the Alberta Teachers' Association;

And This Charter shall entitle the said Local Association to all rights, privileges and benefits of a Local Association under the jurisdiction of the Alberta Teachers' Association.

In Witness Whereof, We have subscribed our names and affixed the seal of the Alberta Teachers' Association this First day of March 1938

M.E. Lazerte
PRESIDENT

John W. Barnett
GENERAL SECRETARY TREASURER

to belong to the same Local, but it was many years before this state of affairs was achieved in Edmonton and Calgary. In both cities there existed teachers' groups antecedent to the incorporation of the Alberta Teachers' Alliance in 1918. In each city, one association consisted of teachers in the public (that is, elementary) schools; the other, those who taught in the high schools. Heirs of what for Alberta was a long tradition, they saw no reason to demolish their organizations at the behest of the upstart ATA. Since they were employed under differing salary schedules, they did not even see the necessity to unite for the purposes of collective bargaining. However, when legislation required the school district after 1941 to adopt "a salary schedule," they did join forces, but for negotiation purposes only. It was only after some years, considerable intergroup tension, and much pressure from the executive council of the ATA that they gave up their separate identities to become the Locals of the Edmonton and Calgary public school districts in fact as well as in name.

In December 1936 the executive council of the ATA resolved: "That Charters be issued to all City Locals recognized as at December 31, 1936, and that no further Charters be issued in the Cities; and further that there be a definite statement of policy that as far as possible the Executive should encourage only one local for each City school board."[2] In 1938 the council further enunciated its policy in its resolution: "That we re-affirm our position as being opposed to the granting of a charter or certificate to locals or sub-locals based on sex lines."[3]

Apparently it was one thing to affirm a position; another to maintain it. In December 1938 the council received a Calgary delegation contending that an AGM statement of policy disapproving the establishment of components of the ATA on sex lines was not intended to apply to Sub-Locals, but the general secretary reported that an AGM resolution on the matter had been tabled for a year; in other words, the matter was still under advisement. The Calgary group wanted three Sub-Locals for the public school district in that city: elementary, junior, and senior high school, "and that any group made up of not less than 50 teachers be allowed to form a fourth sub-local,"[4] an obvious reference to the desire of the male teachers to have their own component. The council

[2]ATA Ex., Dec. 29-30, 1936.
[3]*Ibid.*, April 18, 1938.
[4]*Ibid.*, Dec. 28-30, 1938.

reacted in a typically Canadian fashion; they attempted to straddle the issue by resolving: "That this Executive reaffirm the principle of issuing only one charter to teacher employees of the Calgary School Board No. 19 and this Executive goes on record as stating that they will consider recommendations from any body receiving a charter regarding the formation of one or more sub-locals and the issuance of certification thereto."[5]

Nor was the executive council able to hold to its position that all teachers employed by any one employer should belong to the same Local. In 1941 it came to the council's attention that one Local, the Edmonton Teachers' Association, had not in fact been acting as such since 1938. Apparently, in fact, and unconstitutionally the Sub-Locals had been receiving from the Association the capitation grants which should have been going to the Local. Accordingly, it was therefore decided that ". . . this Executive will not authorize in future any constitution whereby money is paid directly to Sub-Locals,"[6] and a new constitution was ordered.

Two years later the situation was still not settled, for H. C. Clark appeared before the council to argue that case for an Edmonton high schol Local, on the grounds that the existing Local was not representative of the secondary school teachers. He noted that the negotiated cost-of-living bonus applied only on salaries to $2,200, whereas some or most high school teachers were above this figure. Further, with the recently proposed single rather than positional schedule, the high school teachers were apprehensive that, since they constituted only a minority of the staff, their interests would not be protected. T. D. Baker, on behalf of the Edmonton Local, admitted the fact that the high school contingent were a minority of the staff, but could not recall that their interests had ever been sacrificed. The nub of the high school teacher's request was that they wanted Local status so that they could negotiate with the Edmonton public school board on their own behalf independently of the other teachers. The council resolved: "That this matter be referred to the Edmonton Local and sub-locals and that they attempt to arrive at a satisfactory conclusion and that all groups notify the Provincial Executive in regard to their opinion."[7]

Despite its previously stated position opposing the chartering of more than

[5]*Ibid.*
[6]*Ibid.*, Dec. 29-31, 1941.
[7]*Ibid.*, Dec. 28-29, 1943.

one Local for one employer, the council apparently reversed its field and granted the request of the Edmonton teachers, for the following year it unanimously approved the granting of Local status to the system's intermediate (that is, junior high) school teachers. One cannot help but feel that the council was following the dictates of expediency bowing to the pressure exerted by a large and influential group rather than enunciating a defensible principle, for in 1939 it had refused to grant Local status to teachers in Red Deer and Drumheller, even though these two groups were seeking to follow the pattern of "one Local, one employer," the reverse of the "one employer, one Local" coin.

Shortly after the end of World War II the ATA was faced with another constitutional problem. In the early thirties it had encouraged the formation of ATA Districts, each encompassing all the Locals in a particular inspectorate, but with the formation of school divisions during the period from 1937 to 1942 these bodies became obsolete, becoming in effect the new-model Locals. By 1945 the District had reappeared when council member A. O. Aalborg requested that council agenda be sent and grants made to the District Council of Central Eastern Alberta. Both requests were refused, the latter because there was no constitutional provision for such grants; the former because it was regarded apparently as an attempt to limit the council in its constitutional authority.

However, the problem would not go away. The following year the Calgary District Council requested copies of the executive council minutes and payment of transportation expenses for persons attending its meetings. This time the executive council referred the matter to the Association solicitor and received the opinion that it would be unconstitutional to grant the requests. Apparently this opinion agreed with the council's sentiment, for the request was refused. The ATA would continue as it always had, a federation of Local Associations (formerly Alliances) with its executive council elected by the direct franchise of its individual members.

Other Locals which did not fit the pattern included optional rather than statutory members. Two of these were organizations of the Edmonton and Calgary normal school students, the only Locals whose members did not have at least the minimum licence to teach in Alberta. Perhaps it was for this reason, after the normal schools were closed, that these Locals were subtly phased out of existence. Another Local, that of the Correspondence School Branch, consisted entirely of optional members. It was organized in 1941 at the suggestion of the then director of the Branch. He felt that it could do a number of things for its members, such as press for portability of pension rights between the Teachers' Retirement Fund and the Alberta government's scheme, an objective achieved some years after the government authorities explained that it was quite impossible. The director also felt that membership in a Local of the ATA would heighten the sense of professional identity of the correspondence school teachers, who by the nature of their employment tended to be rather isolated from their colleagues in the classrooms. Since the correspondence teachers were civil servants, they were not able to use their organization to negotiate salaries, but the Local was and is active in making representations to the government on such things as pay rates, educational leave, attendance at annual teachers' conventions, and the like. The Local also devotes considerable attention to purely professional aspects of teaching. Its success, despite the voluntary nature of its membership, is witnessed by the fact that in 1966 it celebrated its twenty-fifth anniversary with a well-attended tea.

ATA Locals have a very definite function in the provincial direction of the Association. From the beginning, the annual general meeting, now known as the annual representative assembly—"the parliament of the ATA"—has consisted of delegates sent from the Locals. Locals are also grouped to form the constituencies which choose members of the executive council.

Reconstructing the Locals to parallel the employment pattern did not lead immediately and inevitably to collective bargaining as it is known to Alberta teachers today, although the teachers tried to use their Association for this purpose as soon as the divisions were established. Like every other right they enjoy, they had to win this one in a struggle that extended over a period of some years. First step towards collective bargaining between teachers and school divisions was made through the legislation which established the new units. This required each divisional board to prepare and adopt a salary schedule applicable to all of its teachers; however, the statute neither required the schedule to be adopted as a result of collective bargaining nor did it define what a salary schedule was. As Hall notes, "This procedure of merely specifying salaries on the basis of certain qualifications was apparently interpreted as 'the preparation and adoption of a salary schedule.' "[8] The qualifications included

[8]Hall, "Salary Payments," p. 120.

such factors as certificate held, grades taught, experience, and teaching load. In 1937 the new Berry Creek school division adopted a schedule which paid teachers either $620, $640, or $675 a year, except that the high school staff were passing rich at $720.[9] In 1941 the School Act was amended to require districts as well as divisions to adopt salary schedules.

If the unilateral adoption of schedules did not commit school boards to collective bargaining, it at least eliminated the unprofessional act of underbidding for jobs which advertisements reading "State salary expected" had encouraged. With its newly won disciplinary powers the ATA was equipped to cope with this type of behaviour on the part of its own members, but not on the part of teachers from other provinces and elsewhere, since they were not ATA members until they started teaching.

Salary scheduling principles developed slowly. It was not until 1938 that the policy of paying increments for experience, especially in other school systems, was generally adopted. In this matter, legislation lagged behind common practice; not until 1942 did the School Act, by defining salary schedules, require that they must stipulate the number and amount of increments.

Since the School Act did not require that salary schedules be adopted as a result of collective bargaining, teachers soon sought to achieve this goal under other legislation. A 1937 statute, The Freedom of Trade Union Association Act, granted trade unions the right to collective bargaining. Both the Associations' legal counsel and the attorney-general's department of the provincial government were of the opinion that teachers might be considered as employees within the meaning of this act, although this contention was never tested in the courts. In any event, the following year this statute was replaced by The Industrial Conciliation and Arbitration Act, "but general opinion appeared to be that the Act was inapplicable to teachers or trustees."[10] However, 1941 amendments broadened the scope of the act to include teachers and made collective bargaining obligatory under the threat of penalties for employers who refused to engage in it. The changes also provided for appointment of a conciliation commissioner and appeal to an impartial board of arbitrators. At the same session of the legislature, "The School Act was also amended to state that teachers of a division would negotiate a salary schedule applicable to all teachers

[9] *Ibid.*
[10] *Ibid.*, p. 125.

within the division. Further amendments limited the power of the Board of Reference to dealing only with dismissals, as labour legislation now established authority for negotiation and collective bargaining."[11]

There were still two problems. Just as the earlier legislation had not defined "schedule," the more recent did not spell out what was meant by "collective bargaining," nor did it require school boards to reach an agreement with teachers before the adoption of a schedule. Some boards were naive enough apparently to believe that for them to make an offer (knowing beforehand that it would probably be rejected) constituted collective bargaining, and that upon its rejection they were free to adopt schedules unilaterally. Such action left the teachers free to invoke the remedies available under the Industrial Conciliation and Arbitration Act.

During the early 1940's, adoption of salary schedules was affected by two circumstances: the statutory minimum of $840 still applied, as it had since 1918, and many school boards in their own opinion (and apparently that of the minister of education) were not able to pay it. Before the introduction of the school divisions and the legal requirements for salary schedules and collective bargaining, the problem had usually been resolved by the minister's giving permission for the district board to pay its one (or occasionally two) teachers less than $840 a year. But to approve payment of a salary of say $700 on the part of a single little impoverished district for one individual teacher, and that for one year only, or at most a year at a time, was one thing. To authorize a large system to pay many or most of its teachers less than $840, especially when the system was required to adopt a schedule with increments for service, was something else. On the one hand, the ATA had never conceded that a minimum below $1,100 was acceptable, let alone one below $840. On the other hand, many school trustees seemed to be psychologically incapable of accepting a minimum above $700, a figure which they had used for more than a decade. Furthermore, even in the early 1940's Alberta was only slowly and painfully emerging from the depression which had hung like a blight over the foothills province since the late twenties.

In a number of divisions the dilemma was solved by the adoption of a schedule based on an $840 minimum plus increments and other adjustments, but less an over-all percentage reduction which in 1941 averaged 8 per cent for

[11] *Ibid.*, pp. 125-26.

19 divisions. In this way the teachers did not accept a sub-$840 minimum as anything other than a temporary expedient, while for the time being those 19 divisional boards were not required to pay at a level which they felt their taxpayers could not afford.

Becoming somewhat more realistic in settling their acceptable minimum, in 1942 the ATA abandoned their previous aspirations for $1,100 and instead adopted minima of $1,000, $1,100, and $1,300 for elementary, junior, and senior high school levels, an interesting example of its tacit acceptance of the principle of positional (that is, grade level) schedules. The Association pushed very vigorously for these levels, both in their negotiations and in publicity directed to their own members, to the legislature, and to other interested parties. They were not wholly successful, but in 1943 the legislators did raise the statutory minimum to $900, the first time in twenty-five years that it had been above the original $840. Contrary to the ATA's experience in the 1920's and 1930's, this time around it was supported by most metropolitan dailies, although a number of small-town weeklies were opposed.

At this period, the development of collective bargaining was affected by two war-inspired measures of the federal government. One was a prohibition of wage increases to industrial workers, coupled with requirements for the payment of cost-of-living bonuses. The teachers immediately sought and often received such bonuses, but many school boards interpreted the wage freeze as a prohibition of any increases, including annual increments. Such action, of course, the teachers protested, claiming that increments for experience were contractual obligations, outside the intent of the wage freeze order. Hall concludes: "The request for inclusion of teachers in the Order-in-Council may have been ill-advised as it invited application of other features of the order prohibiting salary increases."[12]

The other war-time measure which affected collective bargaining was an order-in-council dated June 17, 1943, freezing teachers to their profession. The order was not absolute; it did not prevent a man from joining one of the armed forces, for example, or a woman from going into an essential industry such as aircraft inspection. The order had been passed at the behest of the various ministers of education, who were dismayed at the exodus from the classrooms. The teachers bitterly resented the order, for it froze them to a low-paying

[12]*Ibid.*, p. 139.

occupation where salary levels were also frozen. Hall mentions another objection to this order:

> The freezing order had been issued in June but applied only to those who had been teaching in April; thus teachers-in-training or others need not accept teaching positions. Requests for amendment or repeal of the order were rejected although the retroactive date was changed to the third week of June. A year later in answer to continued protests a proclamation was issued ". . . a permit to leave the teaching profession might be granted if it should be shown that lower salaries were resulting from this order."[13]

It was only after considerable pain and travail that school boards learned that collective bargaining meant that school boards had to go right down the line to agreement with teachers before they could adopt a salary schedule. Apparently, although certain school boards knew that teachers could strike—they had done so in Edmonton as early as 1921—they did not seem to believe that it could happen to them. They rationalized that male members who had vested interests in the communities where they lived, for example, ownership of their own homes, would not place themselves for trivial reasons in the position of having to sell those homes and move to new positions. They could not credit that married women teachers tied to the community by their husband's occupations would for trivial reasons vote for strikes and put themselves out of work, since they could not well move to other positions. In this conclusion the trustees were right; what they did not understand was what constituted trivial reasons. They did not realize that it was usually not a matter of $100 a year more or less in their salaries that brought teachers to the brink of strike action. The issues as the teachers saw them and as the trustees did not were professional solidarity and the principle that the teachers should have as much voice in what would be the rewards of their labour as did their employers. Perhaps the trustees might have grasped the point more quickly if the ATA motto of "Magistri Neque Servi" had been proclaimed in a tongue less recondite than Latin. In any event, many school boards reacted with a distinct sense of shock when they learned that members of their instructional staffs, who in their opinion were being well treated, voted in favour of strike action by majorities of more than 90 per cent. Such results hurried many school boards back to the bargaining table.

[13] *Ibid.*, p. 140.

But not all. A vote in favour of a strike is not necessarily followed by strike action, and in 1942 no Alberta classroom had been closed by withdrawal of teachers' services. The Edmonton high school strike of 1921 and that in Blairmore a few years later following a lock-out did not close the schools. Perhaps it was a feeling of false confidence that in the spring of 1942 led the small Mundare school district to reject an arbitration award covering the 1941-1942 school year, and then, in the face of threatened strike action, to concede only that it would pay at the arbitrated figure for the remaining three months of the school year, but would reserve the right then to dismiss all teachers and adopt a new schedule. On May 1 the teachers struck; three days later the school board accepted the arbitration award unconditionally.

In the fall of the same year a much more prolonged shut-down occurred in Vegreville, when the school board reneged on its commitment to accept an arbitration award. The 62 teachers, as a result of a 55-3 vote, went on strike on November 10; the school remained closed until January, when intervention by the department of education resulted in a settlement close to but somewhat under the arbitration award. Hall comments: "The strike may have served as a test case to test the support of the Association and the application of the labour legislation."[14] Certainly it proved the first contention: members of the ATA supported their colleagues in their walk-out to the extent of a voluntary contribution of $1 per member per month for the duration of the strike and one more month. The striking teachers were assured of an income rate which would equal that of the final settlement. In all, the teachers were out for 33 teaching days.

Although the Association was ever mindful of the climate of opinion in which it sought to bargain for a better deal for its members, it did not forget or allow its members to forget that negotiations were conducted not with the public or the newspapers or even the department of education, but with school boards one by one. Every agreement, even every proposal, had to be examined to see that the boards were not violating or seeking to violate the spirit of the legislation, even though they might be adhering to its letter. Some attempted to rob Peter (the tenant) to pay Peter (the teacher) by charging exorbitant teacherage rentals and/or by charging for unused teacherages. *The ATA Magazine* for March 1942 advised teachers on teacherage rentals as follows: (1) the ATA and the department of education would investigate complaints; (2) rental

[14]*Ibid.*, p. 151.

charges are subject to ministerial approval; (3) the teacher is under no liability if the teacherage is not used; (4) School boards have no right to deduct rental from a teacher's cheque without prior agreement.[15]

The following month the editor revealed other schemes that some nefarious trustees were attempting to concoct, for instance, adopting a schedule but deferring its implementation to some future (and unspecified) date, or granting a cost-of-living bonus in lieu of rather than in addition to promised increments.[16]

The following year the executive council gave some attention to an escape clause submitted by school boards in Wheatland school division and elsewhere to the effect that the board reserved the right to place any teacher on its staff on any step of its schedule or at any specified salary. In the opinion of the Association's solicitor, adoption of such a clause abrogated the whole schedule. It did, in fact, tie the teachers to an agreement, but permitted the school board to violate it (in one direction) at their will. The council recommended as a replacement clause: "In case any teacher newly appointed to the staff is engaged at a rate of salary higher than the salary of the class of teachers to which the appointee belongs, the schedule with respect to that class of teachers shall automatically be raised for all."[17]

By the time World War II had ended, both teachers and trustees pretty well understood the nature of collective bargaining. They were negotiating agreements the baroque complexity of which was in sharp contrast to the relatively Doric simplicity of today's contracts. Allowances were made for all kinds of factors besides those of professional preparation, experience, and administrative responsibilities, which are the heart of present agreements. These allowances were for such things as special certificates "if used," for example, in music, drama, typewriting; special subjects taught, such as home economics and industrial arts; heavy teaching load; cost of living; responsibility for dependents; occasionally type of certification, which usually affected the number of increments for which a teacher was eligible rather than basic salary. Grade level taught was often a factor also, high school teachers either receiving a bonus on

[15]*The ATA Magazine,* XXII, 7 (March 1942), 5.

[16]*Ibid.,* XXII, 8 (April 1942), 1-3.

[17]ATA Ex., April 29, 1943.

the basic salary or being paid according to a schedule entirely different from that which applied to other teachers.

The year 1947 saw completion of the evolution of legislation governing salary negotiations between teachers and school boards, when the Alberta Labour Act was passed. This act consolidated all labour statutes administered by the board of industrial relations. "Henceforth, teacher–school board relations proceeded on the following levels: local bargaining agent, conciliation commissioner, and conciliation board. If no agreement is reached at this level, teachers may take a strike vote, but even after such a vote or after a strike has begun, negotiations may continue through mediation on the part of the Board of Industrial Relations."[18] Thereafter, although salary schedules have changed, and in respects other than that of salaries to be paid to teachers in different classifications, the method of reaching agreements has not altered.

Statutes other than those which affected salaries and collective bargaining also appeared early in the Social Credit government's legislative programme. In 1937, legislation was passed which has formed the basis of teacher tenure in Alberta ever since, and except in one respect it has remained, despite numerous amendments, almost unchanged for over thirty years. In summary, the legislation provided that no teacher could be dismissed except for cause or disappearance of his position, and that each dismissal, before or after being made, was subject to review or appeal. Specifically, the legislation did the following:

1. Replaced all term with continuous contracts. (With the advent of collective bargaining, individual contracts were replaced by group agreements. The prescribed formalities for appointment became an offer of employment by a school board, acceptance by the teacher, and board confirmation of appointment, all in writing.)

2. Notice of resignation on the part of the teacher or of dismissal by the school board was required to be submitted by specified dates near the end of the school year.

3. Teachers could appeal dismissals to the newly reconstituted Board of Reference, and pending that Board's decision, the teachers' positions remained open.

4. Teachers could be dismissed for cause at any time during the school year

[18] J. W. Chalmers, *Schools of the Foothills Province* (Toronto, 1967), p. 455.

with the permission of the minister of education, rather than that of the school inspector, as formerly, on thirty days' notice.

5. Teachers could be dismissed summarily for cause at any time during the school year, subject to appeal to the minister.

6. No contract with a teacher might require him to perform janitor or other non-teaching duties. (Those might, however, be arranged through a separate contract.)

7. The minimum salary of $840 remained, with trustees personally as well as corporately responsible for its payment.

The one important change since adoption has been a 1962 amendment which withdrew tenure from teachers during their first year of service with a school system. This change was sought by ASTA, resisted by ATA. In effect, it is a compromise, the ATA feeling that mature experienced teachers especially should not be subject to loss of tenure when they go to a new employer, who might terminate their employment for frivolous or capricious reasons. The ASTA, on the other hand, holds that a single year may not be long enough to determine if a particular teacher is unsatisfactory to the extent that he should be dismissed, since possibly a transfer to another position or increased experience or supervisory help might be all that is needed to convert an inadequate into a competent teacher. Yet under the present legislation the school board may be reluctant to continue that teacher's appointment into a second year and so give him tenure. The trustees have therefore continued to press for what is really a probationary period of two years.

However, it was one thing to enact amendments to the School Act which gave teachers the security of tenure that they had so long sought; it was something else to persuade school boards that the legislation meant what it said. The result was that for a few years there were a great many appeals against end-of-year dismissals. *The ATA Magazine* in October 1937 reported that in 57 appeals to the Board of Reference, the teachers had been sustained in 41 cases, and at least another 20 notices of dismissal had been withdrawn.[19] Within a few years, however, school boards realized that they had to have strong and verifiable grounds for dismissals, and appeals dropped virtually to the vanishing point. In some recent years there have been only one or two cases; in others none at all.

[19]*The ATA Magazine*, XVIII, 2 (Oct. 1937), 23-24.

The idea that security of tenure applied to all teachers was equally one that trustees found difficulty in grasping. As late at 1943 they were advocating that school boards be given authority to dismiss women teachers when they married. Apparently the proposal received little consideration, probably because the growing shortage of teachers discouraged trustees from seriously suggesting that a board dispense with the services of any qualified and able teacher willing to serve. The idea was actually a hangover from the days of the Great Depression when there was a surplus of qualified personnel in Alberta and a strong feeling that no family should have two bread-winners when others had none, and that married women who were teaching were preventing single ones from entering the profession for which they had been prepared.

Another example of proposed sexual discrimination occurred when one school system attempted to retire all female teachers at the age of 60 instead of the usual age of 65. On a test case the Board of Reference ruled that the school system had no power to make such a regulation.

Although as a result of the 1937 and subsequent amendments to the School Act, Alberta teachers probably have greater security of tenure than any other teachers in Canada, this security is not absolute. A teacher may be summarily dismissed for "gross misconduct, neglect of duty, or refusal or neglect to obey any lawful order of the Board."[20] A teacher may also be suspended from duty for the same reasons or because "the presence of a teacher is detrimental to the well-being of the school for reason of mental infirmity."[21]

The Board of Reference is given considerably more latitude in sustaining a school board in a year-end notice of dismissal. The pertinent legislation reads as follows:

Where the board of trustees purports to terminate the contract, if the Board of Reference is satisfied that

(a) the board of trustees in terminating the contract did not act as reasonable persons should act in the discharge of their duties as trustees, and

(b) the contract was not terminated

  (i) because of the misconduct or inefficiency of the teacher,

  (ii) by reason of anything in the mode of life, character, or disposition of the teacher of a nature calculated to make the retention of the teacher detri-

[20]Alberta School Act, (RSA 1955 and amendments), Sec. 350(1).

[21]*Ibid.*, Sec. 350a (b).

mental to the proper and efficient conduct of the school for which the trustees are responsible,

(iii) because of circumstances necessitating a reduction in staff, or

(iv) for the reason that the termination of the contract is conducive to the general welfare of the district and the betterment of the educational facilities therein,

the Board of Reference shall disallow the action of the board of trustees.[22]

In two special fields there have been no improvements in tenure legislation over a period of thirty years. These are concerned with changes in the designation of principals and vice-principals (in effect, demotions) and in the transfer of teachers. A school board, having appointed a teacher to be a principal or vice-principal, may not terminate such an appointment, other than in July, except with the approval of the minister of education. If such termination becomes effective in July, the administrator may request a hearing before the school board. If the board persists in its decision, the principal or vice-principal may then appeal to the minister of education. Upon appeal, the minister must cause an investigation to be made and may then confirm or disallow the termination of designation. Termination of such designation does not mean dismissal as a teacher.

The ATA would prefer to have appeals against terminations of designation made to some independent tribunal such as the Board of Reference, rather than to the minister, who may be an interested party, especially, for example, if the school board is one of his school inspectors whom he has appointed as official trustee. But even so, a demoted principal is in a better position with respect to appeal than is a teacher who is transferred from one classroom or school to another. Such a transfer may be made at any time during the school year, and the only appeal is to the school board which made the transfer in the first instance—a tribunal hardly likely to reverse itself. The only thin consolation is that the board may, but is not required to, pay all or part of the teacher's removal expenses. The ATA objects to the procedure because it permits a school board to transfer a teacher for reasons which may have nothing to do with the calibre of service that the teacher is providing and because the transfer may entail considerable material and other hardship for the transferee. In such transfers, as in terminations of designations, the ATA would prefer to have an appeal to the Board of Reference.

[22] *Ibid.*, Sec. 355 (3).

The last major Social Credit legislation to affect the welfare of Alberta's teachers was not enacted until 1939. This was the Teachers' Retirement Fund Act. As Kratzmann has indicated, "Despite persistent pressures being brought to bear upon legislators year after year, Alberta was actually the last unit of the British Commonwealth to establish a pension plan for teachers."[23] In its original form, the Act provided something less than affluence for pensioners: a mere $25 per month. During the nine years after 1939 the only change in benefits, introduced in 1944, was to increase them to $30 per month, an escalation not large enough to keep even with the war-time increase in cost of living. Other provisions of the original act were as follows:

1. Teachers and school boards each contributed 3 per cent of the teachers' salaries, deducted by the department of education from provincial grants to the school systems. The latter in turn deducted the teachers' contributions from their cheques.

2. One-sixth of teachers' contributions for the first five years were pre-empted to provide pensions for newly retiring teachers.

3. The provincial government provided office space and paid one-half of the pensions.

4. The fund was controlled by a board of four administrators, two of whom were to be nominated by the ATA.

First representatives of the Association were two able mathematicians and prominent leaders in the ATA: C. O. Hicks and A. E. Rosborough. The executive council also had its own committee to render advice on pension matters. H. C. Clarke, member of this committee, in 1938 had the privilege of reporting to the council on the details of the government-accepted scheme which later became the statute.

First pensions paid under the new Act went to those teachers who retired on December 31, 1939, after contributing to the new fund for a mere four months. It is altogether likely that they extended their teaching careers to New Year's Eve primarily to qualify for their pensions. In March 1940 *The ATA Magazine* published a list of the first eight pensioners under the Act, with pictures of three of them.[24] They had all retired on or after the crucial December 31 date.

[23] A. Kratzmann, "The Alberta Teachers' Association: A Documentary Analysis of the Dynamics of a Professional Association," unpublished doctoral dissertation, University of Chicago (1963), p. 52.

[24] *The ATA Magazine*, XX, 7 (March 1940), p. 28.

Since the contributions standing to the credit of the early pensioners were far from adequate to finance the allowances paid to them, these were paid half by the provincial government and half by the reserve fund. By 1944, the reserve fund's revenue was coming from the following sources: (1) ½ per cent from the salaries of all teachers for the first five years, that is, 1939 to 1944; (2) ½ per cent of teachers' salaries contributed by city, town, village, and consolidated systems, but not by rural districts or school divisions; (3) pensioners' accumulated 3 per cent contributions from 1939 to date of retirement; (4) retentions from contributions of those who left the teaching service; (5) the reserve fund's share of investment earnings.[25]

Pensions were raised from $25 to $30 per month effective January 1, 1944.

The same year saw a request from teachers in certain private schools to be included in the teachers' pension scheme. Their request was rejected through such a *non sequitur* as occasionally startles one in educational non-thinking: that these institutions are operated for private gain—even though education is a matter of public concern.

At first, some attempt was made to preserve a logical relationship between a teacher's contributions to the fund and the pension he drew from it; in other words, to keep the fund on an actuarially sound basis. After 1948, the attempt was abandoned. Teachers' contributions were raised to 4 per cent of their salary for a maximum of 35 years, while benefits were computed on the following formula: (Number of years taught between ages 30 and 65) x 1½ per cent of average salary during last five years of service. This arrangement provided teachers with a maximum pension of 52½ per cent of their salaries averaged over the last five years of teaching service. The provincial government undertook to guarantee pensions at these rates, even though the teachers' contributions would not carry half the cost, as originally intended.

Although these changes were greatly to the benefit of retiring teachers, the ATA was still not content, as the provincial civil servants' scheme was still better. Their contributions were at the rate of 5 per cent of their salaries but their benefits were based on 2 rather than 1½ percent, that is, the maximum pension could be as much as 70 per cent of the average five-year salary. Within a few short years, however, the teachers' obligations and benefits were made equivalent to those of the public servants.

25*Ibid.*, XXIV, 7 (May 1944), p. 25.

Other changes since 1948 include the following: (1) contributions may be continued to age 68 years if necessary to achieve maximum benefits; (2) average salary to be used in computing pension is highest rather than last five years; (3) reciprocal portability has been effected with provincial and federal schemes as well as those of several other provinces; (4) the government no longer contributes to the pension fund as such, but provides from general revenue the funds that are required to meet commitments to the retired teachers. More recently, the teachers' pensions have been integrated with the Canada pension plan. A number of options have been introduced, such as last survivor, etc.

With the introduction of automatic membership in the ATA, collective bargaining, security of tenure, and adequate superannuation, teaching during the ten or fifteen years following the election of the Social Credit government has achieved the external attributes of professional status.

What about the internal?

We Sinais Climb

THE DECADE or so which followed the election of the Social Credit government was an era of great achievement for the ATA. It met the changing conditions attendant upon the introduction of the school divisions by remoulding its structure while preserving its basic principles of organization. It learned and used the techniques of collective bargaining. It defended the security of tenure which its members had so suddenly achieved. It persuaded the government at last to adopt a superannuation scheme, and then assisted it in working the bugs out of the first model. Finally, it melded into the Association a great number of new members reluctant or indifferent to the ATA. Yet during those climactic years the Alberta Teachers' Association did much more.

First, it converted Alberta teachers from being adherents of a voluntary, welfare-oriented body into being full members of a professional organization, not only privileged to enjoy the benefits of such membership but personally responsible, willingly or otherwise, for their professional obligations. This feat was accomplished largely through implementation of disciplinary by-laws which established enforceable standards of a teacher's conduct not only in his relations with his colleagues but also with respect to his employers and his pupils.

The disciplinary powers of the ATA were based on by-laws which were approved by order-in-council. These powers included that of holding hearings and requiring witnesses to attend and give evidence under oath, of assessing part or all of the costs of such hearings against offending teachers, even of recommending to the minister of education that he suspend or cancel a teacher's certificate—recommendations which the minister has always accepted.

An example of inter-member relationships which the disciplinary committee (and ultimately the executive council of the ATA) has had to consider occurred as early as 1937. This involved a case wherein a teacher was charged with bargaining individually with trusteess rather than through the Local Association, "which led to his receiving individual consideration by the Medicine Hat School Board."[1] The council appointed a committee to get in touch with the teacher and to advise the council whether it should be pursued. However, as no charge was laid and no proof presented of any preference being gained through individual bargaining, the matter was apparently allowed to drop.

Then, as now, the Association each year had to deal with cases of "contract jumping," in which a teacher accepted an appointment with a school system and failed to appear on the date of school opening, or resigned without giving service, or, if already employed, resigned after the latest date specified in the School Act. Often, perhaps usually, the teacher felt that his actions were justified, as his assignment had been changed to another school or classroom or subjects other than those which he understood he had been engaged for, or living or working conditions were not as represented, or salary was not as promised. Sometimes personal or family emergencies precipitated such action. And sometimes the teacher broke his contract simply because he was offered a more desirable position elsewhere. Whatever the cause, if a complaint was registered, it had to be investigated; if disciplinary action was in order, it had to be taken. In some cases the offending teacher neglected or refused to pay assessments towards costs of the disciplinary committee when they were assessed against him. In one 1937 case, the minister of education was asked to suspend a teacher's certificate until the costs were paid. Two years later, two teachers were given dead-lines; if they were not met, their ATA memberships were to be suspended and the minister was to be asked to suspend their teaching certificates. In 1940 the council directed that a letter of admonishment be sent to one transgressor. It also decided to take up with the department of education the matter of including in the normal school curriculum "a proper professional attitude with regard to contractual obligations, particularly with respect to acceptance of appointments."[2] The same year the council resolved: "That some publicity be given the Discipline Committee inquiries and that a notice be placed in the Magazine to the effect that action has been taken against

[1]ATA Ex., July 13, 1937.
[2]*Ibid.*, Nov. 8, 1940.

teachers who have failed to meet their contractual obligations; that no particulars be given and that the entirely confidential nature of the proceedings of the Discipline Committee be stressed."[3]

A somewhat different teacher–school board problem appears in the council minutes in 1938. According to the council records:

> The President laid before the Executive a charge that [the teacher] allegedly entered into a contract with a school board and actually commenced teaching in grades in which he was not qualified to teach. It was felt that this was a case in which the contract could be terminated summarily without notice, if the facts were as alleged, and that it be left to the Department insofar as it lay within the jurisdiction of the Department to deal with infringements of their regulations and insofar as the teacher's conduct might be unprofessional the following resolutions was passed:
>
> Resolved: That the General Secretary make a preliminary investigation into the charges laid and report later.[4]

Only rarely did unprofessional conduct in the teacher-pupil relationship come to the attention of the executive council. One 1941 case involving proven homosexual behaviour—euphemistically described as indecent conduct towards pupils—resulted in expulsion from the Association and a recommendation that the teacher's certificate be revoked.

The ATA had to learn by experience the extent and limitations of its disciplinary powers. In 1942 its solicitor advised that it had no power to discipline a teacher who accepted a position at or above the statutory minimum salary of $840 a year but below the Association's approved minimum of $1,000. It also discovered that the long arm of the ATA was thwarted when an offending teacher ceased to be a member of the Association, for example, through marriage or other change of occupation. The Association therefore decided to ask the executive council of the provincial government for a by-law change by which such a teacher would be deemed to be a member of the ATA "until his case is disposed of by the Discipline Committee of the Association."[5] Some years later this change was made.

If the ATA was not always sure of its own disciplinary powers, it did know where they did *not* reside. In 1943 the council devoted considerable discussion to one division's salary schedule, by which a teacher guilty of unprofessional

[3]*Ibid.*, Dec. 28, 1940.
[4]*Ibid.*, Dec. 28-30, 1938.
[5]*Ibid.*, March 16-17, 1946.

conduct would lose annual increments. The council's consensus was that the clause was *ultra vires,* as discipline for unprofessional conduct was not within the power of a school board.

With its growth in numbers as a result of automatic membership and its increased responsibilities and activities resulting from such new legislation as the amendments to the School Act establishing school divisions, the Teachers' Retirement Fund Act, the Labour Act, and the Teaching Profession Act, as well as an increase in professional functions, the Association found that more and more time was required for ATA business. The executive council met more often, and for longer periods, but the Locals and the AGM also had more to do. The particular job of the latter was to build policy for an educational world of accelerating change. By 1936, although it was still a joint operation of the ATA and the Alberta Educational Federation, and still included sessions on curricula, examinations, teaching techniques, and educational finance, the Easter convention was becoming more and more a teachers' gathering, to the disgruntlement of some at least of the school inspectors. Perhaps they were suffering from what one Alberta educator has called the separation trauma when they learned that all committees were convened by teachers.

By 1937 the AEF seems to have disappeared entirely from the Easter convention, although strictly educational topics were still on the agenda. Any ATA member was free to attend the convention, and introduce and discuss resolutions, but only delegates from the Locals were privileged to vote.

It is interesting to note that special plans were being made for the 1938 Easter convention to mark the 21st birthday of the ATA. The 1968 conference is considered as marking the golden or 50th anniversary.

The executive council at a meeting in January 1940 made arrangements to bring in one prominent speaker from the United States to address the Easter convention. On the occasion of this council meeting, "Mr. [A. A.] Aldridge voiced strongly the view that the present development of Fall Convocations was initiated in order to clear the deck for Association business at the Easter AGM and that we should proceed to clear the deck forthwith. But it was felt that such a radical change in the character of the Easter meeting could not be made overnight. . . . 'Four days of undiluted AGM *would* be pretty grisly, wouldn't it?' "[6] In 1967 the ARA (née AGM) lasted for four days.

[6]*The ATA Magazine,* XXI, 5 (Jan. 1940), 11.

In 1941 the executive council again considered the proposal that the Easter convention be devoted wholly to the AGM, but the proposal was tabled.

As the Easter convention eventually became exclusively a teachers' gathering, the question eventually arose as what to do about the non-teaching people, professional and otherwise, who had once attended as members of the AEF or AEA. At a 1944 executive council meeting the general secretary reported: "The Deputy Minister suggested that Superintendents, Assistant Superintendents, or other supervisory officers, whether Departmental employees or School Board, might be privileged to have fraternal delegates attend our AGM."[7] The council approved such attendance, except for *in camera* sessions.

At the 1917 and 1918 Easter conventions the teachers of Alberta had revolted against the province's educational establishment to create the Alberta Teachers' Alliance. In 1943 and 1944 a new generation of teachers was again in revolt against an educational establishment, this time that of the ATA itself. Executive council members were criticized for abuse of expense accounts, for example making long distance calls when ordinary letter correspondence would be adequate, staying overnight in the city for personal reasons and charging expenses to the Association, and in other ways abusing the privileges of their position. That such criticism was rather widespread is implied by an admission in the council minutes of July, 1943, that there was general unrest in the ATA.[8] One can infer, however, that these criticisms of the executive council were symptoms only of a deeper *malaise,* an unhappiness with the way the council seemed to be administering the Association's affairs without due regard to the expressed wishes of the members. In June 1944 the president's column of *The ATA Magazine*[9] was devoted to an explanation of the function of the AGM, which, according to the writer, C. Sansom, exercises its control only through by-laws and not through resolutions. The latter are but suggestions to the executive council and are not mandatory in effect. Even control through by-laws is subject to limitations which the AGM has imposed on itself to prevent hasty and ill-considered action. The following month Sansom returned to the same theme when he wrote, "The AGM is mainly an advisory body."[10] The real

[7]ATA Ex., Dec. 16, 1944.
[8]*Ibid.*
[9]C. Sansom, "President's Column," *The ATA Magazine,* XXIV, 8 (June 1944), 4-5.
[10]*Ibid.,* XXIV, 9 (July 1944), 6-7.

power is in the executive, he contended, which is elected directly by the members and is responsible neither to the president nor to the AGM.

The 1945 annual general meeting was the last large one which any teacher who felt so inclined could attend, and where he could submit resolutions and enter into the discussions and debates. Thereafter, according to Sansom, the AGM would consist of elected councillors, far fewer in number than the appointed delegates. Another effect would be "to relieve the so-called 'district representatives' on the Central Executive of their duties as 'representatives' of their respective areas, these duties to be taken over by the councillors in the Locals."[11] The executive council would become essentially a provincial and executive body, and the AGM would fulfill the functions of a legislature. "The members of the Executive will continue to be elected directly by the teachers, and to be 'responsible' only to the teachers who elect them. As in the past, the AGM will exercise no direct authority over the Executive."[12]

Even before the ATA had taken over full responsibility for the Easter gathering, it had begun to show increasing concern about the local conventions. Heretofore these had been organized and administered by the school inspectors working closely with the teachers concerned, but with the establishment of Locals corresponding in jurisdiction with the new school divisions, the ATA assumed the rôle of the voice of the profession. As early as March, 1937—the year in which the first eleven divisions were erected—the executive council took steps to assume control of these local meetings. The word went out to the faithful that they should introduce resolutions at each convention to turn over its control to the ATA, although the inspectors were to have the same position as heretofore, an interesting example of non-logic, apparently designed to placate those august gentlemen. By the fall of the same year the Association seems to have achieved its aim with respect to the local conventions, and with the full concurrence of the department of education. The inspectors, or superintendents as they soon came to be called, were not ignored; they were and are valued resource personnel at local conventions, and their assistance has at all times proven of great value in planning and running these affairs.

The two high school conventions, in northern and southern Alberta, were anomalies that continued to perplex the ATA for some years. Their organization

[11] *Ibid.*, XXV, 5 (April 1945), 2.
[12] *Ibid.*

did not correspond to any ATA boundaries. The problem was that if teachers of the high school grades attended conventions designed to assist them in their own work, they would not be entitled to attend the local gatherings and their services would to a large extent be lost to the Locals of which they were members. The dilemma was recognized as early as 1941, and in the executive council "it was decided something should be done towards holding the high school conventions at the same time and place as the rural conventions."[13] This suggestion apparently proved unworkable, probably because it would have meant the replacement of the two high school conventions with fifteen or eighteen local ones, each too small to be effective or to bring together enough teachers with common interests in such fields as English, French, science, mathematics, or social studies, for example. Three years later the problem was still unsolved, for in 1944 the AGM resolved that the minister of education be asked to grant the high school teachers two extra days to permit them to attend local conventions. This move did not find favour with the trustees, who tended to regard all teachers' conventions with somewhat jaundiced eyes, considering them principally as assemblies wherein the teachers plotted against the school boards for higher salaries and expensive fringe benefits. The following year the executive council resolved: "That a committee of the Executive be appointed to work with officials of the Northern and Southern High School Teachers Conventions Associations with a view to establishing more harmonious relations."[14]

Probably a number of factors led to the disappearance of these bodies shortly after that date. Wartime rationing of gasoline discouraged avoidable travelling. School centralization and resultant greater retentivity of the schools increased the size of non-urban secondary institutions, so that local conventions could bring together enough high school teachers to make sessions on their particular problems feasible. Finally, the pupil transportation facilities which arose to serve the school centralizations made it awkward and expensive to have some classrooms of the school open and others closed on convention days, as occurred when some teachers attended conventions at one time and the rest at another time.

One hall-mark of a profession, at least a "learned" profession, is that its

[13]ATA Ex., Oct. 4, 1937.

[14]*Ibid.*, April 18, 1941.

members normally receive their professional preparation in universities. Although not necessarily, the reverse of this thesis would seem to follow: that practitioners of a calling who have learned their craft in a university are therefore professionals. The ATA had long accepted this principle in its advocacy of a school or faculty of education at the provincial university and had been successful in that such a school was opened to students at the University of Alberta in 1929. However, this was only limited recognition of the professional nature of teaching, since the new School of Education prepared teachers only for the secondary grades. Nor did it prepare all of them; the first class teacher's certificate granted after attendance at a normal school was and is a valid licence to teach in any grade from I to XII. And even after the School of Education was established, its graduates had received most of their preparation in another university faculty, since admission requirements to the new institution included a bachelor's degree from a university. The ATA therefore pressed for a programme wherein the high school teachers-in-training would be registered for the whole of their university career in the School of Education. This objective was achieved in 1939 when the School became the College of Education and its director, M. E. LaZerte, was elevated to the dignity of its principalship. Thereafter, future secondary school teachers could register in education as soon as they entered the university, taking all their courses with an orientation towards their future careers and earning a B.Ed. rather than a B.A. or a B.Sc. degree. No longer were their studies strictly segregated into two categories: cultural or general, followed by a year of exclusively professional courses. No longer could Education be labelled derisively a "trade school," although why such an appellation should be applied to an institution for the training of teachers any more than one for the preparation of physicians, dentists, engineers, or pharmacists was never made very clear.

At the same time, the former route to high school teaching—graduation in arts, science, home economics, agriculture, etc., plus a year in education—remained open and still does.

The next logical step in the development of a university programme for the training of teachers was to elevate the college to the dignity of a faculty, a development which occurred in 1942, with LaZerte as its first dean. The new faculty's offering consisted at first of a three-year programme leading to a B.Ed. degree and a teaching certificate, but shortly it was extended to four years, except for World War II veterans, who were permitted for a limited time to register for the three-year degree. It also offered the graduate degree of M.Ed., which replaced former graduate programmes leading to the M.A. in Education and a B.Educ. granted after a bachelor's degree in some other faculty. Control over the education curriculum was placed in the hands of the Faculty of Education council rather than that of the Faculty of Arts and Science. The interests of the ATA in teacher preparation were recognized by inclusion of a representative of the Association on the faculty council.

From school to college to faculty was enough progress to achieve in fifteen years but it was hardly spectacular. Ontario, for example, had long been preparing its high school teachers in the University of Toronto's College of Education. The ATA wanted more; it wanted not just the high school but all teachers to receive their preparation in the university. This was a hurdle of considerable height to surmount, for it would mean the demolition of the normal schools as such, the surrender of immediate control by the department of education of the curriculum and staffing of the major teacher-training institutions, the loss of status and position for the normal school principals, the displacement of normal school instructors and their absorption into a university milieu for which they were neither oriented nor qualified, if one considers a Ph.D. degree the journeyman's ticket for a university professor. And on the other side of the fence, many university professors had grave doubts as to the suitability of a university's trying to prepare primary teachers for their careers. "Oh, oh. Look, Sally, look. See Bobby jump. See Bobby jump up," hardly seemed to belong in the same institution as Chaucer's *Canterbury Tales* or Plato's *Republic*.

Nevertheless, in 1943 it was announced that plans were being implemented to transfer all teacher preparation to the University of Alberta. Credit for this development goes to a great many different institutions and people: to the Alberta Teachers' Association, which had long pressed to have all teacher education taken within the university, to teacher-premier William Aberhart, to his deputy minister G. Fred McNally and his supervisor of schools H. C. Newland, former ATA president, under whose immediate direction the normal schools operated. Without the dynamic and able leadership of the forceful LaZerte the transfer of the normal schools would have been delayed for years, perhaps for a generation. Nor should the co-operation of the normal school principals be overlooked, for they submerged their own interests, giving up important positions where they were monarchs of all they surveyed to take less prestigious if not less remunerative positions with the Faculty of Education.

First step towards the New Order occurred in 1944, when the university took over from the department of education the control and direction of the summer session, granting credit towards a university degree for courses (or their equivalents) which formerly had counted towards special certificates but had not been previously accepted as academic legal tender. The following year the normal schools went out of existence as such, and Alberta became the first province to place all teacher education under university control. For the normal schools it was a metamorphosis rather than a demise. The Edmonton institution, located on the campus of the University of Alberta, simply became the new home of the vastly expanded Faculty of Education; its staff members found themselves wearing the new dignity of academic rank and responding to the title of professor instead of looking over their shoulders to see who was being addressed. The Calgary Normal School became the Calgary campus (Calgarians frowned on the designation of "branch") of the same university.

For teachers and student-teachers, the changes had even more profound implications. Providing always that they had met or could meet subsequently the university's matriculation standards, the former were eligible to receive one year of advance standing towards the B.Ed. degree in their normal school training and up to three credits (about one-half a year's work) on department of education summer courses. With such a leg up, many teachers went on to university graduation who formerly would never have considered such a course. The student-teachers found themselves attending the same institution as did aspirants to other professions; they were no longer categorized, however mistakenly, as attending some sort of sub-standard post-secondary training institution.

The appointment of an ATA representative to the Faculty of Education Council was not the first formal relationship between the university and the Association. After presentations extending over a number of years, in 1937 the university granted the teachers representation on the university senate. First incumbent was G. D. Misener, veteran of the ATA and early president of the Alliance.

University preparation is one hall-mark of a profession; control over admittance to practice by the profession itself is yet another. Traditionally and constitutionally in Canada such control has always been exercised by the provincial governments; for teachers, by the departments of education. And, Paton points out:

> In the vital field of teacher education and certification there is no effective consultation anywhere in Canada between official teacher representatives and provincial boards or officials who determine entrance requirements and standards of interim and permanent certification. This means that the teaching profession has no control over who enters its ranks and under what conditions. It is true that no association of teachers employed in state-supported schools anywhere has such control, but when the organized group speaks for all teachers in the system, and has accepted responsibility in other matters such as ethics, curriculum, and professional development, the disability is not one to be accepted with resignation. When, in addition, this organized group has no means of removing the incompetents from its ranks, and the public is increasingly critical of poor teaching and is inclined to blame the profession rather than the provincial board of certification, a particularly galling situation is created, for which the profession must find alleviation.[15]

Thus the ATA—and all other provincial teachers' organizations—are a long way from exercising control over admittance to their membership and into the teaching profession. Paton states that only in the three westernmost provinces do the teachers' associations have any representation on teacher certification boards.

Although the ATA had always been interested in certification of Alberta teachers, after the passage of the Teaching Profession Act in 1935 and the automatic membership amendment the following year, it spoke with a new sense of authority and responsibility. In 1937 the executive council discussed the necessity for special qualifications in such subjects as drama, art, typewriting, industrial arts, home economics, etc. They were also concerned with the need for summer school up-grading courses for "rusty" teachers, and the limitations which might be placed on the certification of teachers with second class certificates. Although the Association consistently pressed for higher standards of certification, it was firmly opposed to the down-grading of those which had already been issued. Thus when the department of education wished to limit the validity of second class certificates to Grades I to X, the ATA pressed to continue their validity to Grade XI. In December 1937 the executive council resolved: "That this Executive go on record as being opposed to any regulation

[15]J. M. Paton, *The Rôle of Teachers' Organizations in Canadian Society* (Quance Lectures, 1962), p. 24.

of the Department which is, in effect, retroactive as far as the certification of teachers now certificated is concerned."[16] At the same meeting, the council also resolved: "That the matter of Certification rest in the hands of a board on which the ATA shall have representation."[17]

The ATA was always concerned when it discovered professionally unqualified persons being appointed to senior supervisory posts or specialized positions for which they did not hold any trace of teacher certification. At different times in the same city system a supervisor of music and an instructor in printing were given positions and allowed to earn their teaching certificates after appointment. Normally, to teach school the School Act requires one to hold a valid teaching certificate, these two cases to the contrary notwithstanding. Yet no such qualification is deemed necessary for a school superintendent. However, when one Alberta urban system appointed a lawyer to this position in 1940, the ATA went into a state of shock. The Association had the general secretary report on the case "and his recommendations that representation be made immediately to the Department of Education requesting regulations insisting upon the proper qualifications of persons whose duty presumably it is to supervise and report on members of the teaching profession were read and approved."[18] A few years later the council was urging that the Board of Teacher Education and Certification recommend as appointees to the Faculty of Education staff only those with Alberta teacher certification or eligibility for such certification.

The teaching profession, like many others, is characterized by the fact that a practitioner must hold a valid licence to practise issued by a government-designated authority. But whereas in such professions as law and medicine a licence, once issued, is valid, unless revoked for cause, during the life of the holder, the same is not true in education. Each tyro teacher starts his career with a temporary or interim certificate clutched in his nervous little hand. Differing requirements have had to be met in Alberta before such a certificate may be made permanent, but they have always included a minimum period of satisfactory service as vouched by a school inspector or superintendent. Although this is one of the many controls exercised over the schools by the depart-

[16]ATA Ex., Dec. 27-29, 1937.

[17]*Ibid.*

[18]ATA Ex., Dec. 27-31, 1940.

ment of education, why such a requirement should be imposed on teachers and not on physicians or clergymen, who bear responsibilities equally heavy to those of the teacher, has never really been made clear. Occasionally teachers have become somewhat exercised over this apparent inequity, but usually their concern stops at an interest in what type of service counts towards permanent certification. Such concern was indicated in a 1941 report to the executive council that satisfactory performance in the department of education's correspondence school would be treated as the equivalent of school service for permanent certification.[19] A few years later the editor of *The ATA Magazine* was attacking correspondence education as "the most inefficient as well as the most expensive education,"[20] entirely without any supporting data for his charge. At the last moment he apparently remembered that most of the correspondence teachers were members of ATA Local No. 61, and closed his editorial with a tribute to "the efficient and loyal staff of that Department."[21]

That the Association regarded the difference between interim and permanent certification as arbitrary and largely meaningless is indicated by an editorial in a 1943 number of *The ATA Magazine*[22] rebutting the idea that normal school graduates should not receive annual increments until they achieved permanent certification.

The Alberta Board of Teacher Education and Certification was established when the University of Alberta assumed responsibility for all teacher education. But, although the university prepared the neophytes for their chosen calling, it was still the minister of education who issued them their licences to teach. A liaison body was therefore necessary to reconcile any differences between the minister and department of education on the one hand and the university on the other. Each nominated five members to the new board. The sympathetic government honoured the claim of the Alberta Teachers' Association to representation on the board and gave the ATA's dear enemy, the Alberta School Trustees' Association, the same consideration. Thus the ATA ended with three representatives on the 16-member body. As Paton observes: "This, on the surface, looks like under-representation of the professional organization, but

[19] *Ibid.*, Dec. 29-31, 1941.
[20] *The ATA Magazine*, XXV, 8 (May, 1946), 1.
[21] *Ibid.*
[22] *Ibid.*, XXIII, 6 (Feb. 1943), 1.

reliable sources claim that the practical results have been good from the standpoint of the teachers. . . ."[23]

If the results have been good, as Paton suggests, perhaps it is because virtually all the university and departmental representatives have been former members of the ATA, and at least some continue their relationship with the Association as associate or optional members.

The fact that the ATA has done as well as it has in securing representation on the provincial certification board, in comparison with other provinces, is perhaps because the provincial government was headed by a premier and minister of education who was a school principal, that several members of his cabinet had been teachers, and that a number of backbenchers were also professional educators.

The ATA has always been interested in the in-service as well as the pre-service education of its members, although by its nature the former is less highly structured than the latter. It is also less significant in building a public image of teaching as a learned profession. It is also costly to the ATA, and was especially so in the years before 1936 when it had to spend a great proportion of its income on annual membership drives. Nonetheless, when the Alliance as early as 1920 began publication of *The ATA Magazine,* it, in addition to being a house organ, from the beginning included a great deal of technical and professional material ranging from articles on teaching techniques to summaries of research studies, educational news from Canada and abroad, and critiques and summaries of educational thought in North America, Europe and elsewhere.

The Easter and local conventions, over which the Association and its Locals ultimately assumed control, were also in-service institutions of considerable significance. Other early projects were the establishment of Alberta School Week, begun in 1927 primarily for the edification of the general public but of significance to practising teachers, sponsorship of summer sessions on the psychology and supervision of reading and of arithmetic, and the founding of a professional library. In 1938 the Association set up trusts funds for library, scholarship, and research, placing $1,000 in each. These were almost token guestures, but their importance as precedent-setters is almost impossible to over-estimate. The scholarship trust fund was slowly increased until 1947, when

[23]Paton, *Teachers' Organizations,* 63-4.

the first award in the amount of $300 was made in the name of the recently retired and deceased John Walker Barnett.

The ATA's early concern for the production and publication or research, greatly hampered by lack of funds, has been mentioned in a previous chapter. Its most significant research project during its first quarter-century was the preparation and publication of a monograph on Alberta vocations, which appeared in 1938. It is no coincidence that this volume appeared during the Association presidency of M. E. LaZerte, then director of the School of Education at the University of Alberta, an educator long known in Canada as an ardent advocate of educational research. Some 300 teachers assisted in gathering data for the project, and the co-operation of people in many different occupations was enlisted in checking the assembled information. The final writing was done by two graduate students at the University of Alberta, Dorothy Deakin, who made a minor contribution, and F. T. Tyler, "who compiled and organized the data and wrote most of the report."[24]

The resulting hard-cover volume of about 450 pages appeared under the ATA's imprint. Entitled *Choosing Your Life Work,* for a number of years it was a source book in Alberta high school group guidance classes, but its use was discontinued in the end as its content became more and more obsolete. After a lapse of thirty years, it would seem to have gained a new and historical significance as a picture of how Albertans lived and worked in those fast-receding depression and pre-World War II days. Even the illustrations are informative. From them one gleans the knowledge that farm tractors had just begun to wear rubber tires, that airplanes, or at least some of them, still had two sets of wings, that horse-drawn binders were still in use in the Peace River country, and automobiles still sported fenders. And railway locomotives, equipped with cow-catchers, still burned coal. Women's skirts reached half-way between the knee and ankle, and hats adorned their pretty little heads even when they were shopping. Business and professional men, and even university students (male) regularly wore vests. The cloth cap was still a common head-gear for men. Small boy's pants often came down only as far as the knee. Hospital gowns were still white. Banks and public libraries imitated classical Greek temples on the outside; their interiors seemed to follow a neo-mausoleum school of

[24]Alberta Teachers' Association, *Choosing Your Life Work* (1938), p. v.

architecture. Office furniture represented the last vestige of the mission oak style, heavy, graceless, humourless.

The book's textual material is equally interesting. For example, labourers in Calgary in 1935 earned 25¢ to 35¢ per hour. Skilled tradesmen's wages varied betweent 75¢ and 90¢. Professional people were much better off, as usual. In the year ending June 1, 1936, the average earnings in a few professions in Edmonton and Calgary were: accountants, $1,635; electrical engineers $2,000; lawyers and notaries, $1,925; physicians and surgeons, $1,710; teachers, $1,565. Stenographers usually started at $50 a month, with a top of about $150 and an average of $75. Bank "juniors" began at $600; ledger keepers and tellers earned from $800 to $1,000. None of these positions was open to girls.

From the perspective of thirty years, *Choosing Your Life Work* seems an applied research project of considerable impressiveness. Nor was this effort wholly unique; in 1938, the year in which it came off the press, the Association made a grant to Isadore Goresky in the amount of $500 to assist in his study of the early history of Alberta education. Completed in 1944 as a University of Alberta master's thesis entitled "The Beginning and Growth of the Alberta School System," this work has become a standard reference and source book for all subsequent students and writers in the field. But another twenty years were to pass before the ATA could boast of comparable achievements in the encouragement of educational research.

Now Lettest Thy Servant Depart

THE DECADE or so following the election in 1935 of the Social Credit government was, as the immediately preceding chapters have shown, a most significant era for the ATA, both with respect to the material betterment of teachers in salary, tenure, and superannuation matters, and to the development of teaching as a profession. During the same period a number of other things happened which merit at least passing attention.

For example, the matter of teachers' civic rights—what the university community might more pompously have deemed academic freedom—concerned the ATA. As early as the 1920's the general secretary was largely responsible for beating off an Edmonton-based attempt to deprive teachers of the right to serve as aldermen, perhaps because Labourite C. L. Gibbs was proving a burr under the saddle of the Edmonton business interests when he was elected to the capital city's council. Early in 1935 the ATA's executive council felt it necessary to come to the defence of four Calgary teachers whom it regarded as being persecuted for the out-of-school and in-school expression of ideas not acceptable to certain school trustees. The exectuive council protested the action of the Calgary school board in:

"1. Restricting or attempting to restrict the members of the teaching profession from exercising their full rights as citizens and their duties as teachers.

"2. Adopting a policy of selection and discrimination against certain members of the staff whose views, presumably, do not coincide with the majority of the members of the Calgary Public School Board.

"3. Casting aspersions on the integrity of the members of the teaching profession by implying that they prostitute their positions as teachers to promulgate party policies in the classroom."[1]

The August election the same year, resulting in the seating in the legislature of a teacher premier, other teacher cabinet members, and still other educators on the back benches seemed to decide for all time that teachers have the same political rights as do other citizens; furthermore, that it behooves school boards to allow them the necessary leaves-of-absence to discharge the duties for which their fellow-citizens have chosen them. Since that time, teachers have regularly served as councillors and mayors in small and large Alberta centres with no objection from either school or municipal authorities. In the ATA's jubilee year, only one restriction remains: a teacher may not serve as a trustee in a school system even through he is teaching in an altogether different one.

One consequence of the implementation of automatic membership in the ATA was that, since all teachers would be receiving *The ATA Magazine,* it served as a perfect medium for the publication and distribution of the department of education's Official Bulletin. The *Magazine* accordingly began publication of this feature in April 1936. Ironically, its editor was H. C. Newland, whom J. W. Barnett had displaced from the position of editor of the *Magazine* about ten years or so before.

The ATA status of members of religious orders took most of a decade to resolve. In April 1936, the executive council discussed their position and concurred that ". . . the ultimate aim would be to eliminate any distinction being made between any members of the teaching profession."[2] In 1940 the council was still concerned that action be taken to include each religious as an individual member of the Association, but it was not for another four years that any further progress was made. In 1944 the general secretary was instructed to confer with Archbishop Macdonald of Edmonton on the matter, and if he had no objections, an amendment to the Teaching Profession Act was to be sought to remove the religious from their special category. This change was apparently effected in 1945.

As previously indicated, the ATA had recurrent difficulties with its agents,

[1]ATA Ex., June 29, 1935.

[2]*Ibid.,* April 13, 1936.

who were chronically short in their returns to the Alliance. The renamed Association for a while fared little better in this direction. In 1938 the coucil was concerned with the accounts of its advertising solicitor. The minutes of its meeting on July 2 and 3, 1938, read in part as follows:

> Resolved: That the Executive instruct the General Secretary to advise Mr. V. . . . that they have reviewed the situation insofar as his business and account is concerned with the Association or the ATA Magazine and that they are very much disposed to recommend his dismissal and that the matter is therefore placed in the hands of the General Secretary to take whatever steps are necessary to put the account in a proper and sound position and that should there by any further delinquency disclosed, Mr. V. be dismissed forthwith.[3]

By the end of the year the agent had made some progress in clearing his overdraft, but the situation remained so unsatisfactory that in February 1939 the council resolved: "That the action of the General Secretary be ratified and that [the agent] be dismissed, any further course of action to be decided later."[4]

Another vexatious business matter that the Association inherited from the old Alliance concerned The ATA Publishing Company, its affiliated Bureau of Education, and sale of the latter to the Western Canada Institute. In 1936 and 1939 the Association made offers to buy the shares in the publishing company owned by W. Rogers and J. T. Jones. Apparently these offers were accepted.

Also in 1936 the ATA appointed the general secretary as its representative to attend a meeting of the shareholders of the Institute and vote for himself as a member of the board of directors. Three years later the council was informed that the board of directors had not met in some time. Finally "it was resolved that the Association write to the WCI and offer to sell the shares, entirely without prejudice, for $500 cash. . . . "[5] That this deal was consummated is evident from a minute of a later meeting that year: "Resolved: that we place the $500 received from the WCI in the staff trust. . . ."[6] And apparently that was the end of the Western Canada Institute as far as the ATA was concerned.

A project to which the Association gave a great deal of attention was the preparation of a brief to the Rowell-Sirois Royal Commission on Federal-Provincial Relations. The ATA's principal concern was to establish a case for

[3]*Ibid.*, July 2, 3, 1938.
[4]*Ibid.*, Aug. 2, 1939.
[5]*Ibid.*, July 5, 1939.
[6]*Ibid.*, Dec. 27-30, 1939.

federal aid to education, an aspect of federal-provincial relations arising from the allocation of education in the BNA Act to the provinces. The brief was published in full in *The ATA Magazine*[7] and was duly signed not only by the president and the general secretary of the ATA and by other teachers but also by urban superintendents of schools, normal school principals, the principal of the Calgary Institute of Technology and Art, and professors from the University of Alberta's School of Education. Yet the project in the end proved a disappointment. In 1940 an editorial in *The ATA Magazine*[8] expressed the ATA's acute disappointment that the Commission had completely ignored the need for federal aid to education.

Because William Aberhart had done so much for the ATA, the Association regarded this remarkable man with a strong proprietary interest. It was therefore understandably bitter in 1941 when the senate of the University of Alberta by a one-vote margin decided not to award the premier an honorary LL.D. This action seemed a particularly gratuitous snub since the senate committee had made the recommendation that Aberhart be asked to give the convocation address and receive the degree, and the university president had informally but without secrecy extended the invitation. The senate's disavowal of its committee and the university president was well known to have come from the professorial members of that august body. Nor was the ATA alone in its condemnation of an obviously vindictive and petty display of spite by the professors; its *Magazine* quoted Edmonton *Bulletin* editorials at length in support of its position.[9]

A direct consequence of the university senate's disregard of propriety was a rewriting of the University Act and the reduction of the senate to an innocuous rôle as a public relations body. In 1942, J. W. Barnett was appointed to it to represent public education. Apparently a university degree was no longer *de rigueur* for a university senator.

Not every aspect of the ATA's business in those distant days was vexatious, disappointing, or embarrassing. In 1940 the executive council without any recorded comment or explanation passed the following resolution: "That the

[7] *The ATA Magazine*, XVIII, 8 (April 1938), 17-25.

[8] *Ibid.*, XX, 10 (June 1940), 1.

[9] *Ibid.*, XXI, 10 (June 1941), 1-3.

General Secretary be authorized to take what action he deems best in the matter of the purchase of a guillotine."[10]

During World War II many Alberta teachers joined the armed forces and served their country with great gallantry. Yet the most distinguished honour awarded any Alberta teacher was earned by a woman who did not even leave her school yard to display her heroism. The incident occurred when an RCAF training plane crashed into the yard of the Big Bend School in the Calgary School Division. Mrs. Frances Walsh risked her own life in an endeavour to rescue the pilot from his burning aircraft. For this feat she was awarded the George Cross.

Although World War II seems to have had little permanent impact on the ATA's structure or functions, a holocaust of such dimensions could not help but affect both individual teachers and the Association itself. The ATA's first published reaction to the war appeared in September 1939 in the first month of hostilities. It took the form of an editorial on the retention of positions and seniority for teachers in the services.[11] The problem was resolved in 1942, when word was received that the Reinstatement in Civil Employment Act, 1942, was applicable to teachers, regardless of whether or not they had applied for leave of absence, regardless also of whether or not such leave had been granted.

In January 1940 the editor was urging teachers to resist forced contributions to the Red Cross.[12] That it was the principle of the *corvée* and not the object of its benefactions to which the Association was opposed is indicated by the approbation expressed in *The ATA Magazine* on the occasion of the Calgary teachers' donation of an ambulance to the Canadian Red Cross.[13]

In 1940 the magazine published an open letter to the Calgary *Herald* concerning one of its editorials which the Association regarded as cowardly and despicable libel on the teachers of its city. "The Canadian government has interned only two women as enemy aliens since the war started," the *Herald* noted. "It should inquire into the activities of certain woman teachers not of enemy origin."[14]

The war was a constant source of frustration to the ATA in that the federal

[10]ATA Ex., May 4, 1940.
[11]*The ATA Magazine,* XX, 1 (Sept. 1939), 1.
[12]*Ibid.,* XX, 5 (Jan. 1940), 2.
[13]*Ibid.,* XXI, 3 (Nov. 1940), 3.
[14]*Ibid.,* XXI, 1 (Sept. 1940), 23.

agreement on the part of teachers and trustees. This he did by announcing that the committee had no powers whatsoever, to which both teachers and trustees took strong exception. Despite this unpromising beginning, agreement was reached on the following points: (1) any provincial agreement would have to include more than one scale of salaries, to allow for differing local conditions; (2) allowances should be made for varying qualifications and for administrative responsibilities; (3) annual increments should lead to maxima 50 to 60 per cent above the corresponding minima. However, no agreement could be achieved on the basic salary to be paid to a teacher with minimum acceptable training and no experience. The whole idea was therefore shelved but by no means forgotten.

Internally, the war years were shadowed by the prospect of retirement of the general secretary. He had not built the Association single-handedly, but he had been the one indispensable man in the organization. Yet when World War II began, he was 59 years of age. He was not an old man, and if older than his years—which is debatable—it was because he had lavished them unsparingly in the service of his beloved ATA. Still, there was a feeling in the Association that it would be difficult to retire this old war horse to pasture, and since it would probably take several years, it behooved the Association to begin its preparations early. Even in the 1920's an attempt had been made to appoint an assistant general secretary; Barnett had quietly but effectively sabotaged that idea.

One hint of his impending retirement appeared in the minutes of an executive council meeting in 1941: "Resolved: that since the General Secretary has reached maturity he sit for a photo at the earliest opportunity."[19] Barnett was 61. The portrait was approved in December, at which time the council decided to recommend that he be considered by the Senate of the University of Alberta for an honorary LL.D. degree. But the proposal was half a dozen years premature.

In December the executive council considered the resolution of the previous AGM that a trainee for the position of general secretary should be appointed. It was admitted that the question had arisen before and always been evaded by statements such as that the council had the matter well in hand, and the like. The truth, of course, was that absolutely no steps had been taken to implement

[19]ATA Ex., April 18, 1941.

the AGM's wishes. Still, the matter had to be faced, and it was, at least to the extent of establishing some sort of retirement benefits for the incumbent.

The AGM would not be silenced. In 1943 it called for an understudy to Barnett to be appointed with the idea that he would take over as general secretary when Barnett retired. In December the executive council got around to appointing a committee to choose such a person. The committee consisted of ATA president J. Smith and two past presidents, C. Sansom and H. C. Melsness. After three years or so of masterly inactivity the committee reported. The result was a council resolution, "that this matter be left over until a retirement age is stated or until Mr. Barnett signified his desire to retire and if an emergency arises it will be met with emergency measures."[20]

The AGM still would not be silenced. In 1945 it demanded to know why its direction to appoint an understudy (and successor) to the general secretary had been ignored and that a committee of the AGM be chosen to effect the appointment. The executive council unanimously decided not to concur with the AGM's demands, on the ground that the time was not ripe. After all, Barnett had neither resigned nor died, nor did he show any intention of doing either.

The conflict between the AGM and the council is significant in indicating where the real power lay in the Association. Despite token recognition that the annual general meeting was the parliament of the ATA, it was quite unable to control the executive. As long as the executive council was united in its will, the AGM was powerless.

Probably the reason for the conflict was that the council consisted of older members of the ATA who recalled the battles that Barnett had waged during the depths of the Great Depression and against hostile governments and school boards to keep the organization alive. They knew the ATA's debt to John Walker Barnett and, being honourable men and women, had no inclination to repudiate it. But the AGM was made up of younger men and women who felt no personal commitment to Barnett; he had never ridden over ice-rutted roads to save their jobs or even to solicit their membership. To them he was an aging warrior still fighting battles that had long been won, and antagonizing trustees, superintendents, and even teachers in the process. It was time to think about replacing him.

Barnett was never stupid; he must have sensed a growing alienation, not

[20]*Ibid.*, April 9, 13, 1944.

John W. Barnett

Greetings:

A tireless organizer and champion
of Canadian Teachers;
A philosopher deeply grounded in study,
experience and intercourse with other minds.
A lover of fine dogs, diverse books and good music:
A ruthless, intrepid chess-player;
A virtuoso of billiards whose mastery few of us
(but still a few) dare to challenge;
A man most happy in his home and garden:
nevertheless, a jovial companion on long
journeys and in strange hostelries;
A strong debater and a councillor of long vision;
A graceful dispenser of cigars—good cigars;
A connoisseur of life's wholesome things—merriment,
duck hunting, rare steak, fine arts, keen argument;
A stubborn Englishman and a true son of the west.

The undersigned are but a few of those who bid you
affectionately Hail and Farewell at the close of
your twenty eight years' service for the C.T.F.
May you live long among us in the enjoyment of
these qualities and enthusiasms which make you our friend.

H.E. Smith

A Greeting to J. W. Barnett from some friends on the occasion of his service with the Canadian Teachers' Federation. (Photo by McDermid Studios, Edmonton)

F. J. C. Seymour. (Photo by Goertz Studio, Edmonton)

between himself and his old compadres but *vis-à-vis* the new generation of teachers who knew not the battles of long ago. In any event, in December 1945 Barnett submitted his resignation. He was requested to continue in office until or after the 1946 AGM, and to accept the position of honorary secretary of the Association as of September 1, 1946, at a stipend of $100 per month, and finally retire at the end of August 1947. It was agreed that he would continue as general secretary until August 31, 1946.

Forecast for his sunset years read "fair and warm." Mr. and Mrs. Barnett were presented with a silver tea service at the 1946 AGM. Even the long-recommended LL.D. was to be conferred on the old warrior at the 1947 fall convocation of the University of Alberta. And then suddenly in the midsummer of that year he was dead.

The Association which he had done so much to build suffered a sense of profound shock. Barnett was not only one of its founders; he was a legend in his own time. Even teachers who did not know him personally, and others who knew him and disliked him, felt that the natural order of the universe had been disturbed. No sooner had the late secretary's body been committed to the earth than his former colleagues created one monument after another to his memory. For several years the March issue of *The ATA Magazine* was dedicated to the remembrance of John Walker Barnett, its cover adorned with the portrait taken after he had reached the years of maturity, and its contents including an article or editorial dealing with his contributions to the ATA. To this day an annual scholarship in education is awarded in his name. A little black-bound volume—*In Memory of John Walker Barnett*—appeared. As told in the next chapter, the ATA built itself a beautiful home and called it Barnett House. In time it proved too small, and was replaced by another, but the name remained. One of its finest decorations is the handsome oil painting, a copy of which serves as frontispiece of this work.

But his greatest monument is the Alberta Teachers' Association itself.

Above the tomb of Sir Christopher Wren, in St. Paul's Cathedral, London, stands a tablet inscribed, "Si monumentum requiris, circumspice"—If you seek his monument, look around you." In a metaphorical if not literal sense, the same epitaph applies to John Walker Barnett.

The Blackstock Caper

THE 1946 retirement of J. W. Barnett as general secretary of the ATA coincided more or less with a number of other developments that were profoundly to affect the future of the Association. It might seem that the battles had all been won; that all thereafter in the story of the ATA would be but commentary. On the economic side, teachers had achieved a pension programme—of a sort. Salaries were rising, albeit too slowly. Security of tenure had been gained which, if not absolute, was unequalled in Canada. The new secretary, E. C. Ansley, former ATA president, might have suspected that he had inherited no more than a routine holding or housekeeping job. Yet such it was not to be.

By the middle of 1946, when Barnett retired, World War II had been ended for almost a year and most of the servicemen in the army, navy, and air force had returned to civil life. Since the armed forces had contained large numbers of qualified teachers, the department of education, the ASTA, and the ATA had anticipated that the teacher shortage which had bedevilled the schools during the previous three years and which had led to the introduction of correspondence education in hundreds of classrooms would soon be sharply alleviated if not altogether eliminated. Instead, the situation grew worse. In retrospect, it appears that the reasons for the alarming increase in the teacher shortage were manifold. On the one hand, the Canadian rehabilitation programme for war veterans, perhaps the best in the world, was persuading teachers by the hundreds to attend university, either to up-grade their teaching qualifications or to prepare for an entirely different profession. In either case, the programme effectively prevented their immediate return to the classroom.

Another reason was purely economic. Since, relatively speaking, they were well educated, teachers had usually held commissioned or non-commissioned officer rank. To their relatively good basic pay had been added such benefits as flying or trade pay, married and family allowances, and free meals and quarters or additional allowances in lieu thereof. It is no wonder that hundreds of them viewed the average Alberta teacher's salary of $1,516.18 in 1946 with a somewhat jaundiced eye. So they turned to the market-place which, starved by a six-year consumer-goods drought, beckoned with the promise of quick and abundant rewards.

Thus the crisis deepened, not only in Alberta but all across Canada. Departments of education reacted as they always have done in time of teacher shortages, by authorizing unqualified or underqualified personnel to take charge of the classrooms. The Alberta department avoided the desperate expedient of issuing permits to wholly untrained people by registering whole schoolfuls of children as correspondence pupils. In this way the actual work of instruction was handled by qualified and certificated teachers in the government's correspondence education branch. In charge of the classrooms, however, were uncertificated persons, usually young men or women with Grade XI or XII education, occasionally more mature farm wives. Known officially as correspondence supervisors and soon to the teaching profession as "sitters," they had the responsibility of maintaining order, distributing lesson materials and assignments returned from the correspondence school, collecting and forwarding pupils' work to that institution, marking the register, occasionally helping the pupils over the rougher spots as their mothers would have done if they had been taking their correspondence courses in their own homes.

The correspondence centre system was first introduced in Alberta in 1944, when 209 schools were included. By 1945, the number of schools affected had risen to 294. The ATA, recognizing the emergent conditions which the war had created, did not object very strenuously, but when the end of the war brought no diminution but rather an increase in the number of the correspondence centres—673 in 1946—it began to wonder if the whole scheme was not being used simply to avoid paying the higher salaries which would have recruited the teachers necessary to staff the schools. The executive council was concerned also about the correspondence supervisors' being allowed to take over teaching functions, "to present subject-matter to pupils, to encourage discussion, to check preparatory work, drill, correct errors."[1] They also regarded the remuneration paid to supervisors, typically $90 a month, so close to what a beginning teacher would receive as to remove any incentive for a young person to qualify as a certificated teacher. In the end it was decided that supervisors would not be welcome at local conventions; these gatherings were for ATA members only.

By the December meeting of the council, the concern of its members had deepened. They viewed with alarm the enthusiasm of certain school superintendents for the "sitter" system and the indifference of school boards to the loss of certificated teachers as indicated by an ASTA convention resolution requesting the same grants for correspondence supervisors as for teachers. The general secretary reported that at Lousana a "sitter" had been appointed as principal of its graded school until the ATA protested. The council felt that "Everything short of forcing the Government to resort to the permit system should be done to discourage the 'sitter' system."[2] "Everything" was interpreted to mean that the ATA should refuse to recognize the work of "sitters" as teaching, should insist on a wide margin in remuneration between them and teachers, that they not be accepted at school festivals and track meets held under ATA sponsorship, or at teachers' meetings, that the superintendents be requested to refrain from treating them as teachers, and that the department of education be asked to formulate a provincial policy with respect to them.

No doubt it was a result of what the ATA regarded as a threat to their profession that led to a much more militant and aggressive attitude on the part of *The ATA Magazine,* that and the fact that the publication had acquired a new editor in the person of the recently appointed general secretary E. C. Ansley. The tone of the *Magazine* is indicated by the following items which appeared during 1947:

[1]ATA Ex., Sept. 7, 1946.
[2]*Ibid.,* Dec. 4, 1946.

WANTED: BY ALL SCHOOL
BOARDS IN ALBERTA
A teacher smart enough to
be worth $200 a month, and
dumb enough to work for
$100 a month.[3]

In a few years
THIS MAY BE NO FAIRY TALE

Once upon a time every school in Alberta had a teacher and every little boy and girl in this great big Province went to one of those schools every day in the week except Saturday and Sunday. At school a nice person, called a teacher, looked after them and taught them to read, to do number work, and how to grow up to be fine men and women. This was a long time ago when your mother was a little girl just like you. Then one day some big bad men drove the teacher right out of the school, and we have never seen a teacher since.[4]

Teachers Wanted—Taken from ads for teachers
Alberta papers—July and August, 1946

"Liberal salary schedule" "Attractive salary schedule"	Probably means a few other schedules are worse
"Excellent week-end service to and from city" "Daily bus to city" "School served by bus and railroad" "On gravelled highway"	Invariably from areas where salaries are lowest, perhaps on the assumption teachers should accept easy transportation in lieu of salary
"High salary"	Doesn't mean a thing
"Exceptionally pleasant district" "Attractive district"	Generally, low salaries go with these schools, the teacher being expected to get the difference in salary in aesthetic enjoyment.
"Good teacherage suitable for man and wife"	Be careful of this one, especially if you have a wife.
"Plane fare paid"	Be sure it is a return ticket.
"Light enrolment"	Means "light" salary also.[5]

[3]*The ATA Magazine,* XXIII, 4 (Jan. 1947), 37.
[4]*Ibid.,* 6 (March 1947), 16.
[5]*Ibid.,* 8 (June 1947), 14.

WE KNOW NOW

That Alberta cannot get teachers by offering $1,200 to beginning teachers

—with average salaries of $2,000

—with a pension of $40 per month

—by declaring another 'open season' on teachers.

—through any recruitment campaign until the salaries in education are comparable with those in other occupations

The teaching profession hasn't recovered yet from the effects of the last 'open season,' during which 4,000 teachers' contracts were terminated every year.

WE KNOW NOW

That Alberta can get teachers

—by paying professional salaries

—by providing adequate pensions

—by conferring on teachers their rightful place in community life.[6]

The battle of the "sitters" raged on. Their status was a matter of concern at an emergent general meeting in February, 1947, at which the executive council introduced this resolution: "Resolved: That the Provincial Executive recommends to the Locals that those schools in charge of 'sitters' be not admitted to Festivals and Track Meets under the jurisdiction of the ATA Locals, and that 'sitters' be excluded from teacher meetings."[7] The resolution was approved.

By mid-1947 the executive council heard a report that refusal of ATA members to include sitter-staffed schools in track meets had resulted in the Neutral Hills divisional board's refusal to approve such events, to the embarrassment of the Local. The council reaffirmed its attitude and directed that Locals be notified of the ATA policy as it affected local conventions. In 1948 the council again stated its policy by resolving "that the Executive authorize the General Secretary to attend teachers' conventions only and that any place where 'sitters' are found, he be authorized to by-pass."[8]

[6]*Ibid.*, XXVII, 1 (Sept. -Oct. 1947), 3.

[7]*Ibid.*, XXVII, 5 (Feb. 1947), 24.

[8]ATA Ex., March 26, 29—April 4, 1948.

Despite the Association's unyielding opposition, the correspondence centre remained an element of Alberta's educational picture for several years to come. In 1950 there were still 288 such centres. Not until 1955 did the number drop below 100; not until 1960 did it reach zero. Even after that date the centres reappeared sporadically.

It is probable that the virtual disappearance of the correspondence centres was due not to the opposition of the ATA but to the closing of the one-room rural schools. By 1966 their number had shrunk to 100, a figure that might be regarded as the irreducible minimum.

Better salaries were important in the post-war years; so were better pensions. So significant did the Association view the matter of superannuation that in December 1946 the executive council authorized the ATA's general secretary to act as secretary also of the Teachers' Retirement Fund Board. Early in 1947 an emergent general meeting was called to consider salaries and pensions; perhaps a result of this gathering was an announcement shortly afterwards that pensions had been increased from $35 to $40 a month—just slightly better than the pension paid to elderly indigents.

In April of the same year for the first time the matter of reciprocity of rights as between the TRF and the provincial government scheme was discussed in the ATA council meeting. Apparently the matter was raised particularly on behalf of divisional superintendents, but many others in the department of education were concerned, such as the correspondence teachers, and others, some of whom were even in other departments. On motion of A. O. Aalborg, future minister of education, the matter was tabled. However, three years later the executive council got around to recommending that the proposal be adopted, but only for persons employed in the public service in the field of education. This was the first step towards the achievement of a wide range of portability accomplished through reciprocal agreements with the Alberta and federal governments and the teachers' pension plans in a number of other provinces.

In 1948 the government introduced new pension legislation to replace that which provided teachers with their flat $40 per month retirement benefit. This was the scheme for which the ATA had honoured the Hon. R. E. Ansley on his resignation as minister of education. As has been described in chapter 8, the new scheme provided retiring teachers with an annual salary equal to 1½ per cent of average salary over the last five years of service multiplied by the number of years of teaching between ages 30 and 65 years. It thus provided a maximum pension of 1½ x 35, or 52½ per cent of average salary for last five years of service. Teachers' contributions were to be 4 per cent of earned salary for a maximum of 35 years. The scheme was an immeasurable improvement over what had gone before, but was still not equal to what was available to provincial civil servants (who contributed five per cent of salary for a pension based on 2 rather than 1½ per cent of average final salary); equality was achieved later.

However, a new pension scheme, like a new model of an aircraft or an automobile, usually has bugs that have to be worked out as a result of field trials. Such was the case with the Alberta TRF. For example, in 1951 the general secretary reported on one problem to the executive council:

> Mr. Ansley gave a summary of the situation in Edmonton and Calgary with regard to the pension paid to retiring teachers. It is customary in both of these cities to raise to maximum the salaries of those teachers who are within five years of retirement and have taught for twenty years or more. As the pension is based on the salary of a teacher during his best five years of earnings, this places a burden on the pension fund which has not been and cannot be provided for.[9]

Another problem arose the following year, although it affected pensions only indirectly. Before 1952, teachers were retired at the end of the school year after they reached their 65th birthday. But the legislation indicated that the school year ended on August 31 each year, so that a teacher who reached the age of 65 in July or August could hold his position for another year whether his employer wished him to or not. As a result of a protest on the part of one particular school board, the government moved the automatic retirement date to June 30 on or after a teacher reached his 65th birthday, an action which made a difference of a whole year for those teachers unfortunate enough to have chosen a July or August birthday, and affected their pensions accordingly. An ATA editorial criticized the government for making this change without consulting or even informing the teachers beforehand. The measure seemed particularly ill-advised, considering the chronic shortage of teachers and the efforts which the ATA had been expending to persuade boards to retain teachers and the latter to continue in service after the age of 65.

During the early post-war years the fight for improvement of the teacher's

[9] *Ibid.*, March 29, 1951.

lot had to be waged on many fronts. Thus in 1948 the "blacklist" of unpleasant memory reappeared in *The ATA Magazine* when it carried the the name of the Medicine Hat school division. The division's transgression was in advertising for teachers in accordance with an obsolete salary schedule while negotiations were under way. West Jasper Place school district was castigated for withholding a day's pay from a teacher absent from school to attend his mother's funeral. Another case, the following year, involved a teacher transfer as a result of a student strike against the teacher. *The ATA Magazine* editor summarized the story as follows:

> From now on teachers in Alberta can handle these strikes, if they work together under a plan devised by one of our Locals last fall. When a number of students went on strike against a teacher and demanded his resignation, the Local asked the other teachers to suspend the strikers. The Board ordered a transfer without, as far as is known, a thorough investigation. The Local then asked all other teachers in the Division to refuse to accept a transfer, even though it meant a promotion. When the situation was stabilized and under control, the Local persuaded the school board to hold an inquiry, at which each of the strikers—now suspended from all classes—would be required to attend, accompanied by one or both parents, and at which the teachers' representatives would have the right to cross-examine the strikers and all other witnesses.
>
> This changed the tenure of the strike. The joke was on the strikers. It was a serious group of youngsters who came to the hearing, which was prolonged and thorough.[10]

One case involving an individual school board was significant in demonstrating once again the futility of attempting to by-pass the duly constituted officers of the ATA and deal directly with the membership, a tactic that one minister of education after another had discovered to be pointless. This case involved the Edson school division, which transferred six teachers and requested resignations from five others, with threats of dismissal if they were not forthcoming. The board then advertised positions which were not vacant at salaries which had not been settled. In an attempt to negotiate directly with the teachers, the board of trustees invited them to a meeting, with transportation provided. Hearing of this ploy, the ATA immediately went on the radio to advise members not to attend. As a result, none of the teaching staff appeared for the meeting, and the school board in the end had to negotiate with its teachers through regular channels.

[10]*The ATA Magazine,* XXIX, 6 (March 1949), 4.

These were problems affecting individual school boards, but some were more general. One involved the matter of compulsory arbitration of salary disputes. In 1948 the ATA executive council resolved to ask the government to make arbitration awards binding upon both teachers and school boards. The department of education referred the proposal to the ASTA for the trustees' opinion; they favoured making such awards compulsory only when they were unanimous. Deputy minister W. H. Swift so reported to the ATA; what was the teachers' reaction? They regarded the trustees' position as ridiculous, probably because it would have made such awards binding only when the trustees' representative on the arbitration board was in agreement. This was a long way from the compulsory arbitration which teachers favoured at that time. During the late forties both teachers and school boards commonly accepted arbitration awards. In the fifties, the bargaining became somewhat more hard-nosed, and more and more often the teachers called on their Association to act as bargaining agent. For example, in 1951 it acted as agent of the teachers in 27 cases. Generally, teachers accepted arbitration awards; in the few cases where the school boards did not, strike action followed, for example, in West Jasper Place district, Newell county, and Clover Bar school division in 1954 and 1955.

Despite the relative job security which teachers had secured, the ATA ever remembered that eternal vigilance is the price of tenure. In 1957, for instance, the ATA investigated nine cases of teachers' dismissals. Three resulted in appeals to the Board of Reference. Of these, one was disallowed on a technicality and one the teacher concerned withdrew. The remaining one was settled out of court. In the same year, the Association investigated six cases wherein principals were removed from their assignments. In one case the school board received permission from the minister of education to give notice of termination of principalship, four cases were settled by mutual agreement, and the Board of Reference granted one appeal. In that case the ATA protested the action of the investigating officer, identified by name, for obtaining evidence other than by a public inquiry, and the fact that he did not make this evidence available to the ATA despite an understanding so to do. The following year *The ATA Magazine* drew to the attention of its readers the fact that appeals against dismissals could be made to the Board of Reference, but those against termination of designation as principal or vice-principal or against transfers had been removed from the jurisdiction of the Board of Reference. Henceforth the first type of appeal would be to the employing board and then to the minister of education. Appeals against transfers could be made only to the employing school board, the body which had made the original decision.

Legal protection against arbitrary and capricious transfers of teachers from one assignment to another is one thing that the ATA has never been able to achieve. But the need for such protection is indicated by a 1955 transfer by Bonnyville school division of a teacher from Ardmore to Iron River, the transfer to become effective on September 13, the day after it was given. The teacher received official notice of the transfer on September 19 and filed a request for a hearing to hear an appeal. The board heard the appeal on September 26 but remained adamant in its decision, although to the ATA's general secretary its reasons appeared specious. The teacher therefore asked for a release and got it; the net result was that the division was short yet another teacher. In a somewhat similar case the teacher was transferred 27 miles from her home. "There is one word to describe this abuse of legal authority," the editor of *The ATA Magazine* stated, "and that is dastardly."[11]

But sometimes teachers have found allies to protect them in their positions. Two such cases occurred in 1958, one involving a rural school in the Leduc school division. There, the parents vehemently protested the appointment of a Negro teacher to an all-white school. The board rightly considered her ancestry to be irrelevant and refused to remove her. In the other case, a teacher was physically prevented from assuming her responsibilities at the school in Vimy because "it was alleged that she could not teach catechism and French,"[12] in short, because she was not a Roman Catholic. This unhappy circumstance arose from the fact that the Vimy school had originally been one that served only a local French-Canadian, Roman Catholic clientele, but when it became the nucleus of a centralization for the Westlock school division, a number of monoglot Protestant children were enrolled. In an effort to maintain the school's confessional nature, some Vimy residents attempted to deny access to it by any except bilingual teachers of their own religious persuasion. Through the firmness of the divisional board they were unsuccessful in this endeavour.

During the late fifties an issue which had troubled teachers for more than thirty years was finally resolved. This was the question of a provincial salary

[11] *Ibid.*, XXXVI, 3 (Nov. 1955), 61.
[12] *Ibid.*, XXXVIII, 1 (Sept. 1957), 48.

schedule, with which was usually associated the matter of compulsory arbitration in the matter of collective bargaining. During the Hungry Thirties the Association had supported the proposal, regarding it as a protection against the apparently endless decline in teachers' salaries. With returning prosperity during the war years and after, the teachers' attitude became much more ambiguous, and with the advent of the Golden Fifties the Association's attitude hardened into firm opposition to the idea.

Perhaps the ATA might have continued to support a provincial salary schedule had it been reached by negotiation between the ATA and the ASTA at the provincial level. This, however, was not the trustees' idea. For one thing, although the ATA was regularly empowered to bargain on behalf of its Locals, its opposite number, the ASTA, had no legal power to commit school boards, and if even one district out of the 200 or so in the province refused to accept a schedule agreed upon by the provincial bodies, the whole concept of a provincial salary schedule would go down the drain. Consequently the ASTA concept of a provincial salary schedule was one arrived at by a government-appointed commission (perhaps including representatives of the teachers and the trustees) that would receive briefs from the interested parties and establish an agreement that would be binding on teachers and school boards alike. This, of course, would remove the teachers' right to strike.

Because of the continuing demand for a provincial salary schedule, in 1957 the provincial government appointed a royal commission under the chairmanship of G. M. Blackstock, Q.C., to inquire into the matter. Specifically, the commission was directed to consider:

(a) the feasibility of establishing a scale or scales for teachers in the Province;
(b) the form or forms which such salary scales might take;
(c) the manner by which such salary scales might be arrived at and altered from time to time;
(d) the effects of the establishment of teacher salary scales upon:
  (i) the local government process in regard to schools,
  (ii) the financing of education both in the Province generally and in particular areas within the Province, and
  (iii) the supply of teachers and upon the quality and morale of the teaching profession generally.[13]

[13]Alberta, *Report of the Royal Commission on the Feasibility of Establishing a Scale of Salaries for Teachers in the Province of Alberta, etc.*, (1958), p. 2.

Many royal commissions, legislative committees, and other groups have from time to time investigated some aspect or other of Alberta education. The Blackstock commission is probably unique in being the only one to be boycotted by the teachers of the province. This boycott arose as a result of the treatment of the ATA by the commission chairman, who apparently had expected to open the hearings with an examination of the Association's brief and witnesses. When he learned that the ATA was not planning to submit a brief, or at least not before the hearings opened, he seemed quite disturbed and virtually accused the teachers of jockeying for position in an effort to establish their own views rather than to assist in an objective appraisal of the merits and demerits of the proposal for a provincial salary schedule. Only after the ATA's executive secretary pointed out that the commission's terms of reference permitted a brief to be presented six days before any one of the scheduled hearings did the chairman agree to hear the ASTA's case first. In Ansley's words:

I think that Mr. Owen [ATA counsel] carried on under the most difficult circumstances. For example, Mr. Owen asked a question phrased almost exactly in the words of one of the terms of reference. Mr. Blackstock told Mr. Hennig he did not have to answer, and went so far as to tell the stenographer not to take down any questions and answers. I suggested to Mr. Owen that he read the specific term of reference. Mr. Owen did not do so and I tossed them aside. A few minutes later a member of the Commission drew Mr. Blackstock's attention to a paper, no doubt the terms of reference, and he said, 'Mr. Owen, you may return to the question you asked before. I do not wish to appear biased'. When Mr. Owen asked the Alberta School Trustees' Association for a copy of their brief Mr. Blackstock interrupted and told Mr. Bruce Smith that he did not have to give the Alberta Teachers' Association a copy but Mr. Smith did quite dramatically. We had no idea what the brief would contain until we heard it read. Mr. Owen had to stall until one o'clock after which time we would be able to go over the brief."

Mr. Ansley quoted some more of the remarks made by Mr. Blackstock. "There were two happenings that really bothered me. On two occasions Mr. Owen had Mr. Hennig cornered. Mr Blackstock came to his rescue once and Mr. Bruce Smith the second time. This kind of thing is just not done. [Counsel or Chairman answering for a witness who has been sworn.] Mr. Blackstock's closing remark was that we had no case. You can imagine that after that we did not know what to do. Mr. Ross and I went to Vimy; the others met in the office in the afternoon. Mr. Ross and I discussed at length the untenable position we seemed to be in and we decided it would be to our advantage to withdraw at once because of the Chairman's attitude and remarks. He seemed to have almost a personal animosity toward us, whether to Mr.

Owen, to me, to Mr. Seymour as individuals or to teachers generally, I don't know—but it was there. The hearing had already become a farce as far as I could see.[14]

The executive council at an emergent Sunday morning meeting endorsed Ansley's suggestion that the Association withdraw from the hearings, and approved a letter to this effect on the part of the ATA's counsel, as follows:

The Chairman and Members
of the Royal Commission
to inquire into the matter of
Provincial Salary Scales for Teachers
GENTLEMEN:

Following the conclusion of the first day's sitting of the Commission, and having regard to the extraordinary manner in which the proceedings of the Commission were conducted, and its attitude towards the teachers of Alberta, whom I represented, I consulted at length with my principals during the afternoon and evening of September 12th.

The day's proceedings were carefully considered. It is apparent to my principals that the Commission has attributed to them ulterior motives in declining to present a written brief at this, the first of several hearings. My opening and repeated statement that a greater contribution could be made by the teachers through oral testimony of qualified persons was rejected as being an attempt to jockey for position and as evidence of a disgraceful attitude.

Counsel's right to conduct his case in such manner as he deems proper, having regard to the interests of his principals and also to the objects of this inquiry, was challenged by the Commission and branded as an attempt to run it. The integrity and motives of the teachers were unjustly impugned.

The Chairman's closing remarks that the teachers had no case made before my principals' case was put in evidence, has aroused grave apprehension that the hearings will not be conducted with the impartiality demanded of a Royal Commission.

In the circumstances, I am instructed to advise you that in my principals' considered opinion no useful purpose can be served in continuing their participation in these proceedings.

It is with deep regret that the teachers are accordingly constrained to withdraw from an inquiry into matters so vital to education.

Yours respectfully,
PETER M. OWEN, Counsel of
THE ALBERTA TEACHERS' ASSOCIATION[15]

The following day the letter was delivered to the commission. Efforts were made by counsel of the ASTA and of the Rural Municipalities Association to

[14]ATA Ex., Sept. 15, 1957.
[15]*Ibid.*

persuade the teachers to return to the fold; they were abortive. The commission's secretary acknowledged Owen's letter, stated that "any impression that your client's case has been prejudged is quite erroneous,"[16] and invited the Association to reconsider its decision respecting withdrawal.

The executive council now had a whole series of problems to wrestle with. The first was whether the Association should reconsider its decision and participate in the hearings. Only after long discussion and the presentation of divergent viewpoints did the executive decide not to reverse the previous decision. This conclusion was embodied in the following resolution:

RESOLVED that the Alberta Teachers' Association take no further part in the proceedings of the present Royal Commission and that its solicitor be instructed to reply to the Commission secretary's letter of September 12th, and that a Committee now be appointed to draft the statement to be made to the Commission in reply to its letter, at the opening of the hearings on Monday, September 16th.

CARRIED[17]

There still remained the problems of informing the public and the Association's own membership as to why the ATA had taken such an unprecedented step as to withdraw from the hearings of a Royal Commission established to investigate a matter that touched teachers so closely. The Association issued press releases to the news media to defend its action. With respect to its own membership its procedure was somewhat more highly structured. As the executive council minutes indicate:

There was a discussion of the problem involved in holding local meetings during the next few weeks. It was agreed that every effort should be made to inform the teachers of the reasons for withdrawal from the Commission hearings and of the Association's opinion about a provincial salary schedule for teachers.

Moved by [one of the members]:

RESOLVED that the Executive assistants prepare a schedule of local meetings, and that they advise the district representatives who will make arrangements with local officers to arrange meetings according to the schedule.

CARRIED[18]

Although deploring the attitude of the ATA, the commission went ahead with its assignment, and in January, 1958, it submitted its report. Its recommendations were fourfold:

[16]*Ibid.*
[17]*Ibid.*
[18]*Ibid.*

1. Creation of an all-powerful three-man tribunal with a full-time chairman, to have complete jurisdiction over teachers' salaries.

2. Adoption of a basic provincial salary schedule.

3. This schedule to include provision for regional differences.

4. Extra remuneration for senior and junior high school teachers—in short, for a positional rather than a single schedule.[19]

Reversing its position on a number of points, the Association published what may be regarded as its mature and ultimate stand on a provincial salary schedule (and compulsory arbitration). This was one of opposition, based on the following arguments:

1. It is a principle of collective bargaining that terms and conditions of work be negotiated.

2. A uniform scale would socialize or nationalize teaching.

3. Control of salaries by the government would become political.

4. Such control would lead to interference with intellectual freedom.

5. Every proposal advanced by the Alberta School Trustees' Association would reduce the effectiveness of the teachers in the bargaining situation.

6. The ATA is opposed to further centralization of government.

7. The present system permits experimentation.

8. Compulsory arbitration is a totalitarian concept.

9. Uniform salary schedules promote mediocre salary scales, for example, in the United Kingdom and in Nova Scotia.

10. Salary disparity is normal.

11. There is no evidence that either teachers or the government expect that a uniform scale would be equal to the best current rates.[20]

Perhaps as a result of the ATA's opposition and that of some school boards, the minister of education, A. O. Aalborg, announced that no legislation would be introduced to implement the commission's recommendations at the 1958 session of the legislature, if ever. In point of fact, no such bill has ever been presented or passed. Thus the achievements of the Blackstock commission would seem to be completely negative, unless one concedes that it resulted in a final resolution of the issue of a provincial salary schedule.

[19]*The ATA Magazine*, XXXVIII, 8 (April 1958), 19 *et seq.*

[20]*Ibid.*

The Ultimate Weapon

NO SANCTION ever applied by teachers, not even the "blacklist" which so exercised minister of education J. P. Smith in 1920, has ever created more consternation among school trustees and the public generally than has the withdrawal of teaching services, especially if it resulted in the closing of the schools. Strikes are so alien to the *mores* of the white middle-class people who place such a high value on formal education, the independent farmers, professional people, merchants, managers—the very group which supplies the nation's teachers—that they react with a sense of shock when teachers walk off their jobs. Factory workers, railroad personnel, truck drivers, beverage room personnel can strike, and the public complains at the inconvenience, but when teachers or nurses strike, their action is regarded almost as a personal affront. Charges of unprofessionalism are rampant, and the teachers' commitment to their calling is compared unfavourably to that exhibited by physicians, lawyers, dentists, architects. Conveniently overlooked is the fact that these groups are paid by fees, not salaries, that they accept or reject any patient or client as they wish, whereas hospital nurses or school teachers have no choice as to their clientele. Nor is it unknown for medical men, when their services become institutionalized, to withdraw those services to gain their ends, just as do nurses and teachers upon rare occasions. They do not call such action a strike, but the difference is difficult to detect with the naked eye. Such a tactic, of course, arouses even more antipathy than does a strike by teachers.

The ATA has of late years adopted the position that the right of teachers to withdraw their services is a fundamental one, although this has not always been the stand. At one time it did favour compulsory arbitration of salary disputes, a position which automatically eliminates the right to strike. At this writing, Alberta teachers are in a more permissive position than those in most or all other provinces. The statutes of most provinces are silent on this matter, neither permitting nor forbidding teacher strikes, although they are outlawed in Manitoba. In Quebec the situation is little better. There the teachers are granted this right, but the first time they used it, with every prospect of being successful in gaining their ends, the legislature stepped in to require their return to their classrooms at imposed and not negotiated salary rates.

Under the Alberta Labour Act definite conditions must be met before a strike can be legal. These require negotiation at increasing levels of formality. If a school board and a teachers' bargaining unit (the staff of a system, usually organized as a Local or Sub-Local of the ATA) cannot reach an agreement, they call in their bargaining agents. Normally these are the ATA for the teachers, the ASTA for the school board. Failure at this level results in the appointment of a conciliator by the minister of labour. If his efforts are unsuccessful, the dispute is taken to a conciliation board consisting of one representative of each party to the dispute plus a chairman, chosen by the other two conciliators or, if they cannot agree, by the minister of labour. In due course the board brings down its recommendations, either by a unanimous or by a 2-1 decision. These recommendations are not binding unless the disputants have previously committed themselves to accept them, a commitment which in practice is rarely made. Since the recommendations usually favour one side or the other (or are thought to do so), at least initially they are frequently rejected by the teachers or the school boards or both. Negotiations, however, continue, and if agreement seems unobtainable, the teachers may decide to ask for a strike vote. This decision, incidentally, is one in which every teacher has a chance to participate. Strike votes are taken under the direction of the department of labour.

Many trustees have faced the prospect of a strike vote with considerable unjustified complacency. Looking at their staffs and the high proportion of members who are tied to their communities by husbands' jobs or the real property they own, these trustees tend to conclude, quite erroneously, that such teachers would never vote themselves out of their positions when transfers to other posts would prove difficult or impossible. They have sadly underestimated the loyalty of their teachers to their profession and their colleagues.

Records of only two strikes by teachers in Alberta before 1942 are available. Both of these have been discussed earlier. The first was the 1921 walk-out of Edmonton high school teachers. A few years later came the prolonged Blairmore dispute, a strike following the school board's lock-out of its staff. Neither strike proved very effective, since the Alberta Teachers' Alliance did not include all teachers, and so was not able to prevent strike-breaking action by nonmembers. The next teacher strike did not come until six years after the 1936 amendments to the Teaching Profession Act made all teachers automatically members of their organization. It did not follow all the steps which later governed the business of requesting and taking a strike vote in accordance with provincial legislation; rather, according to the recollection of senior officers of the ATA, it was virtually a spontaneous action—a wildcat strike—on the part of the small staff of the then-independent Mundare school district.

This 1942 dispute was typical of those which led teachers to the ultimate sanction of strike action. It followed negotiations, which, begun in May 1941, finally broke down the following spring when Mundare school district trustees rejected an arbitration award. Faced with a strike threat, on April 30, 1942, the board surrendered—in a manner of speaking. It offered to pay salaries in accordance with the arbitration award, but only for the balance of the school year, that is, until the end of June. It also reserved the right to dismiss any or all teachers at that time, and stated that April cheques would be delayed. The following day, a Friday, the school did not open as the teachers walked out. Shocked at their apparent callousness about the welfare of their pupils, the trustees on Sunday, May 2, capitulated, and on Monday the schools reopened.

In the twenty-one years following the Mundare altercation, some Local or other of the Association went to strike action seven times—about once in three years on the average. These seven strikes are listed in Table II. Their effect on the operation of the province's schools was negligible. According to the Association:

> The percentage loss is . . . 0.3 of one percent *for those jurisdictions experiencing work stoppages.* Of course, this percentage figure is much smaller when the 82 days

lost are placed against the total number of school days in which *all* Alberta school jurisdictions operated since 1941. A conservative estimate would put the percentage loss over the whole province somewhere near 0.012 of one percent.[1]

Even if the one-day walk-out of Mundare's tiny staff had been included, these figures would have been changed only a very long way to the right of the decimal point.

Industrial strikes occur for many reasons: wages, working conditions, pension rights, seniority rights, and so on. Occasionally such workers walk off their jobs because of jurisdictional disputes or in sympathy with other strikers. But almost invariably teachers' strikes are concerned with but one issue: that of remuneration.

TABLE II
ATA STRIKES, 1942 TO 1963

Year	School system	Nature of conciliation board award	School board action	Teacher action	School days lost
1942	Vegreville S. Div.	Majority	Rejection	Acceptance	33
1954	W. Jasper Place S. D.	"	"	"	5
1954	County of Newell	Unanimous	"	"	0
1955	Clover Bar S. Div.	Majority	"	"	9
1957	Normandy S. Dist.	"	Acceptance	Rejection	19
1960	Leduc S. Div.	Unanimous	Rejection	Acceptance	9
1963	County of Strathcona	"	Acceptance	Rejection	9
					82

Source: F. J. C. Seymour, ed., in *The ATA Magazine*, October 1964, p. 107.

Such a one was the 1942 dispute involving the Vegreville school division. Negotiations went all the way to an arbitration board majority award, accepted by the teachers but rejected on September 18 by the divisional school board. Apparently a number of teachers had accepted positions with the system under the impression that the trustees would accept the arbitration board award when it was handed down. But three weeks after the board's rejection, when the

[1]F. J. C. Seymour (ed.), "Submissions of the Alberta Teachers' Association to the Special Committee of the Legislative Assembly on Collective Bargaining between School Trustees and Teachers," in a special issue of *The ATA Magazine,* Oct. 1964, p. 11.

teachers met in convention, the dispute was still unsettled. At that time they voted in favour of strike action by a majority of 55 to 3, the strike to be called at the discretion of the Local executive. The school board chairman suggested that further action be deferred until the trustees had an opportunity to consult their electors, but as that action could not be taken before December at the earliest, the teachers regarded the proposal simply as a delaying tactic, and withdrew their services. The result was the longest strike in the history of the Alberta Teachers' Association, lasting 33 school days, or more than a month and a half. The ATA assessed the entire membership $1 per month for the duration of the strike plus an additional month and undertook to pay the strikers at the rate of the arbitration award less any earnings during that period. If the strike should prove prolonged—perhaps purposely that term was left undefined—assistance was to be given the teachers in finding other positions. In the end, the strike was terminated by the mediation of the deputy minister, and the teachers went back to their classrooms with most of what they had sought. The final settlement called for a basic salary of $840 per year with a cost-of-living allowance of $76.35, fluctuating as the cost-of-living index rose or fell. In addition, the new agreement provided for experience increments and other allowances. A final footnote was provided by a grant from the executive council in the amount of $100 to the Vegreville Local, which emerged from the conflict entirely without funds.

A strike is a traumatic experience, not only for parents and school trustees but for the teachers also. Perhaps this is the reason why twelve years elapsed before the next one. Certainly it was not because all was peace and harmony between teachers and their employers; the Association considered strike action on more than one occasion.

The year 1954 was in fact marked by two strikes, both of which followed acceptance by the teachers of conciliation board awards and their rejection by the school boards. One, in West Jasper Place, closed the schools for a week. The other, in the county of Newell, is interesting in that it occurred during the summer holidays, when the schools were not open anyway. On the face of it, it might be thought that such action would be futile and pointless. In fact, it was quite otherwise, for it meant that the school system was unable to recruit teachers for the coming term. In an effort to exert pressure on its teachers, the county refused to issue the regular July and August cheques, that is, to complete payment for work already done by the end of June. The Association responded by a decision to pay striking teachers from ATA funds, and the minutes of an executive council meeting dated August 16, 1954, note that legal action on behalf of two teachers had been initiated against the county.

At the same meeting it was reported that striking teachers were being blacklisted by other school boards. Deciding to fight fire with fire, the executive council determined to blacklist such boards in turn if it should be satisfied that any discrimination existed. By the end of August, however, the dispute was settled and the schools opened on schedule. As part of the agreement, the action on behalf of the two teachers was discontinued when the county undertook to issue the cheques for the July and August salaries.

The executive council of the ATA was concerned with salary negotiations not merely when teachers went all the way down the road to strike action but at other times as well. Thus in December 1954 the members approved a set of principles to govern strategy for the coming year. These were: (1) Emphasis to be taken off the raising of minima; (2) emphasis to be placed on raising maxima according to local conditions; (3) qualifications to be emphasized; (4) administrative allowances to be emphasized; (5) size of increments to be emphasized; (6) "laddered" schedules to be approved (that is, schedules where more increments are given for teachers with higher than with lower qualifications); (7) professional pay to be sought for extra duties and responsibilities; (8) approval on restriction of increments for teachers with letters of authority, temporary licences, and interim certificates; (9) endorsation of the principles of sabbatical leaves and cumulative sick leaves.[2]

In 1955 the Clover Bar school division board of trustees rejected a conciliation board award. Minutes of June 10–11 meeting of the executive council contain the following: "Be it resolved, that the teachers of the province of Alberta be informed that it will be considered an unprofessional act to enter into a contract with the Clover Bar School Division if the Clover Bar Board refuses the award of the board of arbitration."[3] Since the school board did refuse the award, the teachers withdrew their services at the end of the school year. In this as in most cases, their action could hardly be considered precipitate; they had taught a whole year without a contract.

[2]ATA Ex., Dec. 9, 1954.
[3]*Ibid.*, June 10-11, 1955.

By the middle of August, it had become apparent that the teachers were not going to back down, and the board of trustees applied to the Board of Industrial Relations for mediation—the good services of a mediator from the Board to act as a catalyst for the achievement of an agreement. However, in accordance with the Labour Act, no mediation was possible unless both sides were willing, so the executive council of the ATA, which was the teachers' bargaining agent, had to consider whether it would agree to such a step. The result of the executive council's deliberations were that one member ". . . said he thought that, if the Executive agreed to ask for mediation, there was danger of establishing a precedent, and that school boards could be expected to ask for mediation in all future disputes. Besides, in view of the wishes of the Clover Bar teachers, he did not think the Executive should request mediation."[4] It was so agreed. The result was that the school board and the ATA executive continued to negotiate face to face. Again according to the executive council minutes:

> At a meeting on August 29 between school board members and [executive members] two offers were made: one in which the board agreed to settle the dispute on the basis of the conciliators' recommendations for September-December 1954 and the arbitration award for the remainder of the school year and the coming year (1955-56), the second agreeing to settle the dispute on the basis of the arbitration award for the two-year period 1954-55 and 1955-56. The first offer was refused by the Executive; the second was referred to the local executive through the president. A Home-and-School meeting was called on September 2, at which both sides were asked to present facts, and [two members] spoke on behalf of the ATA. A resolution was passed asking the School board to accept the arbitration award immediately. It was agreed that a school board meeting was held on September 13, agreeing to accept the award, but no intimation was received by head office until September 16. A meeting was arranged between school board officials and the ATA for September 17 at which the agreement was signed.[5]

The schools had been closed for nine days.

The next teacher-trustee eyeball-to-eyeball confrontation occurred in Normandy school district. This, like other department of national defence districts, is an anomaly, which permits the federal government to operate common schools despite the fact that education is constitutionally and explicitly a provincial responsibility; indeed this arrangement is the particular reason for the erection of such districts. A subsidiary reason appears to be that it permits

[4]*Ibid.*, Aug. 15, 1955.
[5]*Ibid.*, Sept. 30, 1955.

teachers to work in a federal organization without becoming civil servants, and allows them to contribute to the Alberta Teachers Retirement Fund exactly as if they were employed by any other district.

However, since a DND district does not have any residents who are electors as defined by the Alberta School Act, it operates under the direction of an official trustee, normally a senior officer of the armed forces. Yet in practice if not in theory he is not the ultimate authority; behind him stands the commanding officer of the station or base whose boundaries are those of the school district. And what the commanding officer wants the commanding officer gets. Yet in school matters even he is not the end of the line; salary agreements, for example, are subject to a veto of the assistant judge adjutant general, known (but not to his face) as the AJAG.

This administrative organization tends to make the negotiation of teachers' salaries an extremely frustrating exercise. In the first place, the negotiations have to be carried on with an official who really does not have the power to commit the department of national defence; all proposals must go to Ottawa for study and review. Secondly, that department, like all other federal departments before 1967, had no experience in collective bargaining, its functionaries not understanding the essential nature of the process. Its officers tended to regard teachers rather as out-of-uniform service personnel—weren't they members of the officers' mess?—and to expect them to behave as such, that is, to obey orders and not argue with their superior officers.

It is not uncommon for a school system to approach or reach the end of the school year without a current salary agreement; by the spring of 1957 the teaching staff and the official trustee of Normandy school district had not even reached an agreement for the 1955-56 school year. For the first time in history a Local of the ATA rejected a conciliation board award. On May 23, 1957, the Normandy district teachers voted to strike. They had the somewhat grudging support of the provincial organization, as the school district's offer was good in comparison with those of other school systems—an indication that the teachers were more frustrated at the RCAF's handling of negotiations than at the size of the offer. As a result, the school's were closed for the last ninteen days of the 1956-57 term. As the strike dragged through the summer a new factor appeared in the controversy, the official trustee's termination of the designation of the vice-principal, who was reduced to the rank of classroom teacher. When the two parties reached agreement on the salary schedule, the teachers made their acceptance contingent upon the withdrawal of notice of termination of the vice-principal's status. Although for some weeks it seemed that the Normandy classrooms would not be open on schedule, the official trustee accepted the teachers' conditions and school began on schedule at the beginning of September.

The conduct of this altercation demonstrated two home truths: that the ATA was not afraid to take on the majesty of the federal government itself if that body proved unwilling to play the game by the rules laid down in the Alberta School Act and in other pertinent legislation, and that not even the federal government could impose on its teachers the out-moded "hired hand" concept for its schools' professional personnel.

Since every year over 100 salary agreements have to be negotiated between school boards and their teaching staffs, it is surprising, not that there have been so many strikes (less than a dozen in the entire history of the ATA) but that there have been so few. Probably one reason for the small number is that the Alberta Labour Act sets forth procedures which provide many levels at which agreement can be achieved: the local level, bargaining agent, conciliation commissioner, board of conciliation, mediation before or after a strike vote or an actual strike. Yet the very fact that withdrawal of services is a sanction ultimately and legally available to teachers is no doubt a reason why teachers have so seldom had to resort to it. The executive council from time to time has given careful thought to the circumstances which would justify a strike. Thus its minutes for April 24 and 25, 1959, include the following:

> The Association is faced with two types of strikes:
> a) the teachers accept and the Board rejects a Conciliation Board award, and
> b) the teachers reject and the Board accepts a Conciliation Board award.
> A strike in the first instance is almost mandatory.
> The second situation . . . is more difficult. Teachers may reject a Conciliation Board award because it is too low, to prevent the award becoming a pattern-maker for the province, or to prevent violation of ATA policy.

The members of the executive council agreed that the Association faces two types of responsibility, financial and constitutional, to protect the interests not only of teachers on strike but of all teachers.

To clarify the conduct of negotiations following the award of a Conciliation Board, the following procedures and regulations are set forth:

I. When the award is made by the Conciliation Board, the representative of the Association shall discuss it with the Local Executive and the Local salary policy committee.

II. The local teachers must be informed of the following conditions which bear on their decision before they vote to accept or reject the Conciliation Board award. [The conditions were that in general the ATA as bargaining agent takes over full control of the negotiations on behalf of the teachers.]

III. Should the local executive and salary policy committee wish to reject the award of the Conciliation Board, the above terms and conditions shall be read to a local meeting which is called to consider the acceptance or rejection of the award.

The next strike following the adoption of this policy occurred a year later, when the trustees of the Leduc school division rejected and the teachers accepted a unanimous conciliation board award. This time the issue was not salary levels *per se* but the matter of cumulative sick pay, not whether but how much. On this occasion the schools were closed for nine days. As usual, the dispute ended in a compromise.

The year 1963 saw the bitterest, if not the longest, strike in the ATA's history. It occurred in the county of Strathcona, where a work stoppage had happened eight years before, when the system was known as Clover Bar school division. Probably there were many reasons for bitterness engendered by this dispute: the fact that the county, with its rich farm lands and petrochemical industries was the most affluent and therefore perhaps the most conservative rural school system in Alberta, the memory of the 1955 strike, the fact that school committee members felt free to attend a CEA convention in the midst of a very tense period of negotiation, and finally, veiled pressure from the government on the ATA to accept the conciliation board's award, since it was unanimous. (However, no such pressure had been applied to the Leduc divisional board three years previously when it had rejected a unanimous conciliation board recommendation.) While the seven-day strike was still in progress, *The ATA Magazine* carried the following editorial outlining the teachers' position:

THE STRATHCONA STRIKE

It is by now not news that the County of Strathcona's 229 teachers have withdrawn their services and that no immediate prospects of a settlement of the dispute are in sight. On one hand, the county council appears to have arranged a series of meetings at which an official of the Alberta School Trustees' Association and a member of a firm described as economic consultants have been presenting material in support of the county's position in the dispute. On the other, the teachers have refrained from seeking to arrange similar meetings and have instead presented their side of the dispute on request to meetings called by other groups.

The genesis of this grave situation dates back some 18 months when the teachers presented the County of Strathcona with proposals to amend the terms of an agreement which had been in effect since September 1, 1961. The teachers' requests were moderate in that they sought changes to take effect September, 1962 in the salary grid for teachers with three, four, five, and six years of training and totalling about 2.66 percent of the total salary bill. The county countered with a proposal for no increase in the grid and a cut in the administration allowance. In subsequent negotiations, neither side budged from its original position. Both the county and the teachers rejected a recommendation from a conciliation commissioner which would have cost about 1.1 percent and the dispute was carried before a conciliation board. When it became evident to the members of the conciliation board that a negotiated settlement could not be achieved, they brought down a unanimous award providing a $5 increase in the size of the annual increments for teachers with three, four, five, and six years of training, and suggested that the administration allowance remain unchanged. This award which would have cost about .36 of one percent was accepted by the county and rejected emphatically by the teachers.

Subsequently, the teachers voted overwhelmingly in favor of strike action as a means towards achieving an acceptable settlement of the dispute. It is a matter of record that last-minute meetings between representatives of the county and the teachers did not produce a formula for settlement and strike action postponed from October 7 took effect on October 9 in accordance with a unanimous decision reached at a general meeting of the teachers.

Powerful pressure was exerted on the teachers during this period by the Minister of Education who, in a public release, urged them to reconsider their decision because the award had been unanimous. The teachers resented deeply an implication in the release that they have taken an irresponsible and unjustifiable stand on this issue. They hold that it is open to either party appearing before a conciliation board to reject an award, and they are aware that as recently as 1960 the school board of the Leduc School Division also rejected a unanimous award of a conciliation board with the effect that, after a nine-day strike by the teachers, a compromise settlement, less favorable to the teachers than the award, was accepted by the parties. The Strathcona teachers are therefore convinced that their action in this case is neither irresponsible nor unjustified.

What has happened in this particular dispute to bring the teachers to the drastic step of taking strike action? Is it the meagreness of the award? Is it the intransigent attitude of the county council? Is it the interminable delays in the negotiations? Is it the studied misrepresentation of the teachers' position? Is it a suspicion that the teachers are being made the pawns in a bigger game being played by a trustee zone and its advisers?

There may very well be different answers to each of these questions from each of the 229 teachers affected, but a most significant point is that over half of the county's teachers, about 130 of them, who do not stand to gain a cent from whatever the settlement may turn out to be, have supported their colleagues all down the line in this bitter battle. And make no mistake, it is a bitter battle.

The teachers have resisted under the most trying circumstances the urge to rush to press with contradictions of statements made in behalf of the county by its advisers and intend to hold to the position that this dispute will not be resolved by who prints what in newspapers. The dispute will be settled when the parties accept a negotiated settlement. As an earnest of their willingness to move toward that position the teachers made a proposal before the strike was called which represented a compromise of their initial request. They are still waiting for evidence that the county as earnestly seeks a solution to the impasse. As each day of the strike passes and as the county's representatives continue to wage their propaganda campaign, the day of reckoning is delayed, bitterness mushrooms and settlement becomes the more difficult.[6]

After the schools had been closed for seven days, a compromise ended the walk-out, although the teachers' gains were minimum. But the Strathcona strike was to draw a whole series of consequences in its wake. Because it had happened virtually on the government's doorstep, because it had received so much publicity, because cabinet ministers and other M.L.A's had involved themeselves in the dispute, the controversy engendered by the work stoppage lasted long after the teachers returned to their classrooms. Numerous attacks were made on teachers' rights to collective bargaining, tenure, and statutory membership. The Association therefore made certain representations to the government. In the words of the editor of *The ATA Magazine:*

Both the Premier and the Minister of Education are convinced that ATA representatives who sought inclusion of teacher-board salary negotiations under *The Alberta Labour Act* in 1941 gave assurance that teachers would not reject awards of conciliation boards. Both are firm in their view that the government of the day would not have agreed to the teachers' request without such assurance.

The Association delegates reviewed the record of teacher strikes dating back to 1942. Of the seven strikes which have occurred over these 22 years, five have been the result of rejection of conciliation board awards by school boards. Of three unanimous awards which ended in strike action, two have been rejected by school boards and accepted by teachers. Only one strike resulted from a unanimous award

[6]*The ATA Magazine,* XLIV, 2 (Oct. 1963), 4-5.

which had been accepted by the school board and rejected by the teachers. Such a record does not support the view that the policy of the Association is to reject awards.[7]

Apparently the right to strike should be granted to teachers only if they undertake never to implement it—surely as naive an assumption as any Alberta politician has made in this century. However, the ATA was not successful in persuading the government that its hard-won rights were beyond questioning, and in April 1964 the Lieutenant-Governor-in-Council, pursuant to a resolution of the Legislative Assembly, appointed a committee "for the purpose of reviewing procedures for Collective Bargaining between School Trustees and Teachers . . . ."[8]

The ATA's position was explicitly set forth in an item in *The ATA Magazine* in November 1964: "Teachers believe that all employees should negotiate with their employers for salaries and working conditions. If teachers are engaged by school boards and their salaries are determined by some method other than bargaining with those same school boards, the fundamental basis of employer-employee relationships would be denied."[9]

The committee, under the chairmanship of R. H. McKinnon until he became minister of education, subsequently under the direction of A. Ludwig, included members from both sides of the House. It held 13 public sittings in all parts of the province during September and October, 1964, and received 36 briefs, in the main from school systems and teachers. In fact, 23 of the 36 briefs were from the ATA or components thereof.

In the spring of 1965 the committee issued its report. *The ATA Magazine* editor succinctly summarized the recommendations: "The committee recommends that teachers retain the right to strike, that time limits for the various stages in negotiations are prescribed by law, that teachers be removed from *The Alberta Labour Act,* and that a new act, to be administered by the Department of Labour, provide for collective bargaining procedures between school boards and teachers, and that assistant superintendents be removed from membership in the Association."[10] The Association's position with respect to

[7]*Ibid.,* 5 (Jan. 1964), 6-7.

[8]Alberta, *Report of the Special Committee . . . on . . . Collective Bargaining between School Trustees and Teachers* (Sessional Paper No. 85, 1965), p. 1.

[9]*The ATA Magazine,* XLV, 4 (Nov. 1964), 53.

[10]*Ibid.,* 9 (April 1965), 4-5.

collective bargaining had been strengthened in this report. The modifications which the committee recommended have shown no sign of being accepted by the government.

Only rarely have other than economic factors been involved in the withdrawal of teachers' services. A 1964 case that came close to precipitating strike action involved the issue of academic freedom, although not so pretentiously dignified. The "Hertzog case," as it soon became known, involved *Edge,* an irregularly published, off-beat, long-hair magazine of opinion established by certain Alberta professors and others. On November 11, 1964, the County of Strathcona suspended one of its teachers, R. Hertzog, apparently for making available two copies of *Edge* to one of his high school students. This suspension evidently was precipitated by a petition signed by some 550 county residents requesting Hertzog's removal, even though some students earlier had petitioned for his retention. Following its action, the county council then applied to the minister of education for permission to discharge Hertzog on 30 days' notice. The minister appointed an officer to investigate the case. The investigator reported that the termination of appointment was not warranted and the teacher should be reinstated. Strangely, the minister did not act on this recommendation, as he had the power and the responsibility to do so, nor did the county authorities take the investigator's hint. At the end of the year, the *status* remained very much *quo*. Early in January 1965, Hertzog submitted his resignation upon the county's agreement to pay his salary to April 30, 1965, more than half a year after his original suspension. *The ATA Magazine*'s editor commented on the by-now notorious "Hertzog case" as follows:

> What had Mr. Hertzog done to deserve such treatment? He had loaned two issues of a publication to a Grade XII female student at her request and following a lesson during which he had referred to a particular article in one of the issues. . . . Mr. Hertzog was also accused of having ridiculed Christianity, but this charge was never proven to be true and, indeed, it was not pressed during the investigation of Mr. Hertzog's suspension.
>
> The Association's stand would have been simple had Mr. Hertzog elected to continue the fight for reinstatement.[11]

At the annual representative assembly (ARA) in April, ATA president L. Jean Scott further commented on what had became a *cause célèbre* by stating that

[11]*Ibid.*, 6 (Jan. 1965), 6-7.

Hertzog's decision to leave the county "left the Association no opportunity to test the legality of a school board's action in delaying a decision required by statute. It left unexplained the delay of the Minister in ordering the reinstatement of the teacher in accordance with his original recommendation."[12]

Seven legal strikes plus a one-day wild-cat walk-out since The Teaching Profession Act was passed in 1935! Since the Association has so seldom been involved in strike action, there are those who feel that it should be prepared to give up the right to strike, which they regard as a proletarian characteristic indeed for a professional organization to claim. To take this view the seasoned salary negotiator, the hard-nosed ATA bargainer would reply that strikes are so few precisely because the teachers have this right, and boards and teachers, knowing this fact, generally come, soon or late, to an agreement. Legal strikes can usually be avoided; unauthorized walk-outs, precisely because of their illegality, can usually be neither anticipated nor prevented. The Alberta Teachers' Association will never willingly surrender its ultimate weapon.

[12]L. Jean Scott, "President's Report," *ibid.*, XLV, 9 (April 1965), 26.

The Rift in the Lute

As has been intimated in previous chapters, the internal operations of the ATA were not always marked by sweetness and light. Occasionally the rank and file of the Association seemed to be marching to the beat of a different drum from the one which the executive council members were hearing. Thus when the AGM was pressing for the appointment of a successor-elect to the general secretary, the executive members seemed unable to hear the message. And earlier, as Powell has noted,[1] Barnett proved adept at ignoring executive directives not to his liking.

Barnett retained in his own hands a large degree of control over the ATA. This he was able to do because of his forceful personality, his total and recognized commitment to the ATA, his drive and seemingly limitless energy, his undoubted ability, his ever increasing experience in ATA matters, his prestige and status as one of the founding fathers of the Alliance. Yet even during his regime there were murmurs of rebellion and discontent.

With the appointment of his successor, the voices of those who would retain control of the ATA in the elected rather than in the appointed officers became more insistent. When the Hon. Ivan Casey implied publicly that the ATA membership and the executive council were not quite on the same wave length, it was particularly galling because there was more than a modicum of truth in

[1]A. J. H. Powell, "The Alberta Teachers' Alliance," unpublished memoir (1962), p. 31.

the implication. That the two elements of the Association should be marching to the beat of different drums was not unknown. Only occasionally, however, did evidence of such discord come to the surface. First intimation to most members that there was a rift in the lute was the 1948 publication of the so-called "Gimby Report."[2] This was actually the text of a talk given at a September 1948 convention of the Edmonton teachers, at which high school teacher and executive council member Marian Gimby smote the ATA hip and thigh. Specifically, her charges were:

1. The executive council has no roots, its members being responsible neither to the AGM nor to its constituents.
2. The general secretary had too much to do.
3. Her own report to the previous AGM had been censored.
4. Resolutions for AGM consideration were also censored before presentation.
5. A long-promised Barnett memorial edition of *The ATA Magazine* was still not out. (It never was published.)
6. Executive committees seldom met. "I think the General Secretary needs help with the *Magazine* but I'm sure he won't welcome any offers."
7. There were not enough classroom teachers on committees and delegations, nor were there enough women teachers. "I do not like to see the increasing concentration of power in the Executive which means in the hands of the General Secretary."
8. Control over executive members' expenses was not tight enough.
9. "I do not like the way the wheels are greased"—a reference to lavish distribution of gratuities and gifts.
10. Travelling expenses of wives of executive members should not be charged to the Association.

In the expressive slang of the day, that tore it, "that" being not the publication but the speech itself. Before it ever appeared in *The ATA Magazine*, and only two days after its delivery, the council had Miss Gimby on the carpet for her criticism of the executive. In its opinion, she should have raised her criticisms with the executive council before airing them at a convention. It was decided that an open letter on the matter should be sent to all the Edmonton teachers, and be signed by all the council members, that the Report be referred to the Association's solicitor, that it be placed on the agenda of the next AGM,

[2]*The ATA Magazine*, XXIX, 1 (Sept.-Oct. 1948), 6, 8-10.

and of the next council meeting, "with the thought in mind of placing it before the Discipline Committee."[3]

Miss Gimby refused to be intimidated. At the December meeting of the council she read a prepared statement protesting the publication of her manuscript (subsequent to the previous meeting) without her permission or without her having an opportunity to revise it. She claimed that she had no intimation that it was to be published despite her inquiries into the matter. She was no lonely Quixote tilting at windmills; like Horatius at the bridge she had her supporters. This she demonstrated by having read into the council minutes a letter from the Edmonton High School Teachers Association deploring the action of those persons who were responsible for the *Magazine*'s publication of her report, and the action of the past president in commenting on this report in an unprofessional manner. This last was in reference to a reply in the same issue of the *Magazine* which characterized the report as being marked by "suggestion, insinuation, innuendo." The Edmonton teachers' missive concluded by expressing full confidence in Miss Gimby.

At the Easter convention the case of *Gimby vs. the ATA president et al.* again became public knowledge. E. T. Wiggins in his presidential report, speaking on behalf of the executive council, stated:

> On one occasion we have been grossly and unjustly maligned. The implications of the Gimby Report are false and malicious. I categorically deny the charges made and at this Annual General Meeting I declare every detail of Alberta Teachers' Association policy and administration open for your examination and judgment.[4]

Miss Gimby could not be silenced; her strength was as the strength of ten because her heart was pure. In season and out she hammered at two or three main themes: that the general secretary had too many duties, too many responsibilities, and therefore too much power; that the executive council was too lavish with the Association's money in approval of unjustified expense accounts, gifts, and entertainment, that no male teacher should enjoy any perquisite not available to female teachers. If some of her colleagues on the executive council felt that she was a boat-rocker of the worst sort, other teachers did not. Thus in 1951 she became the first woman to assume the presidency of the ATA. But even before her election to that position she was winning support in the council

[3]ATA Ex., Oct. 2, 1948.

[4]*The ATA Magazine*, XXIX, 8 (May 1948), 44.

for at least some of her ideas. In March 1951 one member of the council "felt that Mr. Ansley could not write editorials against the policies of the Department and Government and then make successful representations to them."[5] As a result, it was resolved that the council study relationships between the positions of editor and general secretary. Accordingly, the newly elected executive council gave consideration to the problem and also the matter of the general secretary's acting as the secretary of the board of the Teacher's Retirement Fund. However, no firm decision was reached.

Another problem arose soon after the 1951 AGM, when William Kostash, appointed assistant to the general secretary the previous year, submitted his resignation. Kostash a few years previously had served as a member of the executive council and re-entered the ATA organization after some time spent as a correspondence school instructor. Apparently his resignation was motivated by the fact that he did not know what his duties really were, and was triggered by a rather ambiguous report of a firm of consultants which had been appointed to make recommendations respecting the operation of the ATA office. At an emergency meeting of the executive council, "Mr. Ansley stated that he did not know how the work could have been divided at the time of Mr. Kostash's appointment and that since Mr. Kostash had not been closely associated with ATA work for some, it had taken him some time to become familiar with ATA matters."[6] The newly chosen president of the Association was quite disturbed about Kostash's resignation. "She thought there was something very serious about this matter that the Executive should consider carefully."[7]

In the end, the council decided to advertise for an assistant general secretary rather than an assistant *to* the general secretary. The result was the appointment of F. J. C. Seymour, a former president of the ATA.

Minutes of the executive council thereafter indicate considerable friction between the president and the general secretary. The president did not win all the skirmishes with the general secretary, but she did not lose them all, either, and on some issues where she did not achieve immediate success, her views ultimately prevailed.

Miss Gimby served as president of the Association for two terms, a sufficient

[5]ATA Ex., March 9-10, 1951.

[6]*Ibid.*, May 26, 1951.

[7]*Ibid.*

indication that her well-known views on a number of topics, unwelcome though they might have been to a number of her executive council colleagues, received the endorsation of a substantial proportion of the ATA members. An example of the support which she recruited is found in an *ATA Magazine* article by J. S. Farewell, in which he charged that ". . . the public identifies the ATA with one man. The president and the Executive are teaching in their classrooms, and can give only partial attention to ATA business."[8] He went on to criticize the AGM and the automatic check-off of Association dues. He concluded by suggesting that *The ATA Magazine* editor not be on the executive council and that the president serve full-time on a salary. These suggestions the Association adopted some years later.

At the 1953 AGM Miss Gimby delivered her presidential swan song, reporting that the recently appointed assistant general secretary had been made directly responsible to the executive council (rather than through the general secretary) for salary negotiations, publicity, and editorship of *The ATA Magazine*. But with the Association's penchant for trying to ride two horses at the same time, the council also designated Ansley as managing editor, whatever that meant.

She had some pungent comments to make respecting the organization of the Association.[9] "The President of the ATA is the head of the Association in name only," she complained and wondered to whom that officer was responsible—the AGM? or the executive council? or to the membership only, which elected him (or her)? "Ours is the only teachers' organization in Canada where the president is elected by the members," she pointed out. "He should be the choice of the AGM and the Executive as well. I hope I may be the last president elected to face the open hostility of both."

The retiring president was still unhappy about the lavish expenditure of ATA money. In her words, "It has been said that our ATA fees are 'easily raised, freely spent, and lightly accounted for.' " She was therefore opposed to an increase in ATA membership fees, and tied her attitude with respect to economy in operation to another Gimby *leit-motif* when she asserted:

> Until the Association can find ways and means of assuring that the women teachers are elected to our AGM and our Executive in a reasonable proportion to their

[8]*The ATA Magazine*, XXXIII, 2 (Oct. 1952), 24-25.

[9]Marian Gimby, "President's Annual Report," *ibid.*, XXXIII, 10 (June 1953), pp. 22 *et seq.*

numbers, I shall be opposed to the raising of those fees again in any way for any purpose whatsoever.

In the conclusion of her address Miss Gimby made a plea that the ATA include in its ranks all teachers—those in private schools, schools for handicapped children, Indian schools, provincial schools of agriculture, and others, "many of whom are eager to join us." In the decade-and-a-half since she delivered her peroration, ATA ranks have been opened to all of these groups except teachers in Indian schools, nor will the entry of these be delayed for long.

Marian Gimby was one of the most colourful and controversial presidents ever to head the Alberta Teachers' Association. She was outspoken—but not by many. She had the reputation of being a stormy petrel, yet it was not she who blew up the gale. Rather, she served as a focus for deep-seated unease and discontent concerning the direction in which the Association seemed to be drifting: towards becoming an organization controlled from the top down rather than from the bottom up, an oligarchy dominated by appointed and salaried bureaucrats rather than by the elected representatives of the teacher members. If she did not forever prevent such a dire eventuality, she surely alerted the ATA members as to its possibility. When its threat became imminent a few years later, the Association was quick to meet it.

Interestingly enough, this action occurred during the incumbency of the Association's second woman president, Inez Castleton. It was in 1958 that the ATA resolved the long conflict between the elected officers and the general secretary of the Association. It is perhaps inevitable, such conflict, in an organization like the ATA in which the head of the secretariat or staff holds his position year after year, while elected officers come and go. Gradually the former assumes more and more control over the organization. He more than any other individual has mastered the principles and policies, the practices and routines of the organization. He knows all the precedents—and where every body is buried. He is well acquainted with the elder statesmen of the organization, those who have served in an executive capacity in years gone by, and who, although they no longer hold office, still enjoy considerable influence and prestige in the body. Free to travel throughout the province and beyond, the executive secretary is the confidante of the local leaders. He is on a first-name basis with legislators and with cabinet ministers; he is on friendly terms with outstanding educators all across Canada. But even the most assiduous and successful elected officer hardly begins to achieve comparable influence before he is retired to the side-lines—unless he himself becomes an appointed officer, a staff member of the organization.

The growing power of the ATA's general secretary, John Barnett, has been often noted here. Most of the time, Barnett's will prevailed, bolstered as it was by his genuine friendship with many of the most influential members of the ATA. Another factor which favoured the old war horse was the Association's natural reluctance to wash its dirty linen at the public laundromat.

His successor attempted to follow in the footsteps of the giant, even though the latter's middle initial stood for Walker, not Wenceslas. But Ansley found the footprints a bit warmer than had the good page. According to one observer, he attempted to play both ends against the middle, to metamorphose the metaphor, or at least the AGM against the executive council. When direction from the annual general meeting proved unwelcome, he maintained that he was the servant of the executive council. When he found orders from that body distasteful, he claimed that only the AGM could set policy (which it was his duty to implement). But Ansley was not Barnett; he could not face down or overwhelm the opposition as successfully as his predecessor had done.

At last the moment of truth arrived. In 1958 the salaried officers of the Association had grown to four: Ansley himself, F. J. C. Seymour, and W. R. Eyres, all of whom had held high office in the ATA, and E. J. Ingram. In a move to control the general secretary more tightly, the executive council had made Seymour, assistant general secretary, the editor of *The ATA Magazine* and responsible directly to the council rather than through the general secretary. In the spring of 1958 the council decided to appoint an executive assistant to the assistant general secretary, to work on collective bargaining. No doubt regarding it as a further diminution of his authority, Ansley opposed this proposal. Nevertheless, the executive council went ahead with its plans and appointed J. D. McFetridge to the post.

The following weeks the council members spent (sporadically) in considering many aspects of ATA administration. One was the relationship of the Association to the Board of Directors of the Teachers' Retirement Fund. Legally the two were distinct, although the latter included two nominees of the ATA. In practice, the two were almost as tortuously intermeshed as the old Alliance and its theoretically independent Bureau of Education. The ATA's general secretary was also the honorary (that is, unpaid) secretary of the TRF's Board. His ATA office supervisor was the TRF's chief clerk. Desks of the ATA and TRF personnel were side by side; it is questionable whether some of the office staff were always quite sure of just who their employer was. The whole arrangement was conducive to the concentration of control in the hands of one man. In addition to serving as executive secretary of both bodies, Ansley was also ATA treasurer. In June the council met to discuss, among other things, the interrelationship between the ATA and the TRF, the appointment of an office manager, leaving the then-present incumbent free to devote herself wholly to her TRF responsibilities, and the appointment of an assistant treasurer with power to sign cheques. Eyres was appointed to this position and to the post of office manager in charge of stenographic and clerical staff, effective September 15 following. Further, he was "expected to carry out normal duties in addition to this."[10] At another meeting early in August, the council decided that the division between the TRF and the ATA would become effective September 30, and that the second floor of Barnett House would be made available to the TRF Board of Administrators.

By September it had become obvious that Ansley had no intention of implementing the council's directives. Perhaps he thought that he had the support of the AGM or the membership as a whole, and that a show-down with the council would be a back-down by that body.

This time the general secretary had gone too far. The council met on September 26 and 27, 1958, taking the extraordinary step of excluding the general secretary and other appointed officers from the meeting. The office supervisor's appointment to that position was terminated; apparently the council's action in this direction at its earlier meeting had not "taken." Eyres was appointed to the position, both actions being immediately effective. The council also decided to ask Ansley for his resignation, effective forthwith. This he refused to submit, forcing the council to suspend him from his duties. The poignancy of the moment is suggested by the words of the ATA's president, Mrs. Inez Castleton:

> The Executive had felt for some considerable time an appropriate relationship must exist between the appointed staff officers and the Executive Council but that the management function must reside in the elected representatives.
>
> The fact that Mr. Ansley, a man who had made a valuable contribution to our

[10]ATA Ex., June 12-14, 1958.

organization, disagreed with our interpretation of management was most disappointing. I have never forgotten the moment when, as president, I had to request Mr. Ansley to hand over the keys to Barnett House.[11]

Ansley was given until noon on September 30 to submit his resignation, otherwise his contract with the ATA was to be terminated. In the end, the actual dismissal of the general secretary was to prove a long and painful ordeal with both sides referring the matter to their solicitors. Finally, it amounted to Ansley's recognition of the fact that he was irrevocably out, that he did not enjoy the general support of the membership. This last became apparent to the executive council at one of the most unusual gatherings which the ATA has ever convened. It was a hastily called meeting limited to Local presidents or their designated representatives and to members of the executive council. Its purpose was to explain the reasons for the council's actions. As a result, at least eight Locals submitted resolutions supporting the council in its actions—and Ansley was reduced to surrendering on the best terms he could get. These proved to be generous, at least financially.

With Ansley's departure, other arrangements rapidly fell into place. The ATA's representatives on the TRF Board of Administrators were informed that the Association did not favour Ansley's re-appointment as board secretary-treasurer, and a committee was struck to confer with the minister of education as to a successor to this office. The Association suggested W. R. Eyres, a nomination to which the minister agreed. The president announced that the joint administration of the ATA and the TRF had been terminated.

The council appointed an acting general secretary and advertised for applicants for a permanent appointee. Expenses in connection with Ansley's retirement were transferred to the miscellaneous account. The council regretfully received a letter from one of its honorary members withdrawing his membership in the Association and requesting his letter be published in *The ATA Magazine*. The letter was read and ordered to be filed. At the end of the year Dr. S. C. T. Clarke was appointed to be the ATA's third general secretary.

And a new era began.

[11]Inez Castleton, letter of Jan. 16, 1967 addressed to S. C. T. Clarke.

New Brooms

THE CHRONIC TEACHER SHORTAGE of the war and post-war years was not peculiar to Alberta, which was perhaps not as subject to it as were less prosperous areas. In many parts of North America, especially in some sections of the United States, it became not merely chronic but desperate. The shortage forced salaries higher. Millions of American parents faced with dismay the prospects of upwardly spiralling school taxes coupled with deteriorating instructional services as good teachers became scarcer. With their usual energy the Yankees sought solutions for their problems. For some solutions, in typical and ingenious fashion they turned to their technology which had served them so well in the past. Their experiments, technological or otherwise, had their impact, as always, on the schools north of the Undefended Border. In Alberta as in other provinces, these experiments are still under review, assessment, and implementation.

One of these was educational television, commonly known as ETV. If one teacher can teach 25 to 40 children in an ordinary classroom by traditional methods, by the use of the new electronic marvel, the Americans reasoned, should not one instructor be able to teach hundreds and even thousands and tens of thousands of pupils? And if this were possible, three things could be accomplished. The number of teachers needed for a given number of pupils could be cut phenomenally and the teacher shortage reduced or eliminated. With fewer instructional personnel required, costs could be lowered, as always happens when mass production techniques are fully exploited, and school taxes would correspondingly be cut. And with the great resources of personnel, time, and instructional aids available to ETV, the quality of instruction would be of a uniformly high standard, much higher than could be found in the average classroom.

ETV might seem a threat to the teaching profession, but the ATA refused to be thrown into a panic about it. Instead of blindly opposing it, the Alberta Teachers' Association coolly examined this new phenomenon, as evidenced by articles appearing from time to time in *The ATA Magazine*.[1] In general, the ATA's assessment of ETV, corroborated by the march of events, has been that it is simply another teaching tool like other audio-visual aids such as radio and movies, supplementing but not replacing the classroom teacher. Indeed, ETV has tended to increase and not lower the cost of education.

Another glittering prospect for reducing teacher shortages and lowering costs was that presented by machine teaching, one aspect and component of which is known as programmed learning. A teaching machine is a device containing a teaching programme which the pupil can operate by himself. The pupil does an assignment, corrects his own errors which the machine reveals, relearns where necessary, proceeds to the next assignment. The teacher becomes redundant—or does he? From the educational point of view, the merit of programmed instruction is that it permits pupils, bright or dull, to proceed at their own best speed, not to be forced into a lock-step with others whose learning rates are faster or slower. Errors are immediately brought to the learners' attention before they become habitual. The deleterious effects of unfair competition are removed; the pupil competes only with himself. It was also hypothesized that since no teachers, only technicians, were needed, educational costs and teacher shortages would both decline.

Again this hope proved illusory. On the educational side, it was soon realized that although programmed learning accommodated differences in ability, it did not permit pupils of differing interests to study different material, nor did it provide scope for creative ability. Nor because of the initial high costs of developing programmes was it feasible to use the system for the teaching of material of purely local or regional importance.

However, as programmed learning seemed part of the wave of the future, the

[1]R. D. Armstrong in *The ATA Magazine*, XLI, 3 (Nov. 1960), 11 *et seq.;* T. A. Landman, "ETV, We Need Not be Afraid," *ibid.*, XLV, 8 (March 1965), 21.

ATA gave it careful attention. In 1962, it published a monograph[2] outlining developments in teaching machines, programmed notebooks, and "scrambled" textbooks. ATA staff officers attended conferences on programmed learning lasting up to three weeks, and during the 1962-63 school year, seminars for classroom teachers were held in Calgary and Edmonton. These sessions, each of which took place in two successive week-ends, comprised 14 hours of instruction. The Edmonton series, for example, attracted about 40 participants.

Gradually it became apparent that programmed instruction was another teaching aid, valuable especially for dissemination of material of general rather than local significance, for example, mathematics and science, rather than social studies. It was particularly adapted for material where mastery of content and to some extent of skills was the principal objective, less suitable where appreciation or development of creative ability was the aim. The essential feature of programmed instruction—identical with that of good correspondence education—is that each learning unit is broken down into sub-units, each sub-unit is expertly presented to the pupil, whose learning is immediately tested. Like ETV, programmed instruction has not replaced more conventional educational techniques but has often proved a valuable adjunct to them. An application of the technique, perhaps not fully explored, for small school systems especially is the teaching of atypical children, mentally or otherwise handicapped. Many a school system has too few of such educational deviates to justify special classes for them, yet across a province or a country their numbers are sufficiently large to merit the preparation of special instructional programmes for them.

A side effect of the programmed instruction movement has been a renewed emphasis on the well-known but often disregarded fact that each child learns at his own individual best speed, a recognition that has lead to widespread introduction of the so-called streaming or multiple-track organization of elementary school grades.

Still another innovation emanating from the United States in its efforts to eliminate teacher shortages and reduce educational costs was that of team teaching. This was based on the concept that it is as easy for a teacher to lecture to a hundred pupils, or a thousand for that matter, as to thirty—the same premise advanced by the protagonists of ETV. Thus, the theory runs, with large instructional groups a few teachers could do the work now requiring many,

[2]E. Arnett, H. G. Trout, and S. C. T. Clarke, *Programmed Instruction* (1962).

and could do it better because each teacher could be given far more time for professional preparation than he has now, and even so, fewer teachers would be required for a given number of pupils.

Alas, the hopes of the educationally unsophisticated for the elimination of teacher shortages and the reduction of school taxes again proved false. For one thing, the converse of very large group instruction which team teaching implied was the instruction of very small groups: ten pupils, five, even one or two for remedial work or the catering to special interests. Thus more teachers than anticipated were required. Other problems arose. Team teaching requires large schools with dozens if not hundreds of pupils in each grade or subject-matter level; such schools are not always possible or acceptable to parents concerned, especially if it means that their children must be moved long distances by bus to assemble enough children. Team teaching also requires schools designed for the purpose, with both very large and very small instructional areas, but relatively new conventional plants cannot be discarded and replaced simply because, in the opinion of some, they have become functionally obsolete. Finally and most important, success depends, as always, on the teaching staff. Teachers must have not only the skills and knowledge needed to exploit new techniques and technologies; they must be convinced as to their desirability and effectiveness. For such reasons and others, the period of professional preparation for teachers increases at the rate of about one year in every two decades or so. The lengthened period of professional education affects not only new teachers; their senior colleagues are also having to increase their professional competence by means of formal study at universities, attendance at institutes and conventions, professional reading, and in other ways.

Despite its disadvantages, the ATA did not dismiss team teaching out of hand. In 1964, about thirty teachers, school superintendents, and consultants spent two week-ends examining the concept, and seven Alberta teachers attended a Vancouver conference with representatives from the other three western provinces.

Failure of such schemes as ETV, programmed instruction, and team teaching to reduce the need for teaching personnel and for school tax money, usually promoted initially by business men, industrialists, and other lay people, is founded on a basic misconception: that teaching is simply the dissemination of information. Teachers, of course, know that it is far more, that it includes the development of character and personality, the growth of skills and habits, the acquisition of attitudes, and that as children are individuals and not automatons, education is only partially amenable to mass-production methods.

A more promising approach to the problem of shortages of qualified teaching personnel has been the use of non-professional assistants, usually called teacher aides, perhaps by analogy with nursing aides. Teacher aides are usually persons employed to assist teachers in the performance of non-professional tasks such as marking classroom registers, distributing classroom materials and books, operating audio-visual equipment, collecting various fees, helping small children put on overshoes, etc. By 1959 the legitimacy of teacher aides in the classroom was a matter of concern to the teaching profession in Alberta and a committee, appointed by the minister of education and consisting of T. C. Byrne, department of education, S. C. T. Clarke, ATA, and H. T. Coutts, University of Alberta, was attempting to sort out the various roles of teacher, teacher aide, and school clerk. The committee reached the following definitions:

teaching—contact with children which produces or is designed to produce changes in behaviour.
teacher—a certificated person who initiates, organizes, directs, and performs the teaching process in a specified classroom in a school or schools, or is legally empowered to do so.
teacher's aide—one who may perform, in addition to clerical service, some phases of the teaching process under the direction of a qualified teacher.
school clerk—one who does not operate in a classroom continuously but who has a work station outside the classroom to carry out clerical duties assigned by a teacher or principal.[3]

Following the report of the committee, the Association undertook its own research on the matter of teacher aides. The resulting monograph appeared in 1960. The author, K. I. Kennedy, after examining the evidence from a number of projects, concluded:

The evidence that demonstrations . . . have produced in favour of the use of teacher aides is meagre. Little evidence has been produced to show that the use of teacher aides has any effect on the pupils' academic achievement or adjustment; neither has it been shown that their use changes the cost of education. All of these alleged experiments have some faults in their design and some . . . have many glaring faults, including a poorly designed problem, inadequate control groups, small

[3]*The ATA Magazine*, XXXIX, 7 (March 1959), 47.

samples, and a failure to take all the variables into account. In most cases, little consideration was given to more than the child's academic growth and little evaluation was made of the "quality" of the teaching in these classes. . . . Participating teachers and teacher aides were carefully selected and the typical situation is not represented. If the exact situation in which these projects were conducted could be reproduced, similar results could be anticipated; but the results cannot be applied to the general situation.[4]

The rather unfavourable conclusions which Kennedy reached did not close the door on further discussion. Several years later, in fact, the ATA's Teacher Education and Certification Committee referred the topic to a sub-committee to prepare a statement of general principles. This statement received the approval of the committee and of the executive council of the ATA. The statement reads as follows:

Certificated teachers should not be required to perform non-teaching tasks and non-certificated personnel should not be permitted to perform teaching functions.

A teaching certificate is required:

(a) if the activity performed is teaching.

(b) if the activity in which students engaged is part of the regular school curriculum, i.e., in elementary and junior high schools during school hours and in the high school for credit.

A teaching certificate is not required:

(a) if the instruction provided and the activities which the student performs are a minor part of a series of activities planned, organized and mainly conducted by a certificated teacher,

(b) the activity in which students engage is not part of the regular school curriculum, i.e., in elementary and junior high school during school hours and in the high school for credit.[5]

The 1966 ARA passed a resolution expressing approval in principle of the institutes of "teacher assistants," and expressing the wish that the ATA and the department of education establish regulations governing "qualifications, status, and employment"[6] of such personnel. Within the following year *The ATA Magazine* carried two articles on "teacher-assistants," as the ARA apparently preferred to call them. In February 1968 *The ATA News* (vol. 2, no. 7) carried four stories on teacher aides. Thus in its fiftieth year the Association still considers the issue of teacher aides very much alive.

[4]K. I. Kennedy, *Teacher Aides* (ATA Research Monograph #1), p. 1.

[5]*The ATA Magazine*, XLVI, 10 (June 1966), 62-63.

[6]*Ibid.*, 9 (May 1966), 50.

Under the Dome: Variations on a Theme

THE EDIFICE most significant, at least figuratively, to the ATA is not its own Barnett House, impressive though that structure is. Rather, it is a handsome Greco-Roman building dominating the left bank (find your own symbolism there) of the Saskatchewan River in Edmonton. It was in Alberta's Legislative Buildings (for some reason always in the plural) that in 1918 the ATA received its first charter under The Societies Act, and its second by way of The Teaching Profession Act of 1935, vitally amended the following year. Under the dome of this august structure each year the ATA officers meet the cabinet of the Alberta government to discuss legislative and executive decrees affecting the Association. Here also from time to time the lieutenant-governor signs those documents appointing committees and commissions to study various aspects of Alberta education. And under the same dome each minister of education takes his oath of office.

Tension normally characterizes the relationship existing between the ATA and the government. The teachers are primarily concerned about their own condition, and that of education in general. But the politicians must consider all aspects and elements of society. Frequently, for example, they have to weigh the representations of the educators against those of the school trustees; balance the claims of education against those put forward on behalf of public health, welfare, and other public services. Thus even ministers of education sympathetic to the ATA occasionally find themselves in the opposite camp to that of the teachers.

The death in 1943 of William Aberhart, first Social Credit premier and minister of education, inevitably meant a change in the relations of the ATA and the government. In the education portfolio, Aberhart was followed by a succession of school teacher ministers, educationally undistinguished and more concerned with political than pedagogical success. Aberhart's immediate successor was Solon Low, who shortly thereafter left on the road to political oblivion as federal leader of the Social Credit movement. He was followed by R. E. Ansley, one of the Alberta founders of Alberta Social Credit, and not to be confused with E. C. Ansley, Barnett's successor as general secretary of the ATA. So fundamentalist a believer in Social Credit was the new minister that rather than compromise his beliefs in the face of the economic facts of life which the government had to consider, he left the cabinet and the government to sit on the opposition benches of the legislature as an independent Social Crediter. In ATA circles the Hon. Earle Ansley is remembered as the protagonist of a new teachers' pension plan to replace the interim and inadequate scheme which Aberhart had introduced. For his work in this connection the ATA honoured him with a complimentary dinner and presentation.

Ansley in turn was followed by the Hon. Ivan Casey, a high school teacher and realtor from southern Alberta. The Alberta Teachers' Association welcomed him to his new position in 1948, but soon had reason to experience some disenchantment with him. In 1948 the editor of *The ATA Magazine* complained that in August he had declined to visit an ATA workshop at Banff in order to go on a safari at the oil sands near Fort McMurray. And in the last week of that month he had cancelled his acceptances to five local teachers' conventions so that he might attend the annual convention of the Canadian Education Association. A year later the situation had deteriorated still further as the minister seemed very sensitive about criticism concerning the government's educational policies. At conventions in Red Deer and Calgary, Casey had charged that ATA policy was that of the officers and not of the Association. Apparently he was endeavouring to drive a wedge between the ATA's executive council and its members. In short, he was implying that the elected executive members did not represent the views of their constituents, a somewhat curious position to be adopted by a person who owed his position to the same type of democratic processes. At a meeting of the ATA executive council in 1950,[1] "Mr. [Fred] Sey-

[1]ATA Ex., Dec. 8-9, 1950.

mour [president] emphasized that he took a very serious view of the situation."

In 1950, *The ATA Magazine* editor quoted an editorial in the Calgary *Herald* in turn quoting the minister. "If criticism of teacher training continues," said Mr. Casey, "better relations between the teachers and the Department of Education are going to be difficult to maintain."[2] The reaction of the *Magazine*'s editor was predictable: "It is insufferable that any group, and particularly teachers, should be subjected to this veiled blackmail by a Minister of the Crown."[3] Predictably also, relations between the ATA and the minister did not improve. The May 1952 issue of *The ATA Magazine* carried a criticism of Casey for threatening teachers that if they went on strike, they faced the prospect of compulsory settlement of salary disputes and loss of statutory membership in the ATA. With approval of the Association, Kim Ross replied by asking why teachers should be given the right to collective bargaining if it were to be removed the first time they tried to use it.[4] In September 1952 Casey was transferred to another and less significant portfolio, so abruptly that he was actually attending a meeting of the Canadian Education Association when he and the public were first informed of the change. At the general election which next followed he lost his seat and retired from public life.

Casey was followed by Anders O. Aalborg, an honours graduate of the Edmonton Normal School, who for a score of years had hidden his first-class talents in a tiny school near the eastern boundary of Alberta. But if his name was not a household word in the province generally, it was well known in the seats of the ATA mighty, where Aalborg had sat as a vice-president of the Association. In his new capacity the teachers at all times found him patient, courteous, sympathetic—and tough. Despite, or perhaps because of the hard-headed, realistic bent of this man, relationships between the teachers and the department were probably better than during any other period since the death of Aberhart. Aalborg continued to hold the education portfolio until 1965, when he became provincial treasurer, thus continuing in a cabinet post of great importance to education.

He was succeeded by a personable Edmonton junior high school teacher, R. H. McKinnon. However, McKinnon's tenure was too brief for him to have

[2]*The ATA Magazine*, XXXI, 3 (Nov. 1950), 9. [3]*Ibid.*
[4]*Ibid.*, XXXII, 9 (May 1952), 9.

much impact on Alberta's educational structure, for in the 1967 general election he lost his seat to an attractive young professional footballer carrying the banner of the resurgent Conservative party. McKinnon's successor was the Hon. R. Reierson, first minister of education in over thirty years who was not a school teacher.

Reierson continued as minister of labour also, in which capacity he was well known to the ATA, for it is under the labour ministry that teachers conduct their salary negotiations. Although at first the teachers felt some apprehensions at having a layman as their minister, within a year these were allayed, for during that time Reierson announced a new teacher certification scheme under which all teacher education will normally last a minimum of three years, and permanent certification will require a university degree.

In a very real sense, under the parliamentary system of government, the minister *is* the department. Consequently, relations between the ATA and the Alberta government have always been vitally affected by the character, personality, and temperament of the minister who happened to hold the education portfolio.

The most abrasive contacts between the Association and the government have always included those dealing with the placing of non-professionals in charge of classrooms. Only during the Hungry Thirties have there ever been enough certificated teachers to staff the province's schools; before that dismal era the shortage was always met by the licensing of unqualified young high school graduates and university students. When the shortage reappeared during the latter years of World War II, classrooms by the hundred were placed on correspondence education. For a whole decade, as has been described in an earlier chapter, the nearest approach to a teacher that thousands of rural pupils ever saw was their correspondence supervisor, bitterly known to ATA members as a "sitter." Consistently the ATA exhibited its antagonism to the whole idea of using correspondence instruction, not as a supplement but as a substitute for classroom education. As *The ATA Magazine* editor noted: "If the teaching profession had accepted the so-called 'sitter' system and all its implications with resignation or indifference—which would have been the easier course—the system would now be well on the way to becoming a recognized, if not integral, part of public education in the Province."[5]

[5]*Ibid.*, XXXVII, 6 (March 1947), 2.

After more than ten years of taking up the slack with correspondence supervisors, at the end of which time there were still 163 correspondence centres in operation, the department of education apparently decided that the bars to the teaching profession would have to be drastically lowered. The result was the passage of the Emergency Teacher Training Act in 1954. Under the ETT programme, Grade XII graduates could qualify for a Junior E teaching certificate by attendance at three succesive summer sessions, by teaching for two years, and by receiving favourable reports from the superintendents under whom they served. In fact, continuance in the programme was contingent upon such recommendation, and it was not always forthcoming. During the years in which the ETTP was in operation it is estimated that not more than 165 teachers ever actually completed their training,[6] an insignificant proportion—about 3.7 per cent of the total number of new Alberta certificates issued in the 1954-58 period during which the programme was in operation.

The number of those trained under the ETTP was no threat to the job security of ATA members; the principle of a cut-rate training programme menaced the entire profession. The ATA reacted by invoking the same type of sanctions against the "six-week wonders" as it had against the correspondence centre supervisors, for example, by denying them access to teachers' conventions. The unremitting opposition of the ATA to the scheme was probably as important as the gradual amelioration of the teacher supply situation in leading the government to abandonment of the programme when the ETT Act expired in 1958. But the members of the Association know that only by continuing alertness can they protect the standards for admission to the teaching profession when personnel shortages develop.

The six-week programme was indeed a far cry from the proud 1945 announcement of the Hon. Earle Ansley, minister of education, that thereafter the minimum preparation for a teacher in Alberta would require two years at university. In the face of the serious shortage of qualified teachers and in view of the opposition to the proposal, within a year he was hedging his bet. In June 1946, in *The ATA Magazine*,[7] the minister announced a modification of the programme. Under the new regulations, student-teachers could qualify for an interim or temporary certificate valid in the elementary grades after

[6]J. W. Chalmers, *Schools of the Foothills Province* (Toronto 1967), 146.
[7]*The ATA Magazine*, XXVI, 9 (June 1946), 7.

attendance of only one year at the university. This would be valid for two years, and renewable annually as long as the bearer attended university summer sessions. With completion of two years of university work, the second either by regular or by summer sessions, he would then be eligible for permanent certification after two years of satisfactory teaching service. Thus the principle of requiring two years of professional preparation for a teacher's certificate was not negated, especially as the policy of licensing teachers after one year only of professional preparation was avowedly temporary. However, within a few years the minister of education quietly forgot about the temporary nature of the arrangement and permitted those who had completed one year only of teacher preparation to qualify for permanent certification. The ATA, of course, was quite unhappy with the action of the minister's apparent sabotage of the two-year preparation policy.

The position of the ATA with respect to teachers' qualifications has always been that every licensed teacher must hold a certificate of general validity, that special certification follows and does not precede or replace general certification. This principle is not always followed in other jurisdictions, nor did it always apply in Alberta; at one time a few vocational certificates were issued to qualified tradesmen who had not attended normal school. But the ATA's attitude is that university professors and trade school instructors teach subjects; therefore mastery of content is probably adequate preparation for them. But teachers teach boys and girls; therefore they must have a mastery of the principles of human growth and development, of educational psychology and philosophy, and of many other things. The members of the Association have therefore ever been alert to resist special in place of general certification. In 1948 the executive council viewed with some suspicion a move on the part of the board of teacher education and certification to tie in qualification of shop teachers with those of the apprenticeship board. At the same time it looked with some disfavour on the action of the department of education—actually the supervisor of industrial arts—to establish an Industrial Arts Teachers' Association, apparently viewing it all as a deep-laid plot to establish a cadre of technical or vocational teachers outside the ATA. The plea that the newly organized IATA was really a long-established, if long-dormant, organization did not affect the attitude of the ATA council.

Two years later, it was music rather than industrial arts which provided the field of battle, when the Calgary public school board appointed as its supervisor of music—not as a classroom teacher—a professional musician on the understanding that the minister of education would grant him a certificate when he had met certain conditions, including completion of Grade XII and of some university courses. The protests of the ATA proved unavailing. They were equally fruitless when the Association protested the licensing of a journeyman printer as a vocational teacher in the Calgary public school system, an expedient which had been adopted on the plea that there simply was not a single certificated teacher available anywhere to teach the subject of printing.

Yet in the long run, although the ATA lost a few skirmishes, it won the war—probably because it did fight the minor actions. This fact became obvious in the sixties after the passage of the federal Technical and Vocational Assistance Act and the signing in 1961 of a federal-provincial agreement for vocational high school training. The Alberta government, like those of other provinces, poured scores of millions of dollars into new school facilities and equipment. In other jurisdictions, instructors were found by giving competent tradesmen a quick course in pedagogy and sending them into the schools with a limited teaching licence. In Alberta, largely because of the insistence of the ATA, vocational teachers had to meet the same qualifications as other teachers: full matriculation to the provincial university and a year in attendance at that institution. (They were given a year's credit towards their B.Ed. degree on the strength of their trade training.) At the conclusion of their sojourn in the halls of Academe they were granted a Standard S certificate, as were other two-year secondary-school trainees.

The first class of journeymen teacher-trainees entered the University of Alberta in the fall of 1962. This year was important with respect to the professional education of Alberta teachers in another way; it marked the real beginning of a two-year teacher preparation programme for minimum certification, the first in Canada to require this length of time following senior matriculation.

Just six years later, Alberta's non-professional minister of education, R. Reierson, announced the extension of the period of professional education from two to three years. Furthermore, no new teaching certificate could become permanent until the teacher had completed all the requirements for his university degree.

By no means all contacts beween the Association and the provincial government concerned teacher preparation. A post-war development which caused considerable unease among ATA members and at the same time aligned them with their traditional opponents, the trustees, was the passage of Alberta's County Act. Passed in 1950, this statute provided for the replacement of both the municipal districts and the school divisions by single bodies which would perform the functions of each. Originally, health districts were also included, but these were quickly dropped because of protests of the minister and the department of public health. The rural trustees, the only ones at first affected, were opposed because they foresaw their function and influence vanishing; the teachers were also because they feared that the new bodies would be municipally oriented and indifferent or hostile to the claims of education for the taxpayers' dollars. Better the devil (or trustee) they knew than the one they did not—this seemed to be their attitude. They were also disturbed that they had had no opportunity to discuss with the government a proposal which touched them so closely.

Another continuing concern of the ATA was the Royal Commission on Education under the chairmanship of Senator Donald Cameron, appointed by order-in-council on December 31, 1957. The commission was given a wide frame of reference, being charged to "study and consider the aims and objectives essential to maintain a proper and adequate educational programme for the pupils . . . of the province."[8] The commission's areas of inquiry were then spelled out in considerable detail, embracing the school curricula, teacher education, guidance services, school plants, etc., "but exclusive of any detailed study of the sources of funds for school purposes or procedures whereby such funds are obtained and distributed."[9] To the present day, no other inquiry into Alberta education has ever been so exhaustive as that of the Cameron Commission. In less than two years the commissioners held more than 60 meetings, studied documentary reports from other provinces and countries, examined university theses, conducted six major and a number of minor research projects, called on more than 100 consultants from all areas of public education. They listened to about 600 persons who attended their hearings and considered some 5,000 recommendations in the 189 briefs which they studied. Naturally the ATA was

[8]Alberta, *Report of the Royal Commission on Education* (1959), p. 4.
[9]*Ibid.*, p. 6.

concerned with the work of the commission, especially those terms of reference dealing specifically with teachers and teacher education. The Association presented a comprehensive brief; a number of ATA Locals did likewise. In 1959 the commission presented its report, the most extensive document on Alberta education ever published to that time since the formation of the province, containing no fewer than 280 recommendations. Even then the Association's concern was not ended. Under Clarke's authorship it published in March 1960 *The Cameron Commission: A Condensation of the Report of the Royal Commission on Education in Alberta* as a special number of *The ATA Magazine*. In this manner the findings of the commission were made available to every public and separate school teacher in the province.

Occasionally the Association and the department found themselves on collision courses. Thus a conflict arose in 1958 over the rates paid sub-examiners, the teachers who marked the final examinations in Grades IX and XII. In effect, the ATA attempted to blacklist the department of education until sub-examiners were paid what the Association regarded as a reasonable rate of remuneration, *viz.*, $4 per hour. In February *The ATA Magazine* informed the teachers that the request had been rejected on the following grounds: (1) as recently as 1957 the rate had been raised to $15 per day plus a subsistence allowance of $4 per day; (2) expenditures for examinations greatly exceeded income from examination fees (the issue of whether public education should really be free education was neatly side-stepped); (3) there was no lack of interested and qualified persons at the then-current rate (why pay more than one has to for services?); (4) an additional expenditure of $50,000 per year was not warranted (in effect, a restatement of No. 3 above?).

As a result, the department of education remained on the ATA's bad books, or at least the examinations branch did, and teachers were advised not to accept appointments as sub-examiners. The proscription, however, was apparently ineffective, although by the end of the year the subsistence rate had been raised from $4 to $7 per day. But it is doubtful whether the Association learned the obvious lesson, that you can't fight City Hall, or in this case the Legislative Buildings. In this respect, of course, the teachers were no different from other occupational groups, from medical doctors to letter carriers, who have discovered to their sorrow that strikes against the government, that is, against the body politic, are never very effective.

However, as the Association reached the wisdom and maturity of its first half-century, such tension-creating confrontations between the Association and the government were increasingly rare. Long gone were the days of the 1920's, when the minister of education only grudgingly and intermittently conferred with the Alberta Teachers' Alliance officers. By the 1960's department activity directly affecting the teachers was rarely undertaken without consultation with the teachers' representatives. Such consultation usually was through boards and committees, which dealt with such matters as teacher education and certification, examinations, curricula, audio-visual services, technical and vocational education, high school accreditation, pensions, legislation, kindergartens, etc.

Yet the right to be consulted on matters that affect teachers and their organization is one that cannot be taken for granted. Thus officers of the Association were quietly annoyed in early 1968 when the minister of education, without prior consultation with the ATA, announced an increase in professional education of teachers from two to three years for first certification.

A Home of Fairest Mould

WITH ITS MEMBERSHIP FEE originally set at a modest 35c per year, the infant Alberta Teachers' Alliance was by no means able to rent or buy accommodation for the transaction of its business. Even when the annual dues were increased to 75c, John Barnett, the ATA's first general secretary, at first had to provide an office as well as his services in order to earn his stipend. Even when the Alliance was able to compensate him for the use of his spare bedroom, the situation remained unchanged.

"In the early days John kept office in his home on 107 Street opposite the southwest corner of the Queen Alexandra campus," writes A. J. H. Powell, "where Mrs. Barnett and the four young children took innumerable phone calls for him during his many lengthy absences. After a year or two of this, John moved to a down-town room at the top of the old Imperial Bank building at Jasper and 100 Street. This quaint colonnaded structure dated back to times when banks provided living quarters over their premises for their bachelor employees to keep them out of saloons, pool halls and gambling dens. This custom had lapsed, and John was able to rent first one, and later several rooms, to meet the growing needs of the young Alliance, at little more than a nominal charge. He remained there over twenty years, climbing three long flights of stairs at a speed none of us softer mortals could challenge. . . . He never did see the fine new home of the organization named in his honour, Barnett House."[1]

[1]A. J. H. Powell, "The Alberta Teachers' Alliance," unpublished memoir (1962), p. 5.

Increasing rent rates and endless growth in the need for space as well as perhaps a justifiable self-esteem eventually led the Association to consider the erection of its own building. First tentative step in this direction appears to have been a 1946 suggestion by ATA president H. C. Melsness "that the Association should begin to give consideration to the matter of erecting a building of their own."[2] The following year the council recommended to the AGM that $20,000 be placed in a building fund and that $3,000 per year be added to it until the fund reached $30,000, at which time presumably the new building would be erected. In a relatively leisurely manner the Association proceeded to search for a site, at one time favouring one owned by the city on the south side of the Saskatchewan River. Ultimate choice, however, was a location on the north brow of the beautiful river valley. Its purchase was announced in the December 1948 issue of *The ATA Magazine.*[3] First problem after the site was chosen was to have it rezoned for commercial use. As anyone who has ever been concerned in rezoning problems is well aware, these are usually extremely frustrating experiences; however, the ATA had a friend at court to expedite the process. This was H. D. Ainlay, former president of the Alberta Teachers' Alliance and mayor of Edmonton from 1946 to 1950. In Ainlay's own words "I was in office in the city and was able to get the zoning changed to enable the building to go into this location."[4]

Design of the building went forward during 1949, the architects being Kelly and Ross Stanley, sons of old Alliance veteran and former president T. E. A. Stanley. A model of the building was on display for the 1949 AGM.

The leisurely progress of the ATA towards its objective was suddenly disrupted in 1950 when the Association's landlord gave notice that its lease would not be renewed when it terminated in September 1950. In fact, the Imperial Bank would like to regain possession by April 1 of that year. The reason for dispossessing a quiet and solvent tenant was that the bank had decided to tear down its Greek temple and replace it with a big ultra-modern box. The ATA's building project immediately swung into high gear. In February 1950 a decision was made to call for tenders on a two-storey building so designed as to be able to carry an additional three floors. As usual, tenders came in far higher than

[2]ATA Ex., Sept. 7, 1946.

[3]*The ATA Magazine,* XXIX, 3 (Dec. 1948), 3.

[4]H. D. Ainlay, unpublished, untitled memoir, 3.

Alberta Legislative Building, Edmonton. (Alberta Government Photo Branch)

Barnett House, 103rd Street, Edmonton, the first home owned by the ATA

the estimates. But the project could not be abandoned or even deferred. A re-tender call was issued, and in April a contract in the amount of $113,648 was awarded. Cost of the project, including land and furnishings, totalled about $150,000.

The following month the still-unbuilt roof figuratively collapsed when the city's town planner placed a stop-work order on the project. He had dreams of a scenic road winding along the rim of the valley, and the ATA building would interfere with it. Two months later, the order was rescinded as the proposed road proved to be prohibitive in cost. But the ATA was two months closer to eviction. As there was now no hope of being able to move into the new quarters before expiry of the lease in the bank building, and in fact the Association was being pressured to leave ahead of time, it took up quarters in the Millar Building in Edmonton's warehouse district with a lease to May 31, 1951. In September 1950 the new building was promised for occupancy by February following. However, as anyone who has had anything to do with building programmes realizes, the only thing surer than that costs will exceed estimates is that occupancy will be later than promised. "On June 1, 1951, the ATA staff moved into the new quarters." Ansley writes. "The painters were still busy and a number of other things had not been finished."[5] The building was officially opened on November 24, 1951.

It presented few surprises although it contained and incorporated many new and excellent features in both design and materials. However, according to the architect, K. Stanley:

> One interesting feature of the library is the round steel column immediately behind the glass. During construction, the Steel Company was unable to supply the usual round steel column at the time of erection, and substituted it with a used solid steel ship's drive shaft weighing in the neighbourhood of four thousand pounds. It is undoubtedly the finest piece of steel in the building.[6]

When the Association moved into its new quarters, not only the painting was unfinished. The ATA estimated that it was out of pocket some $8,600 as a result of the delay in construction occasioned by the stop-work order and the additional rent which the organization was required to pay for temporary

[5]E. C. Ansley, "The House that the Teachers Built," *This is the House that the Teachers Built* (19), p. 3.

[6]Kelly Stanley, "Alberta Teachers' Association Building," *ibid.*, p. 10.

accommodation, and also by the need to vacate the Imperial Bank building on short notice. As a result of both factors the Association was also put to the expense of moving twice instead of once. In 1951 the ATA concluded amicable arrangements whereby it recovered a substantial portion of its loss from the city and the bank.

This was not the last financial problem in connection with Barnett House. In 1952 the Edmonton Roman Catholic separate school district requested a share in the school taxes being paid by ATA on its new property. In endeavouring to arrive at an equitable division of its taxes, the executive considered a number of factors, specifically: (1) the number of Roman Catholic teachers in the ATA; (2) the proportion of ATA revenue received from Roman Catholic teachers; (3) the proportion of Roman Catholic school children in Edmonton. Surprisingly enough, it paid no attention to the School Act, which indicates that a corporation may divide its taxes between public and separate school districts in one of two ways: (*a*) in proportion to the ownership of shares in the corporation by Roman Catholics and others—obviously impossible for the ATA; (*b*) "in the same ratio that the assessment of persons, other than companies, for public school purposes bears to the assessment of persons other than companies, for separate school purposes."[7] Instead, the ATA and the two school districts concerned blandly disregarded the statute and agreed that 8 per cent of the school taxes would go to the separate school district.

The splendid new Edmonton home of the Association, with its chilled-steel propellor-shaft column, soon began to reveal some serious inherent disadvantages. The ATA's growing roster of members meant a growing staff and a shortage of space. This shortage was no insuperable handicap; the building had been designed to carry an additional three storeys. More serious were other handicaps. The hillside location and the lack of rear lane and rear access (except over other private property) made deliveries to and from the building awkward and frustrating. Also, the need for parking space for staff and visitors appeared to have been overlooked or insufficiently realized. Thus in 1960, when Barnett House was only nine years old, the AGM decided to proceed with a new building as soon as possible. By September of the same year the planning was well under way. The new Barnett House received its first occupants on January 29, 1962, with the usual official opening on June 16 following. The new

[7]Alberta, The School Act (R.S.A. 1955), sec. 294.

structure, comprising 20,000 square feet, included, in addition to the usual work areas and offices, a spacious foyer which joined the office wing to another that housed executive council chambers and a large auditorium suitable for meetings and dinners. In its move to new quarters the Association brought along as tenants the staff of the Teachers' Retirement Fund Board; it soon added other lessees as the Edmonton separate and public school Locals appointed their own secretary-treasurers. The new Barnett House is located in northwest Edmonton, far from the madding crowd. The first Barnett House was sold to the Alcohol Foundation of Alberta.

If the ATA's first home of its own met the needs of the Association for only eleven years, from 1951 to 1962, its successor proved adequate for an even shorter period. By 1966 the ATA membership had topped 20,000, more than double the number on the nominal roll a short decade before. Therefore in the precentennial year the recently renamed ARA authorized a building programme to provide additional space for the Association, either through an addition to Barnett House, still mint-new, or through an entirely new edifice. Consequently an additional 2.7 acres were purchased from the city, of which 1.7 acres are to provide for a sunken parking lot. The Association implemented plans to add an additional 42,000 feet of floor space, tripling Barnett House's size. The ATA also undertook to expand its building within 15 years, otherwise under a caveat the city can repurchase the 1.7-acre parking lot. The new complex includes a four-storey office wing (with footings to accommodate twelve storeys at some future date) and a separate printing plant.

An interesting commentary on the growing number and prosperity of Alberta teachers resides in the fact that the members of the Association themselves provided the financial sinews for the new Barnett House. Required funds came principally from the sale of a series of debentures offered first to ATA members, subsequently to the public, in denominations ranging from $100 to $1,000 and multiples thereof—a long day from the era of half a century before, when a handful of the founders had pledged their personal credit to $50 limits in order to furnish the infant Alliance with some working capital. With returns ranging from 7 to 8 per cent, these debentures provided an attractive investment to (comparatively) affluent teachers. At the same time by direct sale the Association avoided the cost of brokerage and the possibility of onerous discounts.

By the fall of 1967 the new building programme was well under way.

Infrastructure

UNTIL about the end of World War II The Alberta Teachers' Association was structurally a relatively simple organization. It had begun, very provisionally, with a membership consisting of a handful of bold pioneers in 1917, achieved a viable size about 1920, struggled against the attacks of a hostile government during the twenties, met the vicissitudes of the Hungry Thirties, and survived the turmoil and unrest of the war years. In 1945 it differed but little from the Alliance of a quarter-century before. With 5,541 members it was actually smaller than it had been when the war started, since in 1939 it had counted over 6,000 on its rosters. The basic organization of Locals and a provincial executive with a small secretariat had altered little in the previous decade. But within the first ten years after the war its membership was to reach 8,610; within another decade it had surpassed 17,000; by the time the Association's Golden Jubilee rolled around in 1968 it counted four members for every one on its roll in 1945. The Association's 22,000-plus membership roster included not only teachers active in the province's classrooms but also hundreds of retired, student, and optional (associate) members. And as its membership multiplied, so did its activities, interests, and staff. It is therefore not inappropriate to designate the internal organization of the burgeoning Association by the rather grandiose term of infrastructure.

It is perhaps not surprising that not until 1946 did the ATA come to consider the formulation of a policy on life and honorary memberships, nor that such a policy was not hammered out until two years later. By that time it was difficult to discover who had been granted life memberships or on what basis. However, in 1948 the council established standards to be observed for each category:

These were:

Life Members

1. Teachers must be retired and qualified for pensions.
2. They must have taught for at least 20 years (subsequently modified to ATA membership for the same period).
3. They would have all rights and privileges except to vote on elections for officers and on by-laws.

Honorary (Life) Members

1. This honour would require a two-thirds vote of the executive council.
2. It would be open to both teachers and others.
3. Not more than two honorary memberships would be awarded in any one year.
4. Honorary members would have the same rights and privileges as did other life members.

The matter of posthumous honours was not considered, although in subsequent years a number of such honorary memberships had been granted. First award of honorary membership was made to C. Sansom in 1949; second to M. E. LaZerte in 1950. Both recipients were past presidents of the Association.

The ATA recognizes not only accomplishment in the teaching profession and education generally but also potential for such achievement in a number of awards for younger practitioners of the teaching art and for teacher-trainees. Since scholarships are really gambles based, as bets on racehorses occasionally are, on past performance, it is not inappropriate to say that the Association puts its money where its mouth is. The ATA's first formal award of this nature was the Clarence Sansom Gold Medal in Education. This award originated about 1940, interestingly enough, not in the Association but through the action of a short-lived alumni society of the School of Education, University of Alberta. After this society became an unsung casualty of World War II, the ATA was asked to accept responsibility for the medal, which it did in 1950, at that time changing its name to the present one.

The establishment of the University of Calgary with a full four-year programme in education leading to a degree suggested that a second medal be presented. Thus came into being the Milton Ezra LaZerte Gold Medal in Education, like predecessor named for a previous president of the ATA. No doubt by design recognitions for excellence bear the names of men and women prominent in teacher education as well as in the annals of the Association. Sansom was a principal of Calgary Normal School, which ultimately became the Faculty of Education at the University of Calgary. LaZerte, as previously noted, was first dean of education at the University of Alberta, and before that had been director of the School and principal of the College from which the Faculty developed.

Each medal is accompanied by a scholarship of $500. There are many other such monetary awards granted by the Association. The complete list for 1967 follows, each named for a man or woman prominent in ATA affairs or in Alberta education:

Fellowship in Education ($2,400)	John Walker Barnett
Scholarships in Education ($500 each)	Clarence Sansom
	Milton Ezra LaZerte
	Hubert Charles Newland
	Thomas Edwin Albert Stanley
	William Aberhart
	Harry Dean Ainlay
	William Edward Frame
	Clarence Oliver Hicks
	Donalda James Dickie
	Lloyd Garrison
	Eva Osyth Howard
	Charles Edgar Peasley

Solving or attempting to solve internal problems. keeping an eye on the department of education and all its boards and committees, endeavouring to out-manoeuvre trustees on questions of tenure and bargaining, maintaining fraternal relations with sister organizations across Canada (or should one call them sororal relations?), weighing the implications of new legislation, launching research, library, and other projects, watching public relations, implementing a new pension scheme—all of these matters took time, attention, energy, and money. But even this list of activities is not exhaustive. One new project in the post-war decade was the establishment of what has come to be known as the Banff Workshop, later to be known as the Banff Conference, instituted in 1949. The workshop is held for one week each year at the Banff School of Fine Arts during the period immediately following the university's summer sessions.

Originally three courses were offered, in: ATA policies and administration; curriculum development; educational publicity and public relations.[1] By 1966 the courses were designated as Leadership, Professional Development, Teacher Welfare, and Long-Range Planning. In 1967 there appeared a new programme called Communications. In addition, there was an Economic Consultants' Seminar. According to Kratzmann, the objectives of the Banff conference or short course have been: (1) to study organization, administration, and policies of the Association in order that the services to members may be improved at provincial and local levels; (2) to study methods and problems in curriculum making; (3) to develop an interest in and to study the techniques of educational publicity and public relations; (4) to encourage teachers to write about schools, educational and professional matters.[2]

Besides being the first of its kind in the ATA's history, the 1949 workshop is also memorable as marking the first time that the Association established relations with another professional group. This development arose when the registered nurses' association requested permission to send four representatives to Banff. As the executive council minutes indicate, "General agreement with this action was expressed by the Executive, many feeling that it was a good thing to welcome any such interest on the part of another professional organization."[3]

Normally, the attendance at the Banff workshop is limited to one representative per Local (except for very large Locals) and to executive council members. To these are added resource personnel, ATA staff, and a few fraternal delegates, for example from the department of education, to bring the usual attendance to about 200, as compared with about 60 in 1949.

From its earliest days the ATA had opened windows on the world, maintained relations with educational and other organizations through the exchange of fraternal delegates, co-operation with the Alberta Education Association, and

[1]A. Kratzmann, "The Alberta Teachers' Association: A Documentary Analysis of the Dynamics of a Professional Association," unpublished doctoral dissertation, University of Chicago (1963), p. 212.

[2]*Ibid.*, 211.

[3]ATA Ex., July 25, 1949.

in other ways. After World War II the ATA's external relations expanded in all directions.

One new organization to appear in the immediate post-war period was the Alberta Education Council (AEC), perhaps because the late Alberta Education Association was not quite as expendable as appeared. First established in 1946, within a year the AEC had enlisted support from 21 organizations. *The ATA Magazine* reported its objects to be:

1. To arouse public interest in and to co-operate for the promotion and improvement in legislation relating to all phases of elementary and secondary education in Alberta.

2. To prepare and publicize treatises and papers designed to assist high school boards in providing a greater measure of equality of educational opportunity to the school children of Alberta.[4]

The ATA gave considerable support to the new federation. In 1948, ATA representative E. C. Ansley accepted the vice-presidency. The secretary and the president, Mrs. Mary Butterworth and H. E. Spencer respectively, were chosen from the ranks of the school trustees. Later the same year the ATA made a grant of $500 to the AEC in addition to its membership fee of $5.

The new Council was rather more successful in achieving its first objective than in reaching its second. It took over sponsorship of Education Week, a baby that had been handed back and forth between the ATA and the CTF, and mounted some promotional campaigns designed to persuade the public that education was a Good Thing. However, in 1953 ATA president Marian Gimby charged that "Our handling of Education Week has been spotty. We have let the Alberta Education Council fall by the wayside."[5]

The University of Alberta (and other universities when they were established) also provided opportunities for co-operation on such matters as continuing professional education of teachers, evaluation of teacher credentials, the council of the Faculty of Education, the annual short leadership course for school principals, and the alumni association. Other continuing external contacts were with various bodies concerned with driver education, educational research, private schools and colleges, highway legislation, etc.

By the fall of 1957, ATA president Inez Castleton was able to announce that

[4]*The ATA Magazine*, XXVII, 5 (Feb. 1947), 7.

[5]M. Gimby, "President's Report," *ibid.*, XXXIII, 10 (June 1953), 27.

the Canadian College of Teachers had been established with headquarters at Ottawa. According to her, "The purpose of the College will be to stimulate professional growth of teachers, to improve standards of service to teachers, and to hold before the teaching profession and the public the concept of a good teacher."[6]

It is difficult to see what functions the CCT could perform towards the achievement of its purpose that could not be handled equally well by the already existing CTF. One can therefore be excused for wondering if the real motivation for the college was not to establish a prestigious organization comparable to the Royal College of Physicians and Surgeons (Canada) to reflect lustre on the profession as a whole. This impression is reinforced by the information that its nominal roll would include fellows as well as members.

The ATA gave qualified approval only to the new body. It asked that an equivalent be accepted in lieu of the university degree which was proposed as one of the conditions of membership, and the necessity of writing a book, holding professional office, serving on a community enterprise, or similar conditions be deleted as prerequisites to membership. The Alberta organization also felt that the same person should serve as secretary of the CTF and the CCT. Because of these reservations the ATA therefore took a small amount of umbrage over the solicitation of memberships before membership qualifications had been decided.

All across the North American continent the whole post-war period was one of increased public interest in and dissatisfaction with conventional education. No doubt a number of factors contributed to the general feeling of unease: the continent-wide and apparently chronic shortage of teachers, rising educational costs, apprehension lest the Bad Guys (from USSR) with their advanced missile and space technology would overwhelm Our Side, the Quebecois' quiet revolution and demand for equality of status for their language and their culture. One manifestation of this unrest was the organization of the Canadian Conferences on Education, the first of which was convened in February 1958 under the chairmanship of the distinguished neurosurgeon Wilder Penfield. Over 850 delegates from 35 national organizations assembled for four days to study the crucial problems of Canada's school systems. They were organized into eight workshops, each of which tackled the issues in one of the following fields:

[6]*The ATA Magazine*, XXXVIII, 2 (Oct. 1957), 30.

school buildings and equipment; education for leisure; financing of education; higher education; organization and curriculum; rôle of the home in education; special needs in education; teachers—quality and quantity.

In the opinion of education officer E. J. Ingram, who served as secretary of the Alberta committee associated with the conference (of which the CTF secretary served as director), the most important problems which confronted the conference were money for education and teacher qualifications. ". . . the success of the conference will be measured by change in the attitude of the public towards education," Ingram reported. "This will become the primary task of the conference delegates and the sponsoring organizations they represent."[7]

In 1962 the second Canadian Conference on Education was held along lines similar to those of the first one four years before. Again, Canadian teachers' organizations, including the CTF, supported the conference. But when the question arose as to whether a continuing organization should be established, to hold further conferences in the future (and probably engage in other activities), the teachers took a long, hard look at what sponsorship of such a body would entail and decided that such action posed the threat of making their organizations the captives of a group whose interests were not parallel to their own. Accordingly, the CTF decided not to act as a sponsor of such an organization, explaining its refusal in the following resolution:

> That the teachers are not opposed to the organization of bodies to foster interest in education and that they are prepared to offer professional consultation and advice to such bodies; however, in order to maintain our professional independence and freedom of action, we are not prepared to act as a sponsoring body of any such post-conference organization.[8]

By no means all the ATA's formal relationships with other organizations were limited to those whose primary interest was in education. For example, a 1958 minute of the executive council recorded the appointment of a fraternal—that word again—delegate to attend the convention of the Alberta Association of Registered Nurses.[9]

The nurses, of course, were old friends of the school teachers, but in time

[7]E. J. Ingram in *The ATA Magazine*, XXXVIII, 7 (March 1958), 20 *et seq.*
[8]*Ibid.*, XLII, 10 (June 1962), 37.
[9]ATA Ex., Feb. 7-8, 1958.

other relations were established and other contacts were made with other professionals. The channel of communication was the ATA-inspired Council of Professional Associations. First established in the mid-fifties, it languished and nearly disappeared, to be revived through the efforts of the ATA's new executive secretary, S. C. T. Clarke. Membership in this little-known organization consists of professional bodies which are represented on faculty councils of the University of Alberta. It thus includes the professional organizations of physicians, lawyers, dentists, engineers, etc. as well as of teachers and nurses. The Council meets about twice a year to study common problems such as legislation, annual dues and the collection thereof, discipline of members, etc.

There were other contacts. During the decade leading to its golden jubilee, the Association was represented by active participants in or fraternal delegates to such organizations as the Western Conference of Teacher Organizations, the Western Canadian Conference of Teacher Education Organizations, the Canadian Education Association, successive British Columbia Teachers' Federation workshops, a Salary Conference of the Western Provinces, the Alberta Association of Registered Nurses (a platonic if long-standing liaison), the Alberta Federation of Labour (a half-century old relationship), and the more or less amicable enemies or inimicable friends who constitute the Alberta School Trustees' Association. There was also the Leadership Course for School Principals, a fortnight-long brain-scrubbing ordeal first held in 1957 under the sponsorship of the ATA, the ASTA, the Department of Education, and the University of Alberta. Finally there were two south-of-the-border contacts, with the Association for Supervision and Curriculum Development, and a National Education Association gathering on salary schedules.

The ATA's members were equally busy at home. Thus be 1964 the Association also had eleven standing and four special committees dealing with concerns of the ATA and of teachers generally. The standing committees were concerned with curricula, discipline, finance, honorary memberships, pensions, pensions grievances, professional relations, resolutions, scholarships and loans, and teacher education and certification. There was also one whose rôle was undefined: the table officers committee. Special committees were for the history of Alberta education, international assistance, self-evaluation for high schools, and ditto for elementary schools. In all, some 70 teachers were acting on internal and external committees and organizations at the provincial levels and beyond.

Not all activities of the ATA during the 1960's have been earth-shakers; many have been adjustments to the changing times, or provision of special services to the members. Among the former was, at long last, acceptance of an idea advanced by Marian Gimby when she was president of the Association; that the incumbent of that position be able to devote his full time to the affairs of the ATA without responsibilities for a particular classroom or school or school system. In 1962 the executive secretary announced that such an arrangement had been achieved. Thereafter the ATA presidents have been granted leave-of-absence by their employers, the Association compensating the school systems for lack of services.

Two examples of special services to members my be mentioned. One was the establishment in 1959 of the ATA Savings and Credit Union, Ltd., with W. R. Eyres as secretary-treasurer. Within the first year the union had recruited 162 members. Its assets amounted to $15,000 approximately, and during the first eight months of operation it had made loans of more than $15,000. Another extra dividend available to ATA members since 1960 has been the opportunity to participate in charter flights to England. Three such flights were made in 1966, and four the following year. In 1965, the Association sponsored all-expense air tours to the Orient. In addition, in 1967 the ATA sponsored a centennial flight to Expo 67.

Yet such activities, interesting as they are and welcome as they might be to those intimately concerned, are of but minor significance compared to the major objectives of the Association. These have always included teachers' enconomic betterment and professional development. Although the former has received less public attention than other perhaps more newsworthy and more controversial activities, the Association has never forgotten that unremitting effort is necessary not alone to advance the teachers' economic security, but merely to preserve their present position and to avoid falling behind in a period of apparently chronic inflation. To preserve gains painfully achieved during the first fifty years of its existence, the Association recognizes that it must adopt a hard-nosed attitude in bargaining for new and better salary agreements. It must also train personnel in the principles of collective bargaining, not merely in the textbook theory of the process but in the tactics and strategy which lead to success in eyeball-to-eyeball confrontations. With some 200 school systems in the province, and separate agreements needed for each, the staff of Barnett

House could not be expected to provide bargaining expertise as needed in every series of negotiation, even though the ATA is regularly named as the teachers' bargaining agent and the staff members are available in particularly sticky cases. Accordingly the Association has trained a cadre of bargainers, or rather resource personnel known as economic consultants. These are teachers, characterized by maturity, proven ability, drive, and commitment to their Association, who have attended conferences at Banff and shorter seminars which are held throughout the province, and who either serve on negotiating committees or who advise and assist those who do.

But as the Association enters its second half-century, probably its most important project is its Long Range Planning (LRP) Project. As *ATA Magazine* editor Seymour noted:

> In the fall of 1963, the Executive Council of The Alberta Teachers' Association discussed the idea of long-range planning and approved a proposal that the Association engage in such planning. The Executive Council then presented the following resolution to the Annual General Meeting:
>
> "BE IT RESOLVED, that the Executive Council prepare a statement of long-range objectives for the Association, particularly in the fields of economic welfare, teacher education, and professional development, and an outline of plans for the achievement of these objectives."
>
> This resolution was passed by the Annual General Meeting.
>
> In May of 1964, the Association conducted a survey of teacher opinion on 14 topics: local and sub-local activities, staff officers, ATA functions, conventions, in-service education, teacher education and certification, specialist councils, new developments in education, ethics and discipline, *The ATA Magazine,* ATA publications, salary, collective bargaining, and living and working conditions. During the school year 1964-65, the results of this survey were reported in "The Secretary Reports" column of the magazine.
>
> The next step in the Long-Range Planning Project was authorization by the Executive Council of the production of planning kits which would assist local participation in the development of long-range plans. At the 1965 Annual Representative Assembly planning kits were distributed to local representatives on the following topics: Analysis of Present ATA Policy, Analysis of Present ATA Activities, Analysis of Present Organization and Administration.[10]

Second stage of the LRP Project followed immediately as Seymour has also noted:

[10]*The ATA Magazine,* XLVI, 1 (Sept. 1965), 14.

On Saturday, September 25, in eight widely-separated locations throughout the province, over 500 representatives of local associations will meet in regional conferences to see the second stage in the Association's Long Range Planning Project unveiled. This project, authorized by the Annual Representative Assembly nearly two years ago, started with studies of the internal workings of the organization, and will next expand into studies of curriculum, organization and administration of the school system, teacher education and certification, education finance, and educational planning. The overall extent of the studies, and preliminary considerations will be released in detail during the regional conferences and in the week following, and members of local associations will hear much more about the LRP Project in the weeks and months to follow.

But the important point of the whole project was the decision of the Executive Council to call on local associations to take part in shaping the stand which the Association is to take in the future in the crucial areas of education.[11]

Nearly two years later, at the 1967 ARA, two days were devoted to the 70 resolutions which together formed the ATA's blueprint for the educational future, at least to 1975. If some of the resolutions were extremely general and represented positions to which no one could object (for example, that every child has the right to educational opportunities in a publicly supported educational system), others are specific, controversial, or so new that outside the profession controversy has not had time to develop. ATA editor McConaghy has summarized these resolutions under three general headings: curriculum, educational finance, and teacher education and certification. Because they will cast a shadow far into the ATA's future, this summary is here quoted in full:

On Curriculum

That the choice of techniques and processes for achieving the aims of education is the responsibility of the teaching profession.

That every child has the right to educational opportunities in a publicly supported system.

That the ATA should be adequately represented on all Department of Education curriculum committees and boards.

That matriculation standards be established so that at least 25 per cent of the school population qualify for university entrance; and success in matriculation examinations continue to be a sufficient condition for admission to Alberta universities.

That there be more local autonomy and local participation in curriculum building.

That new curriculum not be introduced unless texts, outlines and guides are available at least six months previous to its introduction as working curricula.

That kindergarten classes be placed under the jurisdiction of the Department of

[11] *Ibid.*, 5.

Education and that a full-time director of kindergartens be appointed.
That all Grade IX departmental examinations be eliminated.
That potential use of paperbacks, possible multiple text authorization, and improvement in procedures for text selection be investigated.

On Education Finance
That the amount of financial support for education contributed by the three levels of government should be directly related to their ability to pay.
That the major part of expenditure in university education, technical and vocational education, adult and continuing education and educational research should be borne by the Federal Government.
That the uniform levy on the equalized assessment of real property for the School Foundation Program Fund not exceed 25 mills; and the Fund be structured so that the major part of expenditure on public elementary (including kindergarten) and secondary education be borne by the provincial government.
That a federal office of education be established which will have as one of its functions continuing research in the problem of educational finance at the national level.
That the ATA oppose expenditure of public funds for either direct or indirect support of private schools which duplicate educational services offered by public or separate schools.

On Teacher Education and Certification
That teachers require only one teaching certificate and all teachers have the same certificate.
That teachers prepared in Alberta require a period of internship and two years of successful teaching experience for permanent certification.
That the professional organization has the right to share in decisions affecting the preparation and certification of teachers, and will share the responsibility for decertification of incompetent teachers.
That instructional services may be carried out by uncertificated persons (teacher aides) providing that all such instructional activities are under the supervision of a certificated teacher; and that the Executive Council, in cooperation with other interested bodies, develop criteria governing the employment of such personnel.
That any teacher who has been out of teaching for a period of five or more years voluntarily complete an adequate period of educational reorientation.[12]

The story of the Alberta Teachers' Association in the ten years or so preceding the celebration of its golden jubilee is one of almost incredible metamorphosis. Yet it is not that the ATA has become a different kind of organization; it still fights for its members' economic betterment, even if fang and claw have

[12]*Ibid.*, XLVII, 8 (April 1967), 24, 26.

been replaced by more sophisticated weapons. It is not that the Association has lost interest in promoting recognition of teaching as a profession and of the ATA as its voice; never has it been more active in securing formal recognition on government and other boards, committees, councils, and commissions, and in requiring those representatives to do their homework before opening their mouths at the meetings of such bodies. But at last it was able to and did pursue its objective of professional growth with vigour and seriousness of purpose never before demonstrated. It had poured time, money, and effort into not one or two channels but such a multitude that an adequate treatment of the ATA's fifth decade would require more space than has been devoted to the first four together.

In half a century the ATA has developed away from a small, tightly knit "band of brothers," in which each member had established personal relationships with a high proportion of the total membership, to whom he was bound not only by ties of common economic considerations but by those of personal affection and respect. It has become something different. The ATA member of today probably knows more colleagues personally and well enough to call by their first names, but yet less intimately, and in any case, their number is a smaller proportion of the 20,000-odd teachers who make up the ATA.

Yet the Association has avoided becoming a faceless, anonymous monolith, dextrously controlled by a self-perpetuating "establishment," and whenever it shows signs of so becoming, enough Young Turks in its ranks stand ready to cut the Pooh-Bahs down to size. That the Association has avoided the dangers of giantism is no doubt owing to the fact that Alberta teachers are the kind of people they are, unwilling to delegate to others the power of making decisions on matters of vital importance to them. It is also owing to the vitality of the Locals, which are more than mere constituencies for the ARA or units out of which convention districts are built. Since they or their sub-locals are the negotiators of and signatories to the collective agreements under which teachers are paid, they are very viable units indeed, and ensure the vitality and democracy of the organization as a whole. Commenting on a study by E. J. Ingram, [13] the ATA's executive secretary S. C. T. Clarke concluded: "... teachers believe in what the Association stands for and, even if they do not participate in the administration

[13]E. J. Ingram, "Member Involvement in the Alberta Teachers' Association," unpublished doctoral dissertation, University of Alberta (1965), p. 167.

of the Association, they feel it is representing the interests of the teachers. One could conclude that while they may criticize how the Association operates on occasion, in time of threat they will support it whole-heartedly. Experience bears out these conclusions."[14]

[14]S. C. T. Clarke, "A Student's Analysis of the Association: Ingram," *The ATA Magazine,* XLVI, 4 (Dec. 1965), 71.

The Flowering of the Sixties

ONE REASON for the Flowering of the Sixties was the appointment of Dr. S. C. T. Clarke as executive secretary of the Association. His two predecessors were organizers, promoters, champions of the ATA and the classroom teacher, aggressive in protecting the shorn lamb from the chill winds of adverse circumstance, and determined to raise the defenceless young ungulant to become, not a prowling predator in sheep's clothing but at least into a full-grown ram with the courage and armament to defend its rights and its place in the economic wilderness. Barnett and Ansley came to the ATA's council chamber directly from the classroom; Clarke is a much more urbane individual. To competent teaching experience he added graduate study in education. To his decade as a high school teacher he had added another as a professor of education in Alberta and California.

In his perceptive study of the ATA, Kratzmann has recognized Clarke's influence, manifested very early in his new term of office. In his words:

> A number of factors appear to bear a relationship to the change . . . waxing strongly in the perception of members of, and persons external to, the A.T.A., was the appointment of Stanley Clarke as Executive Secretary in 1959. All interviewees afforded him the credit for initiating and coordinating the additional service-oriented activities of very recent years.[1]

At the same time, the contributions of the ATA members, especially the Association's leaders and executive council members, to the great leap forward must not be overlooked. In the first place, credit must be given them for their wise choice of an executive secretary. Nor could the new servant of the Association have implemented any innovations in the ATA's programmes without the acqui-

[1]A Kratzmann, "The Alberta Teachers' Association: A Documentary Analysis of the Dynamics of a Professional Association," unpublished doctoral dissertation, University of Chicago (1963), p. 233.

escence and indeed the active support of the executive council and the membership at large. The confrontation of Clarke's predecessor with the executive council of the ATA had firmly established the latter's authority as well as the dependence of the executive secretary on the council for its approval of any major and significant project. Finally, with the best of intentions by executive secretary, councillors, and members in general, without adequate financial resources, the best of planning would have come to naught. But with the burgeoning school population consequent to the post-war baby boom and the buoyant provincial oil revenues after 1947, the number of classrooms (and of ATA members) increased very rapidly. In 1950, their number was 7,106, of whom 6,088 were employed by school boards. Fifteen years later the Association membership had much more than doubled, to 17,160. Of these, 15,327 were the ordinary members who provide the Local, ARA, and executive council personnel and talent, and who contribute to the Association's finances far out of proportion to their numbers—life members (750 in 1965) pay no dues, and others only nominal sums at the rate of $12 per year.

Many ATA projects of the sixties were extensions and expansions of programmes which had originated in the twenties, thirties, and forties. An entirely new movement was that embodied in the establishment of specialist councils. Each council consists of teachers, supervisors, professors, curriculum builders, even administrators concerned with a single teaching area or subject, or with a single field of professional concern. The development of these councils is a sign that the era of the generalist is over, the day of the specialist has arrived. No longer is the elementary teacher a young schoolmarm teaching the whole programme for every grade from I to VIII in a drafty, uncomfortable, isolated rural one-room school. No longer is the high school instructor a harrassed young or older man attempting to cover every subject for matriculation in Grades IX to XI or X to XII—and acting as principal of a four-room school on the side. In the sixties the elementary teacher has one grade only in his or her classroom, which is only one of ten or twenty in a modern, new, functional building. He has become a specialist, in Grade III, or IV, or VI, and would be quite unhappy if asked to take responsibility for two grades.

Still, the more specialized specialists are in the high school; those who labour in the vineyards of English or science or mathematics or what-not, not only in the senior high school grades, but at the VII to IX levels as well. Thus it was natural that most of the early specialist councils were in subject-matter fields. Organized in October 1960, these included councils for English, modern languages, science, social studies, and mathematics. There was one other, established for school principals, primarily, educators who no longer had to spend most or all of the school day on instructional duties, handling their administrative responsibilities after hours or in moments stolen from their teaching function. This last body has been designated as the school administrators' specialist council.

The number of councils grew rapidly. In the spring of 1961 the Alberta Guidance Association at its eighth annual conference changed itself into a specialist council, and new councils were formed for home economics, industrial arts, and business education. By 1963 the number of councils had grown to twelve, the newest groups including fine arts and health and physical education. The languages council had enlarged its scope to include classical (that is, Latin) as well as modern languages. (In deference to some Canadians—or rather *Canadiens*—the nomenclature of "foreign languages" has apparently been abandoned.) With the phenomenal increase in vocational education which followed the 1960 passage of the federal Technical and Vocational Training Assistance Act, the industrial arts specialist council extended its scope to include vocational education.

As their names indicate, most of the councils emphasized school activities at the junior and senior high school levels, although, with increasing departmentalization at the upper elementary levels, these areas of concern were not wholly neglected. Two more specialist councils were established dealing extensively or wholly with the lower grade levels; these were the school library and early childhood education councils.

The councils have emerged as semi-autonomous bodies sponsored by the ATA. Their membership rolls are open to other than ATA members. They determine and collect their own dues, publish their own periodicals and other materials, hold their own conferences. The Association usually provides the initial impetus for their establishment, gives them clerical and professional assistance from its own staff, furnishes financial assistance for special projects up to 50 per cent of their cost and a fixed dollar limit, and devotes a section of *The ATA Magazine* to "Council News," or at least did until a new ATA publishing policy was adopted in 1967, when such material was moved to the new *ATA News*.

The councils' activities are not limited to the publication of materials pertinent to their members' interests. Clarke has summarized their 1966 activities as follows:

In 1966, the Association organized its fourteenth council—the Early Childhood Education Council. Over 300 teachers attended the inaugural meeting. Although membership in councils decreased slightly from last year (the 199 membership was 3,319 as compared with 3,624 in 1965), the activities of the councils increased. Grants for councils increased from nearly $15,000 to $17,000 in 1966. During the same period, total expenditures by councils increased from approximately $30,000 to $43,000.

During 1966, over 80 conferences, seminars and short courses were sponsored by the Association's 13 councils. In addition, 23 different publications were produced. Plans for 1967 are even more ambitious. Although not all councils have established sub-groups, there are now a total of 41 regionals in operation. The problems reported by councils are primarily concerned with regional councils. These include the necessity of revitalizing the regionals each year, stimulating interest and participation, financing, and communications between the regionals and the provincial council with respect to activities.[2]

This summary does not do justice to the scope of the councils' activities. In 1966, the mathematics council hosted a three-day conference of the National Council of Teachers of Mathematics, the reputable United States association. The Conference was attended by 651 delegates, including over 250 from south of the border, and well over 100 from other parts of Canada. Some councils, including those for mathematics and science, have held programmes to upgrade the knowledge of content on the part of their members. The business education council in 1967 sponsored a national invitational conference addressed by business leaders as well as educators from across Canada. In 1966 the science council sponsored a school science fair at the Edmonton Jubilee Auditorium. Some councils have worked with other groups, for example, the library council has co-operated with the Canadian School Libraries Association to choose school districts as nominees for Canadian school library awards. The social studies council co-operated with the Historical Society of Alberta and the University of Alberta to sponsor a centennial conference on western Canadian history during May 1967 at Banff. This gathering attracted some 400 partici-

[2]S. C. T. Clarke, "Report to the Fiftieth ARA," *The ATA Magazine*, XLVII, 8 (April 1967), 40.

pants from eight Canadian provinces and an even larger number of American states. The same council since 1964 has organized a week-long field study at and near Hinton, an interdisciplinary project including in its scope material in geography, history, geology, and other fields. Another 1967 project, this one of the fine arts council, dealt with the matter of team teaching in the arts and involved the Alberta Music Educators' Association and the Recreation and Cultural Development Branch of the Alberta government.

By 1967, all systems read Go—memberships passing the 4,700 mark, grants exceeding $20,000, total expenditures topping $56,000. The 14 councils held 88 conferences in addition to the 52 sponsored by the 47 regional councils.

The specialist council is an agency for professional development organized from the top down and owing its success in large measure to the support and direction provided by the executive council of the ATA. Another developmental agency of concern to the Association, but apparently of grassroots origin, is the teaching internship. This institution is not indigenous to Alberta; internships have been incorporated into United States teacher preparation programmes for a number of years. Alberta, however, appears to be the first province to accept the concept, and even yet it is not widely known or at least implemented outside the foothills province. It appeared spontaneously and sporadically, apparently, in the late fifties in Alberta's rural systems, "partly as a recruitment device, partly as a means to orient new appointees to teaching situations often far different from those they had previously met as students either in the ordinary schools or in the university."[3] Originally the internship consisted of relatively unstructured experience as a helping teacher (or sometimes in emergencies as a substitute teacher) during the six or eight weeks in May and June following the closing of the university term at the end of April or thereabouts. The interns are teacher-trainees who have completed their professional preparation and are eligible for teaching certificates, which, as a matter of fact, are usually issued during the period of internship. At first, interns were given what the armed forces vividly label as "joe jobs," balancing registers, marking end-of-the-year tests, supervising study halls, assisting extra-curricular activities such as track meets and school festivals, etc. Thus each intern's experience tended to be unique.

Interns were (and are) paid for their services, usually at rates lower than

[3]J. W. Chalmers, *Schools of the Foothills Province* (Toronto, 1967), p. 147.

those which apply for members of the regular staff but more than those received by non-professional instructors such as correspondence centre supervisors. Usually their remuneration was based on a daily, rather than on a monthly or yearly rate. The internship has often been confused with student teaching, but the resemblance is only superficial Although the intern might occasionally instruct under the supervision of an experienced teacher, the latter made no formal evaluation of the former's performance, nor was such practice in any way a part of the neophyte's professional preparation. He had already qualified for his teaching certificate.

The institution of the internship soon became more formal, more highly structured as those concerned gave more thought to its functions and potential, and interns themselves were given some orientation to their rôles. As early as 1962 the ATA was promoting conferences of interns for this purpose. By 1963, Clarke had evolved seven features of the internship.[4] These were:

1. Timing—after institutional preparation.
2. Practice teaching—supplements but does not supplant this activity.
3. Remuneration—small, to defray expenses only.
4. Intern's responsibility—not for a specific classroom, except temporarily.
5. Academic credit—none.
6. Sponsorship—by department of education, university, trustees, teachers, and superintendents jointly.
7. Duration—as decided. Ideally, a year.

Two years later, Clarke again gave consideration to the internship when he wrote:

> It occurs after institutional preparation. It supplements but does not supplant student-teaching. The intern is paid. He is not held finally responsible for the students he deals with. Internship does not occur within the preparing institution (the university) but out in the field (the schools); it is not a university course which is marked or graded and for which credit is allowed; and it is jointly sponsored by school boards, the Department of Education, the teachers (locally and through their organization), the trustees' organization, and the preparing institution.[5]

Developments in the internship continue to occur, usually with the concur-

[4]S. C. T. Clarke, "Internship for Teachers," *The ATA Magazine*, XLII, 9 (May 1962), 77.

[5]S. C. T. Clarke, "The Rôle of Internship in Teacher Education," *The ATA Magazine*, XLV, 11 (June 1965), 22–3.

rence of the Association and sometimes as a result of its urging. It is no longer confined to rural systems. Edmonton, for example, has a well-developed internship programme, carefully worked out to give beginning teachers the sort of experience which they will find of greatest value when they take over their Edmonton classrooms the following fall. The staff members under whom they will do their internships also receive direction as to how they can best help their charges.

The teachers' and the trustees' associations agreed that if the internship is to be regarded as an integral part of the teachers' preparation, its costs should be not borne wholly by the sponsoring school systems. Teacher preparation is a provincial function; consequently the province should bear at least part of the cost of internship. The department of education has accepted this viewpoint, and now the intern's remuneration is met at least partially out of provincial revenues.

Further changes can be anticipated. One is that the internship may become one of the prerequisites to teacher certification, just as it is for the licensing of a physician. This change, however, must wait on another development, the growth of enough opportunities so that no teacher-trainee will be denied the opportunity to undergo this experience. It is noted, too, that Clarke suggests that internship should last a whole year, not merely one or two months. However, sudden imposition of this requirement would mean that one whole class of trainees would be withdrawn from regular teaching service for a year, and with staffing problems throughout the province remaining acute, such action does not yet appear feasible. Nor is it likely in the immediate future, since action has now been taken to extend professional preparation for first certification from two years to three.

The interest of the ATA in the institution of the internship is indicated by the fact that in 1962 *The ATA Magazine* announced, "For the first time in Alberta, conferences of teacher interns were held . . . sparked by the ATA. . . ."[6]

Internship is an introduction and orientation to the profession of teaching. Other means are used to introduce neophytes to some particular aspects of their profession or to their professional association. Thus one school system, the Northland school division, regularly or occasionally (for example, in 1965 and 1967) holds orientation programmes of about three days to introduce new

[6]*The ATA Magazine*, XLII, 9 (May 1962), 77.

appointees to their future assignments. This activity arises from two circumstances. The first is that with the exception of two or three schools, its thirty-odd wilderness temples of learning are isolated, usually northern institutions attended predominantly by children of native ancestry who bring to the learning situation a background of experience and a set of standards and values wholly different from those which are the usual mental and emotional baggage of the white, middle-class, urban or semi-urbanized children who attend most of the province's schools. The other circumstance is that especially in the two years mentioned, the Northland system enlisted a high proportion of its new recruits from off-continent sources—are Canadian teachers too timid or are they too sophisticated to serve in the schools of the forest? The Northland orientation programmes involve university, department of education, ATA, and divisional officials. Other systems also hold orientation sessions, although usually their programmes are less extensive than those of the moose division.

In 1960 the ATA began the practice of inducting teachers new to the foothills province, whether so by initial training and preparation or by immigration, into the Association. Purpose of the ceremony, faintly reminiscent of the initiation ritual of fraternal lodges and service clubs, is to acquaint new members with their rights, privileges, and obligations as members of a most important profession. Although the original impetus for the induction ceremony came from the provincial executive council, or at least from the provincial office, it has always remained optional with the Locals, which have remained responsible for mounting the actual ceremony. Despite this voluntary feature, in the first year about half the Locals exercised the option. In 1967, the executive secretary announced that during the previous year over 2,000 induction kits had been distributed to 55 Locals of the 71 then in existence.[7] Each inductee received a certificate of induction into the Association and two ATA booklets. *Membership in your Professional Association* and *The Teaching Profession.*

Since Clarke's appointment to the executive secretaryship of the Association, the ATA's work of professional development has become so important that not only have highly qualified personnel been appointed to devote their full time to it but this department has even had its own publication since 1961, a four-times-a-year *Professional Development Bulletin,* consisting mainly of announce-

[7] S. C. T. Clarke, "Report to the Fiftieth ARA," *The ATA Magazine,* XLVII, 8 (April 1967), 46.

ments and news about professional development programmes, as well as occasional articles.

The *Professional Development Bulletin,* or "pdb" as it is labelled, is not the only new periodical to appear from Barnett House, even excluding those emanating from the specialist councils. Occasionally during the early sixties special letters to officials of the Locals, or to the membership at large, were disseminated to deal with often inflammatory issues by providing a relatively confidential medium for information and viewpoints, and to do so on short notice. These letters were essentially private in nature, as contrasted with the public character of *The ATA Magazine.* From such occasional publications perhaps grew *The ATA News,* which first appeared in September 1965 for distribution to officials of the Local organizations. The first number contained a potpourri of information, for example, on electoral votes, regional conferences, hours at Barnett House, fall and spring conventions, specialist council activities, the ATA credit union, life and honorary memberships, and so on. Thereafter *The ATA News* appeared irregularly, not to replace *The ATA Magazine* but to supplement it. Issue No. 2, similar in nature, did not appear until November, 1965, but December of that year saw two issues. Each was devoted to a single theme, one dealing with a salary dispute involving the Red Deer urban public school district, the other concerned with the evaluation of years of teacher education for purposes of determining salaries. No other issue appeared until February; its subject was also evaluation of teacher preparation, as was No. 8's, which was distributed in March. Numbers 5 and 6 both appeared in February; both were special issues. The latter was devoted to the settlement of the Red Deer salary dispute. The seventh and ninth were also special numbers, the former giving the texts of resolutions for the 1966 ARA, the latter being devoted to a salary dispute with the Three Hills school division. The final number of Volume I was again general in scope and content. Seven of the first ten issues had been special numbers. The ten issues appeared in six different months.

With a new school year the *News* began to appear more regularly; every month from September 1966 to March 1967 saw an issue in the mail. In February, two issues appeared, or rather Parts A and B of Volume II, Number 6. Of the eight numbers (or seven, depending on how one counts that double-barreled number), all except one were labelled as special issues. Further to confuse the picture, with February 1967 the publication's name was changed to

The ATA Report to Locals, and the former name was applied to a new periodical with its own volume and number identifications. *The ATA News* (new series) first appeared in February 1967. It abandoned the multilith format of its predecessor, using letterpress production, tabloid size, with many illustrations. *The ATA News* (old series) was an anonymous publication (except for the ATA imprint); the new organ carried a masthead bearing the names of recently appointed T. W. McConaghy as editor and J. D. McFetridge as associate editor. Three numbers appeared during the spring of 1967; Volume II, Number 1 in September of the same year.

With the beginning of the new school year in the fall of Canada's centenary, *The ATA News* reached maturity, a robust adult at the ripe age of two years, and began monthly publication. Its distribution was to the complete ATA membership. Scope of the new tabloid is suggested by a glance at the contents of Volume I, Number 3 (new series). The lead story, with a cut, was headed "Clarke to leave ATA post," and told that the executive secretary had submitted his resignation, to leave ATA employ on June 30, 1969. Other heads included "Cooperating Teachers Study Internship Program," "Calgary Newsmen Critical of Teachers' Public Relations," "Centennial Conference on the Canadian West," "New Printing wing on schedule" (with no fewer than five cuts), "ATA President concerned about Teacher Turnover," as well as other material: shorter news stories, a cartoon, a question-and-answer column, a few notices, including a plug for ATA debentures to finance the Association's new building programme, and an editorial, "Retention is important too."

With the new publication taking over the function of keeping teachers informed about their organization and knowledgeable about teachers' concerns in general, *The ATA Magazine* began another chapter in its long history. Its new beginning had been anticipated as early as September, 1966, when McConaghy became the chief and full-time editorial officer of the ATA. In the fall of 1967 the *Magazine* abandoned the pocket-sized format it had used for some 35 years to return to its almost-forgotten 8½″ x 11″ dimensions. The *Magazine* had varied from ten to twelve numbers per year; now it began a bimonthly, six issues a year schedule. With Volume 48 *The ATA Magazine* ceased to be a house organ and became a general educational journal.

A continuing object of concern on the part of *The ATA News* during its first two years of publication was the matter of evaluation of teacher preparation.

With the province-wide adoption of single salary schedules and remuneration based on professional preparation as much as on experience, it had become increasingly important that an acceptable frame of reference be established to determine the amount of preparation which a teacher could claim for salary purposes. This question was entirely separate from certification. A teacher's certificate is basically a licence to teach in a province or other jurisdiction, sometimes specifying grade levels or subjects for which it is valid, or attaching other conditions, for example, terminal dates. Thus originally the department of education had little concern with the amount of teacher preparation. However, with changes in school grants and payments from the province's Foundation Programme Plan Fund, provincial support of the school systems to some extent was made dependent on the level of their teachers' qualifications; therefore the department became concerned over the method used in assessing amount of teacher education.

If all teachers in Alberta had received all or even some of their professional preparation in a single provincial university, a simple statement of standing from that institution would suffice. The neutrality of the University of Alberta was beyond doubt; further, its registrar's office had personnel skilled and experienced in assessing transcripts from different institutions of higher learning, be they written in the Cyrllic alphabet or the Latin tongue or even in Chinese ideographs. As long as there was one university only in Alberta—and that a provincial institution—there could be no possibility of conflicting assessments being handed down by competing agencies. Therefore the practice grew up of appealing to the university for such evaluation, ostensibly for the purpose of seeking admission to the provincial halls of Academe. Teachers and school boards accepted the university's evaluations, occasionally with some grumbling, but generally with good grace. Soon teachers abandoned the pretence of intending to register for a university programme. Thus the university found itself in a business which really had little to do with its primary purposes. It established an evaluations committee in the registrar's office and proceded to evaluate thousands of documents for teachers' financial and not educational objectives. To assist teachers, school boards, and others in determining salaries under the collective agreements in effect throughout the province, in 1961 the ATA published an *Appendix to Salary Schedules,* approved by the teachers' and trustees' associations, the department of education, and the University of

Alberta. The *Appendix* indicated the then-current and also obsolete (although still valid) certificates or combinations of university degrees and teacher certificates which would be accepted at each level from one to six years of teacher education. It also dealt with summer school courses, special certificates, requests for reports on certification and evaluation for degree credits, and exchange of teaching certificates, that is, obsolete for current credentials. The importance of the university's rôle in evaluation of teacher preparation is indicated by the following: "The term 'approved' when it relates to university courses or university degrees means approved by the University of Alberta."[8] For a number of years the *Appendix* was a standard addendum to teacher-school board agreements.

Although the University of Alberta had been providing an evaluation service ever since World War II, by 1965 Dr. H. T. Coutts, dean of education, expressed the feeling of university officials concerned with evaluations that the university should discontinue this service. His reasons were:

> "This is not a university function"; evaluation engenders ill-will; the cost is greater than the revenue; a considerable staff has to be used and despite this there are delays; the space is needed for other purposes; with more than one independent university the University of Alberta at Edmonton should be freed from the task; a large number of those whose documents are evaluated never become students at the University of Alberta; there is a better way of arriving at salary entitlement of teachers . . .; and "We do not provide a similar service for other professions."[9]

The university president, Dr. H. T. Johns, informed the minister of education that the university proposed to discontinue the service and rather gratuitously suggested that the department of education pick up the torch as of April 1, 1966. The reluctance of the university to continue to provide the service was not a surprise; it had in fact been apparent for some time. As early as 1964, the ATA proposed to do evaluations for its own members, somewhat as the Ontario Secondary School Teachers' Federation does for its members. However, the ASTA was unwilling to accept such an arrangement, primarily through fear, apparently, that ATA evaluations would be unduly lax and generous in order to raise the salaries of the ATA's own members. With the date of the University of Alberta's withdrawal fast approaching and no generally accept-

[8]Alberta Teachers' Association, *Appendix to Salary Schedules.*

[9]Alberta Teachers' Association, *The ATA News* (Old series), I, 3 (Dec. 1965), 2.

able replacement in sight, in January 1965 the minister of education met university officials. How peremptory the minister was is unknown, but as a result of the meeting it was announced that the university would continue its evaluation service, possibly for another year.

The issue continued to simmer, not quietly, until the beginning of 1966. The university became more and more insistent that it be relieved of what had become an onerous chore; the ASTA became more and more rigid in its opposition to the ATA's assuming a rôle where, it was charged, it could set its own members' salaries; the ATA systematically went ahead with plans to perform evaluations, since no other option appeared on the horizon. The Association's position was set forth in March 1966 as follows:

> The Association is on record that the evaluation of programs and years of teacher education should be based on the principle that teachers who have taken their teacher education outside Alberta should have their qualifications evaluated on a basis no less, but no more, favorable than that which is applied to teachers who have been prepared within this province.
>
> The proposal is quite simple and straight-forward. The Association will administer evaluations within terms of reference to be established by a board on which the universities, the department, and the trustees would have representation. The difference between what is proposed and what now applies is simply that the Association instead of the university would operate an evaluations office.
>
> The Executive Council has taken the stand that it is fundamental that a professional organization assess the professional preparation of its members. It proposes that the Association will be able to attest publicly as to the professional qualifications of its members by assessing those qualifications.[10]

The ATA executive council continued with its preparations to establish an evaluations service following endorsation of its plans by the 1966 annual representative assembly. It budgeted money to establish the service, secured files, appointed personnel, created the machinery of a teachers' qualifications board and an appeal body, and invited its members to use the services.

As the ATA moved ever closer to entering the business of evaluations and the minister of education continued to sit on his hands, the ASTA grew ever more frustrated. It refused to co-operate by nominating representatives to the appeal board—the ATA plan called for two members from each of the Associations, two from the department of education, and the ATA president as a non-voting

[10] *Ibid.*, I, 8 (March 3, 1966), 3.

chairman (except for tie votes). In 1966 the ASTA published a pamphlet entitled *Crisis in Alberta Education,* in which it charged that the whole proposal was a sinister scheme through which the ATA would aggravate the existing teacher shortage to raise the salaries of ATA members at the expense of the taxpayers. It drew a red herring across the landscape by stating that the ATA was deviously attempting to gain control of teacher certification, a proposal that had never been advanced. It inferred that the ATA was trying to usurp from the department of education its legal and inherent right to evaluate teacher qualifications, not for certification but for salary determination—a function which that department had never exercised, and which could be performed by any agency provided employer and employee agreed.

In effect, the trustees' association, having failed to stop the ATA in its attempts to fill the imminent evaluations vacuum, was appealing directly to the public through its own publication, and indirectly through the news media.

Until the fall of 1966 the silence of the department of education on the issue was deafening. Yet such masterly inactivity could not continue indefinitely, as payments to school systems from the provincial foundation programme fund were determined in part by teacher evaluations. Therefore at last, in October 1966, the deputy minister suddenly announced that effective the following November—just three weeks later—the department would establish its own service, ostensibly for the purpose of administering the foundation programme fund, although he conceded, "No doubt use will be made of it in salary agreements as has been done with the university service."[11] Since fund payments are made on the basis of completed years of training, "The Department proposes to evaluate teacher qualifications in terms of total years of teacher education. It does not propose to provide evaluations on fractions of years."[12] The department had been pushed into its decision, reluctant dragon though it was, by the fact that the often-postponed withdrawal of the University of Alberta from the evaluations game had irrevocably been set for October 31, 1966.

The proposed department of education service promised to be unsatisfactory. Not only was the department inadequately staffed and equipped for the rôle it was about to attempt; it was proposing that its evaluations, made, like those of the university, for one purpose, be used for another. Furthermore, many if not

[11]*Ibid.*, II, 2 (Oct.7, 1966), 3.
[12]*Ibid.*

most of the collective agreements recognized partial years of training; therefore the department's evaluation would be of limited applicability.

By the end of October the minister of education faced the moment of truth. The University of Alberta finally withdrew from the evaluations business; the department of education was not equipped to assume the function; the ATA was already performing it. Following a meeting with the teachers' and the trustees' associations, the deputy minister announced the department of education's nominees to the ATA-proposed qualifications board. In effect, the honourable minister had capitulated. Eventually in 1967 the trustees too recognized the facts of life, as the following indicates:

> On Thursday, March 23, the smoke of battle cleared and VE—Victory for Education Day—was declared by the combatants. That evening to celebrate the end of hostilities, the executive members and professional staff of both sides met in joint-meeting and witnessed the signatures of Dr. E. W. Smith, president of the ASTA; Frank Hoskyn, president of the ATA; and Education Minister, R. H. McKinnon to a memorandum of agreement establishing a Teacher Salary Qualifications Board.
>
> The Teacher Salary Qualification Board (TSQB) should not be confused with the ATA Teacher Qualifications Service (TQS). The TQS has been operating since last August and, up to the end of March, had issued 795 statements of qualifications, 973 conversion statements, and 1,710 membership eligibility statements for teachers.
>
> The TSQB will be a neutral board consisting of ten representatives—one each from the three Alberta universities, two each from the Department of Education and the ASTA, and three from the ATA (of which one representative will be chairman).
>
> The main purpose of the TSQB will be twofold:
>
> To develop and establish principles to provide the basis for evaluation of years of education for salary purposes.
>
> To function as a board of final review and appeal in any dispute which may arise concerning a statement of qualifications issued from either the ATA-TQS or the Department of Education Foundation Program Fund Evaluations Service.
>
> The Department of Education will restrict its evaluations service to that required for administration of the Foundation Program Fund. It will not duplicate the services provided by the ATA-TQS but, rather, will accept TQS evaluations for Foundation Program Fund purposes.[13]

ATA publications have by no means been confined to newsletters, handbooks, *The ATA Magazine,* various publications of the specialist councils, and the like. Monographs poured out of Barnett House in several different series, prepared by the ATA staff members or by classroom teachers or administrators on a free-

[13] *Ibid.* (New Series), I, 2 (April 1967), 1.

lance basis. One series, generically labelled *Improvement of Instruction,* included such titles as *The Improvement of Written Language through Action Research.* Others in the same series were *Helping the Underachiever, Inservice Education for Teachers,* and *Modern Concepts in Mathematics.* A research series of monographs included such titles as *Teacher Aides, Teacher Housing, The Professional Load of Alberta Teachers, Trends in Class Size in Alberta Schools,* and others. Still another group of monographs was the *Problems in Education* series, bearing such titles as *Modern Mathematics and the High School, Accreditation, The Cameron Commission—Two years After,* and *Merit Pay in Teachers' Salary Administration.* Miscellaneous publications include *Programmed Instruction* (a monograph), *A Career in Teaching* (a leaflet for high school distribution), an ATA *Library Catalogue* and supplements, *Guidebooks* for conventions and local associations, curriculum and economic handbooks, materials for the assistance of negotiators in collective bargaining, etc.

The most ambitious ATA publishing project since the 1938 appearance of Tyler's *Choosing Your Life Work* was an Association centennial project entitled *Schools of the Foothills Province.*[14] Other special publications, with the exception of the Tyler work, had been devoted largely or wholly to teachers' concerns. This latest venture was much wider in scope, dealing with all aspects of education in Alberta from the Territorial days to Canada's centennial year.

The first section, "Historical Bench Marks," is a chronological account of the development of Alberta's educational system closely linked to the social history of the province. Subsequent parts are entitled "Pupils and Programmes," "Districts, Divisions and Dollars," and "Laymen and Schoolmen." Among the topics considered in these sections are secondary and vocational education, examinations, Indian and native education, pupils conveyance, teacherages, the separate school system, and many others.

First printing was for 4,000 copies, of which 1,000 were offered to the public. The rest the Association presented to the province's school districts and schools, to university, government, and other libraries, to its parliamentarians, ATA past presidents and other prominent Association members, senior educators throughout the province, and others.

Some 500 pages in length, illustrated by about 30 black and white illustra-

[14]Chalmers, *Schools of the Foothills Province.*

tions, the book bears the cachet of the University of Toronto Press and is dedicated to Dr. Milton Ezra LaZerte, a former president of the Association. The dust-jacket carries a coloured photograph of the Weedon School.

This educational institution was a completely undistinguished one-room rural school which once served a farming and ranching community near Cochrane. Its likeness adorns the dust-jacket not for what it is or was, but for what it represents. Built in 1910, it was typical of the school buildings of the era. As such, it was acquired by the Alberta Teachers' Association, which moved it to Heritage Park in Calgary as an educational museum, "to show modern children how different school life was in the early days of the West."[15] Nor does the structure stand in isolated splendour like the last rose of summer; the school grounds contain the original stable and other outbuildings, and even the pristine swings and pump, or reasonable facsimilies thereof. The interior also mirrors the pre-World War I era in its furniture, equipment, books, maps, and pictures, and flag.

The Weedon School project resulted from a 1962 directive of the AGM that a start be made to establish several one-room schools as educational museums. The Weedon school was open to the public in 1964, although the ceremonial opening was not held until July 1, 1965. In 1966, the executive secretary announced hopefully that the second museum would be in Edmonton, but a year later the capital city was not mentioned in this connection. Instead, other projects at Vermilion and Camrose appeared to be in the works.

But "works and bricks," to use World War II service terminology, were not the only or even the most important concerns of the ATA. One which caused considerable discussion was the junior college. In Alberta this is an institution which offers one or occasionally two years of a university-level programme with transfer privileges to the university with which it is affiliated, and possibly other, vocationally oriented courses as well. Most junior colleges have grown out of previously existing high schools, with some instructors offering subjects at the college and some at the secondary school level. Those whose work was wholly at the post-secondary level did not need to have teaching credentials; the others of course, did, and were also members of the Alberta Teachers' Association. This dichotomy naturally caused stresses in junior college intra-staff relations, nor were these wholly alleviated when the colleges became quite separate from

[15]*Ibid.*, dust-jacket.

the high schools. A 1965 amendment to the Public Junior College Act made it clear that certificated teachers employed by a college were automatically members of the ATA, just as were their colleagues who taught in the public and separate schools. Uncertificated junior college instructors, however, are not members of the Association.

By 1967 the situation was receiving the careful scrutiny of the Association. In a December 1966 meeting with the provincial cabinet, representatives of the ATA put forward three recommendations anent junior colleges. These were:

> That junior colleges in the Province of Alberta be organized as extensions of the public school system now in existence.
>
> That the Department of Education ensure that at least one year of teacher preparation, prior to first certification, be taken at a university which prepares other professionals.
>
> That all teachers in junior colleges be required to possess Alberta teaching certificates, to be active members of the Association and to contribute to the Teachers' Retirement Fund.[16]

At the 50th ARA in the spring of 1967, ATA president F. W. Hoskyn conceded that the Association was not a wholly satisfactory organization for the junior college instructors in its current form, but added, "Some consideration has been given to the formation of a junior college local with sub-locals in the various junior colleges in Alberta."[17]

At time of writing, in Alberta the whole matter of post-secondary education, including that offered by junior colleges, is receiving careful scrutiny at all levels of government, from federal to local. With the expiry of the federal-provincial agreement on vocational and technical training, the Canadian government has withdrawn from the secondary level, where since 1961 it has made available massive grants for the building and equipping of vocational facilities. Instead, it has indicated a readiness to underwrite post-secondary education and training, in many fields to the 100 per cent level—but on its own terms. The Alberta government has established a provincial board of post-secondary education under the chairmanship of G. L. Mowat, a professor of education at the University of Alberta and formerly an administrator in the provincial department of education. Local school boards and county councils are studying

[16]*The ATA Magazine,* XLVII, 5 (Jan. 1967), 65.
[17]*Ibid.,* XLVII, 8 (April 1967), 18.

their own functions in the field. The teachers' and the trustees' associations are devoting considerable time at their conventions to post-school education, including the proper rôle of the junior colleges. In the opinion of many, with the erection of new universities at Calgary and Lethbridge, making university-level education more available to a vast number of young people, the junior colleges should emphasize non-academic educational programmes rather than those leading to university degrees, as had been the case hithertofore.

The views of the Association were further spelled out by Clarke as follows: "The Alberta Teachers' Association's view is that teaching is a profession. We believe that all teachers should belong to one professional organization. We believe that the Alberta Teachers' Association is and should be the voice of the organized teaching profession in Alberta. These beliefs are long-standing."[18] The ATA also has appointed a long-range planning committee to study the whole matter of post-secondary education.

The fifth decade of the ATA's history has been marked by a burgeoning professionalism marked by activities in many areas: increased concern with teacher education, both before and after admittance to Association membership, interest in new techniques such as team teaching and the rôle of teacher aides, attention to application of technology to the teaching process, as with ETV and programmed learning, and many other areas. One of these, as has been indicated, is research. From its earliest years the Association has supported research and the publication of research findings to the limit of its modest resources. By the early 1960's the need for research was becoming so apparent in so many directions, because of Alberta's changing educational picture, that it was obviously beyond the resources of any single existing organization or combination or organizations, to meet. Consequently the ATA, the ASTA, and the Alberta Federation of Home and School Association began to press the government to enter the field of educational research, just as it had so successfully the area of physical research through the agency of the Alberta Research Council. The government at first was reluctant to do so, pointing out that it was indirectly supporting educational research through its support of the University of Alberta, and that graduate students in education were required to embark on research projects as part of their graduate programmes. The writing of a large number of masters' or doctoral dissertations, however, by no means implied that a

[18]S. C. T. Clarke, "Junior Colleges," *ibid.*, 9 (May 1967), 29.

systematic and co-ordinated attack was being mounted against the urgent and current problems of the day. By 1967 the weakness of the government's rebuttal was implicitly recognized when the provincial legislature made provision for the establishment of the Human Resources Research Council, of which education was to form a part. The ATA viewed this response to the demand for government support of educational research with some misgivings, fearing that the claims of education would be scanted. It therefore pressed for the appointment of an educationist as director of the new agency. This request was realized in the summer of 1967 with the appointment of Dr. L. W. Downey, a former professor of school administration at the University of Alberta. Chosen as chairman of the council itself was R. H. McKinnon, former minister of education, who had lost his seat in the 1967 general election. Whether such an obviously political appointment would be adequate to the needs of the position remained to be seen.

The Association begins its second half-century in a lead-from-strength position. Its finances are sound. It has the unwavering support of its members. It is an organization characterized by youth. In a way, it always has been. In "the olden days," to use a phrase from the teen-agers' lexicon, teaching simply filled the hiatus between school and marriage, or a life-time career. But by the late sixties our whole population had taken on a youthful tinge as a result of wartime and post-war baby booms; the teaching profession mirrored the ethnographical composition of Alberta society.

The province's teachers are bright, inquiring, better educated than ever before, probably healthier, and committed to the discipline to which they have devoted a large part of their as-yet short lives. Their organization is equally vibrant, dynamic, prepared to cope with the stresses that lie in the future.

That there will be problems is indisputable. Executive secretary S. C. T. Clarke has submitted his resignation, effective at the end of 1968, in the feeling that after a decade at the head of the ATA's secretariat it is time for him to be replaced for the good of the Association. The executive council, on the advice of a selection committee, had appointed to the post Clarke's compadre and its assistant general secretary and former president, F. J. C. Seymour. Then in February 1968 Seymour abruptly died, victim of a heart attack suffered while he was on an assignment for the Association. Thus the organization was faced with the consequences of a double loss: Clarke, the former professor, the philosopher, the one who never lost sight of the ultimate aims of the ATA, and Seymour, who never forgot that now—whenever now was—the Association's immediate objective was a better deal for its members, better salaries, better working conditions. Clarke the strategist, Seymour the tactician—the ATA was losing both within the same year.

Yet the Alberta Teachers' Association will go on to new achievements. Perhaps in the future it will have to depend even more on its able elected officers for the leadership it must and will have—not an inappropriate outcome for such a body as the ATA.

Interlude

Tribute to F. J. C. Seymour

In the late 1950's there was a good deal of confusion about the boundaries of required membership in the Alberta Teachers' Association. Persons in top administrative positions were concerned about conflict of loyalties to either the Department of Education or school boards and to the profession. They felt that membership in the Association had little to offer, and feared punitive action from its discipline committee if they recommended demotion or dismissal of teachers. Others did not share these doubts, or if they did, felt that loyalty to the profession and the benefit to education of professional solidarity far outweighed any difficulties in them being members.

These were the circumstances surrounding the Association's calling a meeting, at its expense, of all superintendents and assistant superintendents. The Chief Superintendent of Schools, then Dr. T. C. Byrne, was not invited until the last minute. Graciously, he consented to attend, but his appearance came as a surprise to some of the officials of the ATA. One of them was Fred Seymour. Dr. Byrne remarked that, despite his surprise, Fred introduced him with unfailing courtesy, and made him welcome.

This incident illustrates one of Fred Seymour's salient characteristics. He was a true gentleman. In eighteenth-century England he would have been taken for a "blue blood." It was part of his very being to be courteous at all times, to all people. Part of his genius, and his tremendous success in collective bargaining, was his ability to differ, to express forcefully the points of difference, yet ever to respect the other person and to act with unfailing courtesy. This did not prevent him, on occasion, doing a most effective job of "cutting someone down to size" when this action was required.

However, he did this infrequently, and with such an absence of personal rancor, and with such a focus on the issues involved, that it seldom or never created ill will.

These characteristics were well known around the province. Many school boards enjoyed bargaining with Fred. They knew that in the bargaining process they would have to concede more than they wanted to, and they seemed to relish the prospect of this happening at his hands, in his gentlemanly manner.

His courtesy and consideration were bone deep, and was also anchored in well-thought-out and firmly held convictions. For this reason his advice was widely sought and his opinions were valued. His command of language was such that he could talk for extended periods on matters of principle. On one occasion, the story goes, he talked to a conciliation board for ninety minutes. This same talent could hold large audiences of teachers spellbound. Persuasiveness was another of his characteristics.

As a working colleague he was unsurpassed. He meticulously "did the right thing" — because it was natural to him. He consulted colleagues before making decisions. Because of his unfailing courtesy, contrary views could be freely expressed to him. He would listen attentively and consider carefully all points of view. When once he had made up his mind, he was solid and unwavering in his stand as the Rock of Gibraltar. These qualities made him an excellent member of a working team.

His unfailing courtesy and consideration caused him to be universally liked. He had hosts of friends — even among the enemy! He was a true gentleman. He was firm in his convictions. As a working partner he was unsurpassed. Above all, he worked literally day and night, in devoting these extensive talents to the teaching profession. This dedication to service advanced the cause of teachers, and contributed to his early death.

S. C. T. Clarke

III

The Federation

ATA vs. CTF: A Love-Hate Syndrome

HARDLY had Canada's teachers begun to think provincially than they recognized the desirability of a national organization. The concept apparently was first mooted in a letter from the Ontario Teachers' Association (later the Ontario Educational Association) to the Provincial Association of Protestant Teachers of Lower Canada proposing such an organization for the whole Dominion. The idea was pursued for a couple of years, then reluctantly dropped as not feasible, an understandable outcome when one considers the country's tiny population spread over an immense area, and the great expense and difficulty of convening a nation-wide conference of any sort. Even today, with a population multiplied many times and tremendously improved transportation facilities, the facts of geography which must be overcome by any Canada-wide organization are still daunting.

Not until 1890, therefore, did the feasibility of establishing a country-wide teachers' organization again become a live issue. In that year the Quebec Protestant group felt it had received enough encouragement through correspondence and as a result of visits of its representatives to Ontario and the Maritimes to push for the organization of a national body. In 1891 a propitious occasion arose, a meeting in Toronto of the National Education Association of the United States, attended by a large number of Canadian teachers and other prominent educationists from all across the Dominion. The gathering unanimously passed the following resolution: "That in the opinion of the representatives from the different provinces of the Dominion present, it is advisable that an association for the teachers of the Dominion of Canada should be formed to be called The Education Association of the Dominion of Canada."[1]

The conference then chose a provincial council consisting of provincial superintendents or acting ministers of education, presidents of Canadian universities, principals of the teacher training institutions, and presidents of all provincial teachers' associations. In turn, the council chose the Honourable G. W. Ross of Ontario as president, various superintendents or acting ministers as vice-presidents, a clergyman as secretary, and a treasurer. As F. K. Stewart summarizes:

> This, then, was how the Dominion Educational Association was provisionally established in 1891. It was formed as the result of strong efforts of teachers' organizations to unite for the advancement of education. In this undertaking they obtained the support of ministers and superintendents of education, who assumed the responsibility for the organization, an arrangement that the teachers of that period both favoured and took for granted.[2]

Although no doubt they did not realize it at the time, the teachers, by acquiescing in the composition of a council and an executive whose personnel were predominantly administrators, had already lost control of the organization which they were instrumental in founding. Even at the first sessions in 1891, any reference to teachers disappeared from its name. Yet the first convention in 1892 seemed to auger well for Canadian education and Canadian teachers. A number of important resolutions were passed, or at least the problems with which they dealt were significant. One such problem was the preparation and publication of a history of Canada (to sell for not more than 50¢) which would be authorized by all or most of the seven provinces. Every provincial government contributed to a total of $2,000 for prizes. Fifteen manuscripts were entered in a competition, and by 1897 the book was published and adopted by several provinces. Unfortunately, within a few years it was regarded as out-of-date and its use discontinued.

After 1892 the Association met about every three years until 1913, irregularly thereafter until 1941, and annually since then. President for the first two conventions was the Hon. G. W. Ross, Minister of Education for Ontario.

[1] F. K. Stewart, *Interprovincial Cooperation in Education*, p. 9.
[2] *Ibid.*, p. 10.

Later, its destinies were guided by administrators, usually deputy ministers of education or equivalent, occasionally the head of a teacher training institution or some other member of the educational establishment. As Stewart indicates,[3] not once in the period covered by his study, 1892 to 1956, did a classroom teacher serve as either president or secretary of the organization now known as the Canadian Education Association. In time, it came to be irreverently called "the deputy ministers' club," for those worthy public servants eventually came to possess collective and even individual vetoes over almost any significant proposal by the Association, or at least on any controversial one. This power did not arise from their regular elevation to the presidency—that was a symptom rather than a cause of the malaise. Rather, it sprang from the fact that most of the Association's revenue came from provincial department of education grants, and the organization certainly was not going to cut off its pecuniary life-blood by antagonizing any of the provincial education ministries. Thus the association which had originated in the action of bodies wholly or largely made up of teachers rapidly became an organization for the discussion and implementation of administrative policies. Teachers have served on its board of directors, and continue to do so, but in time the teaching profession had to establish its own Canadian Teachers' Federation in order to have a national organization which would and could speak to the Canadian nation on their behalf.

The establishment of a national organization exclusively of and for teachers had its beginning at a 1919 national conference in Winnipeg, primarily not for teachers but for lay people, on "Character Education in Relation to Canadian Citizenship." The story of this conference, given at length in *The Report of the Tenth Annual Convention of the Alberta Educational Association,* is not really part of the story of the Alberta Teachers' Alliance. However, because two resolutions seem to have particular cogency in view of recent political developments in Canada, they are quoted herewith. These were:

13. That this conference recommends to the Federal Government the adoption of a distinctive Canadian flag.[4]

14. That to the end that both English and French speaking Canadians may not

[3]*Ibid.,* pp. 163-6.

[4]J. G. Taylor, "Report on National Conference on 'Character Education in Relation to Canadian Citizenship,' " in AEA *Report on the 10th Annual Convention,* p. 11.

continue to lack interpreters of the good will of each to the other, the study of both English and French should be encouraged in all Canadian Universities.[5]

This conference did not lead even indirectly to the establishment of the national organization of teachers; it simply provided the occasion for the secretaries of the four western provincial organizations to plan a future meeting. These were H. Charlesworth, of the British Columbia Teachers' Federation, "a dynamic and forceful leader,"[6] John W. Barnett for the Alberta Teachers' Alliance, J. K. Colling of the Saskatchewan Union of Teachers (soon to be renamed the Saskatchewan Teachers' Alliance), and E. K. Marshall, representing the Manitoba Teachers' Society. Charlesworth was apparently the originator of the idea. The group planned a further meeting, which was held in Calgary during the summer of 1920. Its purpose was to organize a Western Canadian federation of teachers' associations. All four provinces were again represented, with a delegate from Ontario as an observer. As a result of his presence, sights were raised and a national organization emerged, with Charlesworth as their first president and Barnett as secretary. The following year, ATA president H. C. Newland reported progress to the AEA convention:

> Let me first refer to the formation of the Canadian Teachers' Federation, which, as you will probably know, is an organization which was formed in Calgary last summer, consisting of the provincial organization, beginning with the British Columbia Federation, the Alberta Teachers' Alliance, the Saskatchewan Teachers' Alliance, the Manitoba Teachers' Federation, the Ontario Secondary Teachers' Federation, the Ontario Men Teachers' Federation, the Ontario Women Teachers' Federation, and the Quebec Federation of Teachers' Associations. I may add that the latter organization has been received into the fold since the formation of that body last summer in Calgary, and taking all these organizations at the present time I think we are safe in estimating that the total membership amounts to approximately 25,000. It may be more, but I think it is at least that number.
>
> This Federation has been formed for the purpose of guiding the teacher organization movement throughout the Dominion, and I may say that it has already begun to function. The constitution has been very clearly put before you in a number of cases, but it is interesting to note that the clear constitution came from an official organ of the Quebec teachers, in which there could be no mistaking their interest and good wishes in the work that is being done by that organization. The constitution is simply this, that every organization or teachers' alliance in Canada which

[5] *Ibid.*

[6] J. M. Paton, *The Rôle of Teachers' Organizations in Canadian Education* (Quance Lectures 1962), p. 37.

will come in may come in and contribute members to the executive. The executive at the present time consists of members representing all the alliances which are included at the annual meeting to be held next year either in Saskatoon or Toronto. It will be the privilege of each affiliated organization to send delegates. These delegates will then constitute the executive for the following year, and will initiate such legislation and measures as will be found to be in the interests of the organization. An interesting point about the constitution, and the fundamental basis of the organization was that it should begin from the ground and build upward. Each provincial organization maintains its own identity, and its own individualism, and it is only by a unanimous vote of the executive that any regulation may be passed, so the interests of the teachers in the various Provinces are protected, and in this way there is the possibility of finding common ground in which we may all work together.

The organization is functioning. Telegrams have been received not more than two weeks ago from the Secretary, Miss Arbuthnot, of Toronto, ensuring the teachers of Edmonton their "sympathy and support." Those were the words. Mr. Charlesworth, Secretary of that organization, after adjustment of the affair in New Westminster, sent a similar telegram full of encouragement, and showing clearly enough that the organization is on the job. The organization in Ontario has been active. There have been some lively affairs staged at Fort William. A similar affair, I believe, has been taking place in several parts of Ontario. There has been a dispute in Ingersoll. We have also, coming nearer home, the fact that the Saskatchewan Alliance has been working. There has been trouble in Moose Jaw, and also at Regina. Thus we find that throughout the country the various organizations are actively functioning.[7]

The optimism which Newland felt for the new organization has not always been justified, and several times it has come close to breaking up through regional differences in attitudes among the provincial components of the Federation, usually between Ontario and the West. Nevertheless, it has survived and now includes all provincial organizations and that of the North-West Territories. The only groups of significant size remaining outside the organization consist of the 1,500-odd teachers employed across Canada by Indian Affairs, and the French Catholic teachers of Quebec.

The CTF, as Newland shows, began as an aggressive labour-union type of organization primarily concerned with the economic well-being of Canadian teachers. However, in time it became something different. Paton indicates the kind of association which it developed into: "Gradually, as was inevitable, the

[7]H. C. Newland, "Report of the ATA to the AEA," in AEA *Report of the 10th Annual Convention*, pp. 20-1.

CTF came to see its proper rôle as co-ordinating information and promoting co-operation among the provincial affiliates. This rôle it has played most effectively through the years; for example, in assisting Saskatchewan teachers during the drought of the thirties, in the Winnipeg floods, in the problems of the Nova Scotia Teachers' Union in the fifties, in the growth of the Research Division, and in the sponsorship of national workshops and seminars."[8]

One seldom-noted (perhaps because so obvious) hall-mark of a profession is the establishment of a national organization to which all practitioners can belong. Creation of a viable national organization is particularly difficult when the nation is small in population, when it spans a continent, and when, as in Canada and the United States, it is governed according to the federal principle, with licensing at the state or provincial rather than at the national level, and according to varying standards across the nation. It is particularly difficult when the nation is divided by its bilingual nature into two solitudes. Nevertheless, teachers of Canada during the 1920's worked very hard, often against heavy obstacles internal and external, to build an organization comparable to the Canadian Medical Association and the Canadian Bar Association.

Through the twenties, the ATA must be counted as among the strongest supporters and severest critics of the fledgling organization. Note has already been taken of the ATA's disappointment with the CTF for its feet-dragging response to the Edmonton high school strike. The controversy over its meagre contributions to the Edmonton strike fund illustrated a basic difference between Ontario on the one hand and the West on the other respecting the function of the Federation. At least in the beginning, Western teachers seemed to regard it almost as an extension of their provincial associations, an organization which would fight for the economic welfare of individual teachers wherever they might be threatened, and in return the teachers and the provincial organizations would give it their unswerving loyalty and complete financial support. The Ontario organizations, on the other hand, appeared to regard it as a loose and voluntary organization with no authority over its affiliates. And of course Ontario was perfectly correct. They also seemed to feel that the Federation should confine itself to such innocuous activities as exchange of information and the betterment of education in general rather than the amelioration of the teachers' condition in particular. From this position it was but a short step to the attitude that the

[8]Paton, *Teachers' Organizations*, p. 42.

fees which they paid to the Federation were not really dues but donations. Therefore, regardless of the CTF's reaction, they could be varied in size at the will of the affiliate, depending on the availability of funds at the moment and the degree of approbation with which the affiliate regarded the general or specific purposes for which the money was being expended.

The Western organizations regarded the Ontario attitude as condescending, arrogant, and infuriating, especially when they paid in full the CTF assessment on the basis of their membership while the Ontario group did not. Instead, they used their financial power as a club to beat the other associations into line, the only weapon they could use since the CTF constitution did not give them the number of voting members on the directorship which their large number of teacher members would seem to entitle them to. In 1923, sources of CTF revenue were:

British Columbia		$ 664.90
Alberta		860.00
Saskatchewan		350.50
Manitoba		787.00
Ontario		
Secondary School Teachers' Federation	$ 598	
Federation of Women Teachers' Association	1,000	
Public School Men Teachers' Federations	62	
		1,660.00
		$4,302.40

Despite earlier optimistic prognosis, the Federation had not been able to establish a beachhead in *la belle province* or the Maritimes.

Probably the Western affiliates tolerated the Ontario behaviour for two reasons. In the first place, the prospect of losing about 40 per cent of the CTF's revenue must have been daunting, even though the eastern province's $1,660 was somewhat less than its fair share, less in proportion to what the West was contributing. Secondly, the Western organizations were genuinely anxious to extend the domain of the Federation to embrace all teachers from sea to sea. But if the West was the importunate suitor, the East was the reluctant object of its attentions. At the 1923 annual meeting, held in Montreal, all member organizations were represented, with observers from Quebec, which despite earlier expressions of intent had not joined, and from Prince Edward Island and Nova Scotia. Apparently in 1924 the Federation's beachhead was pushed as far east as Quebec, although only to the extent of capturing the comparatively small Provincial Association of Protestant Teachers. The Roman Catholic teachers, lay and clerical, English and French-speaking, who constituted the great majority of Quebec teachers, still remained uninterested. By April, 1925, the Nova Scotia Teachers' Union had evidently expressed its intention of joining the national organization; in October of the same year it was still going to do so. Another convert was the small Saskatchewan Secondary Teachers' Association, destined to become a part of the Saskatchewan Teachers' Federation which was established on January 1, 1934, to include all previously existing teachers' organizations in the province.

If the CTF as a body was not promoting or even condoning teachers' strikes among its affiliates, it was active in other areas, at least for some of the time, under the leadership of Alberta's H. C. Newland, who assumed the presidency in 1923. The following year the Federation issued its first news bulletin, which dealt with excursions for teachers, the Imperial Conference of Teacher Associations, special trains to the CTF annual meeting in Victoria, affiliates' publications, annual meetings of those affiliates, and their officers.

Despite such evidence of vitality, the September 1924 issue of *The ATA Magazine* found weaknesses in the Federation; that it was run by correspondence rather than by face-to-face discussions, that there was a frequent change of officers, that differing fiscal years of the affiliated organizations led to confusion with respect to fees, that to obtain comparable educational statistics from province to province was very difficult. It is not easy to understand how this last could be considered a weakness of the Federation, although it was most surely a problem. However, it was to cope with just such problems that the CTF had been organized.

On the other side of the ledger, the Federation claimed a modicum of credit for the fact that there was no serious problem in any of the provinces, whatever that statement implies. Perhaps a serious problem was one involving the threat of or overt strike action. A serious dispute in Brandon had been settled. The Federation had been successful in arranging special CNR or CPR trains to its Vancouver conference, 40 travelling by the former and 170 by the latter carrier. Evidently in those days when the Canadian Teachers' Federation held a conference, any teacher could get into the act. Finally, most of the affiliates showed increases in their memberships. The ATA's roster indicated 2,196, up 166 from the previous year despite a decline in student members at the normal schools.

Such was the information published for the teachers. The following year, however, in August the executive council devoted considerable time to a discussion which originated in the cost of affiliation to the CTF, some members regarding it as excessive in view of the benefits derived. In the end, it was decided to continue the relationship for the time being since the CTF was still a young and developing organization and presumably had not had time fully to show its potentialities. Accordingly, the council voted to oppose a Saskatchewan motion which would have split the Federation in two, presumably at Manitoba's eastern boundary. Such action would have created a western organization such as the 1920 gathering in Calgary had been convened to establish. Other issues on which the ATA differed from its sister organizations arose in 1926, when the Alberta group expressed opposition to the establishment of permanent headquarters for the CTF and to the publication of a "Dominion Magazine." Perhaps nervousness at the instability of financial support from Ontario inspired the caution on the part of the denizens of next year's country.

The following year, 1927, was of special significance to the CTF, which played host to the World Federation of Educational Associations on the occasion of its second triennial meeting, held in Montreal. Delegates attended from continental United States, Hawaii, Japan, China, Ireland, Scotland, England and Wales, as well as from the host country. The Alliance and the Alberta Education arranged jointly to send three representatives. At the CTF meeting, topics under study included: advance of teacher training, board of conciliation and arbitration, improvement of educational journals, interprovincial exchange of teachers, collection of statistics on educational costs, relationship of universities and high schools, and many others. The Nova Scotia Teachers' Union was still on the verge of joining the Federation.

Two years later the teachers from Prince Edward Island sought support from the CTF in their controversy—successfully concluded—to obtain high salaries from the provincial government. With heavy-handed irony the editor of *The ATA Magazine* commented as follows:

> While congratulating the Prince Edward Island teachers we must congratulate the Canadian Teachers' Federation also, for it would be unreasonable to suppose

that the telegrams sent to the Provincial Government of Prince Edward Island and to Prince Edward Island Teachers' Federation from the different affiliated provincial organizations . . . had no effect upon the Prince Edward Island Government.[9]

Perhaps the 1929 CTF meeting was memorable for two things: attendance by teachers from beyond the Canadian boundaries, specifically, Newfoundland, and from the English-speaking Roman Catholic teachers of Quebec.

The 1930 CTF conference returned to Calgary, the Federation's birthplace, and it is therefore appropriate that on that tenth anniversary its first secretary, J. W. Barnett, assumed the presidency. The teachers' growing economic distress resulted in special attention being paid to measures which would alleviate the stringency of the times, such as raising the standards for normal school entrance, and seeking federal government help from its unemployment relief fund for teachers out of work. Such was the tenor of CTF business during the early thirties, until in 1933 the annual meeting of the Federation was cancelled, to the indignation of the ATA. Its executive council moved: "That we ask the officers of the CTF to justify the decision not to hold a conference, and that the attitude of each province be made known to all, this to be a condition precedent upon payment of capitation fees."[10]

By 1934, however, the CTF was again able to devote some attention to other than economic issues affecting teachers. It decided: (1) to set up an educational research and statistics bureau; (2) to sponsor a dominion-wide education week; (3) to initiate a publicity campaign to disseminate information about its aims and activities.[11] Results of these decisions were soon apparent, in a page in *The ATA Magazine* contributed by the CTF director E. K. Marshall dealing with national and international news and sponsorship of Alberta School Week, formerly under the wing of the ATA. Both of these developments occurred in 1935. In that year the CTF had not yet established itself as a national force in education; that day was many long years away. But it had survived the Depression, still at a stage of unparalleled severity, and its future, though clouded, was assured.

During the decade or so following the election of the Social Credit government and the 1936 amendments to the Teaching Profession Act, the ATA

[9] *The ATA Magazine*, IX, 9 (May 1929), 19.
[10] ATA Ex., July 3, 1933.
[11] *The ATA Magazine*, XV, 3 (Nov. 1934), 22-3.

faithfully continued its not uncritical support of the Canadian Teachers Federation. Alberta's representative brought back word that the 1935 conference had been attended by representatives from all nine provinces and from twelve teachers' organizations, that the CTF's bureau of research, established the previous year, was co-operating with the Dominion Bureau of Statistics, that the national body was concerned with the over-supply of teachers, the large unit of school administration, and the need for federal aid to education. Dissatisfaction with the Federation is apparent in ATA president E. C. Ansley's report to the 1937 AGM, which reads in part as follows:

> It was our opinion that Alberta and other provinces could have made contributions to a study of the problems confronting certain provincial organizations which would have been of value to teachers of these provinces, but problems of this nature were summarily disposed of, in favour of numerous voluminous and exhaustive reports on phases of education, which, if not entirely removed, were at least some years distant from our professional interests.[12]

At the 1937 CTF conference, the large unit of school administration was naturally a matter of increased interest, for Alberta had just established the first eleven school divisions. Other topics which received attention were the financing and administration of education in English-speaking countries, educational opportunity in Canada, and school statistics. The Federation was also pressing for the establishment of a dominion—how quaint that adjective now sounds—research council for the social studies. At the following year's conference, Alberta's M. E. LaZerte was chosen as president.

By 1940, the CTF's membership totalled 36,678, including honorary, associate, and student members. Some 49 per cent of the paid membership was in the three westernmost provinces. Saskatchewan and Alberta, with automatic membership in their provincial organizations, counted 100 per cent of the teachers in the Federation. For some other provinces the corresponding ratios were: British Columbia, 77 per cent; Quebec Protestant, 74 per cent; Prince Edward Island, 75 per cent. And it was reported that some teachers were still out of work in Ontario, Nova Scotia, and Saskatchewan, despite the impact of World War II.

The influence of that struggle appeared in the 1941 business of the CTF, when it suggested to the minister of national defence that male teachers be

[12]E. C. Ansley, "Annual Report of the President," *The ATA Magazine*, XVII, 8 (April 1937), 3.

considered indispensable, and therefore exempt from selective service (that is, conscription or part-time military training.) The result was resoundingly in the negative. Teaching might be an essential industry, enough so to justify freezing teachers to the classroom, but it wasn't all that essential.

The ATA's almost chronic dissatisfaction with the CTF was evident in the 1941 deliberations of the Association's executive council. There was a feeling that perhaps the ATA should withdraw from the national body, but instead it sent its usual delegation to the annual conference with instructions on such things as regional conferences (suggest them), entertainment (cut it down), federal aid (press for it), and teachers' salaries (a more aggressive approach is needed). In September the CTF president reported that a campaign to raise $50,000 as a war contribution had fallen short of its goal, but enough had been raised to purchase a mobile canteen for Canada's soldiers.

In 1943 the burning question was whether the CTF should appoint a full-time secretary. The ATA was suspicious of the proposal, fearing that such an appointment would reflect eastern viewpoints, but the West would have to pay most of the cost. The feeling was that if a national office was established, it should be in the west, but the matter was finally tabled.

In 1945 the CTF used powers of persuasion to intervene in a dispute in one eastern city. ATA president H. C. Melsness reported the case to the members as follows:

> This year the influence of the Federation was used to help effect a settlement of the teacher crisis in Montreal. The case of the 1,400 teachers there who had been dismissed *en masse* by the Central School Board was still unsettled when we met at Vancouver. Strongly worded resolutions were sent to the Chairman of the Board in Montreal, which were followed by the eventual withdrawal of notices of dismissal, and a settlement was made that was satisfactory to the teachers.[13]

Nevertheless, the executive council felt that there was considerable unrest over the fees being paid to the national body, and it was decided to publish a statement in *The ATA Magazine* as to the work of the CTF. This action was not enough to silence the criticism, for the matter was repeatedly discussed by the executive council. This entry appears in the minutes for a March meeting: "The Executive felt that there was no reason why Alberta should continue to support the CTF to the fullest extent unless and until the other provinces showed an

[13]H. C. Melsness in *The ATA Magazine,* XXVI, 1 (Sept.-Oct. 1945), 11.

inclination to do likewise, and paid their share. They agreed that for the present no further payments of fees should be made to the CTF."[14]

Shortly thereafter, the problem again received an airing:

> Mr. Seymour expressed the opinion that the ATA representatives to the CTF Convention should bring up the question of capitation fees for 1946-47, pointing out that the ATA had always borne its share of the costs of the CTF (except for one year), but it appeared that two of the Provinces were delinquent in paying their share. He felt that some proper basis for allocation of fees should be set up until all Provinces had paid their full assessment.[15]

The council directed the representatives to raise the question.

In September 1946 the executive council learned that a proposal for a Dominion teachers' magazine and a national office had both been rejected because of lack of funds. Its members probably took a certain amount of smug satisfaction on being informed that a CTF-approved national policy on education was behind what had already been achieved in Alberta. Other information forthcoming from the Federation was that it was pressing for teacher representation on the Canadian delegation to UNESCO, and that affiliation with the Canadian and Newfoundland Education Association was being examined to discover what such affiliation implied. (This matter had been under examination since the previous year.) Evidently the teachers were rather chary about a body which they regarded, quite correctly, as representing the educational establishment. Apparently, however, their fears were allayed, for in December it was announced that Dr. Willoughby had been appointed to represent the CTF on the CNEA directorate.

Thus the Federation survived its first quarter-century, and the ATA, one of its founders, was still a member. But all tensions between the two bodies had not yet been allayed.

The post-war period was one of change for the Canadian Teachers' Federation. As early as 1947 it had taken the decision, previously opposed by the ATA, to establish a national office, and was advertising for a secretary-treasurer. For the services of the right man the Federation was willing to pay up to $5,000 per year. At this time the idea of a national magazine was renewed, but the ATA's

[14]ATA Ex., March 16-17, 1946
[15]*Ibid.*, June 29, July 4, 1946.

position, that it was premature, received sufficient endorsation to defer the project.

The establishment of a national office seemed to infer that the CTF should have its own building. Each provincial affiliate was requested to pay $1 per teacher to a building fund. The ATA took the position that Alberta would pay its share, probably over a five-year period but faster if necessary. On January 17, 1948, the Federation opened its national office, but not in the west as the ATA had once advocated, but in the more logical location of the national capital. First permanent secretary was George Croskery. The Federation's aspirations, as usual, were out-running its income, and for a while its activities were hampered by lack of funds or were financed by special appeals.

One such was a Parcels for Britain fund, whereby Canadian teachers were asked to send food parcels to their still heavily rationed British colleagues. Locals and individual Alberta teachers contributed generously to this appeal. Another humanitarian appeal to which the ATA responded occurred as a result of the disastrous 1950 Red and Assiniboine River floods. The Association withdrew $2,000 and remitted it to the CTF to be forwarded to the Manitoba Teachers' Society for flood relief purposes. The circuitous route which the contribution followed indicates that the ATA was meticulously observing protocol and carefully avoiding any appearance of by-passing the national body. The same routine was followed two years later, when the Association approved a donation of $2,000 to the Nova Scotia Teachers' Association for the relief of striking teachers, and appealed to Locals and individual teachers to make their own contributions as well. In February 1952 the executive council took steps to set up a "Strike Fund of the ATA"[16] and finance it.

As previously noted, early in the CTF's history the ATA had seriously considered supporting a Saskatchewan proposal to withdraw from the national body and establish a western federation. With its proclivity for having jam on both sides of its bread the Alberta organization eventually enjoyed—or perhaps experienced—the advantages of both a regional and a national body. The first western conference of teacher organizations met in Edmonton early in 1948 under the aegis of the CTF, which away back in 1920 had also held its first meeting in the foothills province. All four western provinces were represented by presidents and general secretaries, a total of seven delegates being in at-

[16]*Ibid.*, Feb. 25, 26, 1952.

tendance. The agenda included the expected topics—salaries, pensions, tenure, teacher training, and the like. The second conference made some comparisons among the provinces and concluded that the best salaries were being paid in British Columbia. Alberta had the best pension scheme; British Columbia and Alberta jointly claimed the laurel for the most satisfactory teacher tenure. Alberta was admitted to have the best teacher training system, but was the only one where a teacher could be transferred at the whim of a school board. In general, there were too many varieties of teachers' certificates, Saskatchewan alone having almost twenty. The conference also adopted a model salary schedule with an initial salary of $1,600 ranging up to $2,800 for a teacher with but a single year of preparation to $2,800 to $4,800 for one with five years of preparation.

The third conference raised all figures by $200 and also provided for positional (that is, grade level) schedules, although it noted a trend to single schedules. The report to Alberta teachers noted, "Not one association in the western provinces is in favour of a provincial salary schedule—there is too much provincial control now."[17] Although all four provincial societies were able to report that they had the right to collective bargaining, none claimed to have a satisfactory degree of tenure security, and two of the four had none at all.

The third conference also studied interprofessional relationships. "All four provinces reported that there is something fundamentally wrong in the relationships between superintendents and principals and teachers. Something must be done to bring teachers, principals, and superintendents into partnership."[18] Was it perhaps this conclusion which some years later led to an amendment of the Alberta Teaching Profession Act that opened the doors of ATA membership to school superintendents?

By 1950 the western conference was firmly established as part of the educational picture. The precedent which it set was then followed by the establishment of an eastern conference. Writing some years later, Kratzmann thus assessed the conference:

> An analysis of reports of the fifteen conferences during the 1948-1962 period shows that special attention has been given to salaries, teacher shortages, tenure, pensions, teacher training and certification, publicity, taxation and school grants,

[17] *The ATA Magazine*, XXX, 5 (Jan. 1950), 27.
[18] *Ibid.*

contracts and collective bargaining . . . ATA officers have considered these regional experiences to be of more direct value to the Association than the contacts and experiences made through the parent organization.[19]

Thus the western conference supplemented but did not replace the meetings and activities of the national body, which in 1950 chose as its president E. T. Wiggins, past president of the ATA.

In 1955 the ATA was granted the right to send four delegates to the CTF, rather than three, as previously. As usual, the Federation's actions continued to annoy the ATA, but not to the extent of its raising the threat of withdrawal from the organization. At the 1955 meeting, for example, the CTF approved an increase in the annuul fee from 80¢ to $1 per teacher per year, but took no steps to match expenditure to income; in other words, to adopt a balanced budget. For that year a deficit of $4,000 was anticipated. In the opinion of the ATA's representative, there was "much talk about several school problems; no suggestion of action."[20] Yet this verdict was perhaps too harsh; business completed during the session included the following: an ATA resolution that any affiliate in arrears on dues be suspended was adopted; a decision that policy resolutions should be tabled for a period of a year on the request of any affiliate; further consideration of the establishment of a Canadian College of Teachers; striking of a committee to consider the matter of a CTF magazine—a hoary chestnut still not sufficiently browned to snake out of the fire.

At the 1955 meeting it was announced that Ontario had at last decided to assume the responsibilities of full membership and allow its representatives to hold office in the CTF. A reasonable enough decision; after all, 35 years had passed since the Ontario representative had met with those of the four western representatives in Calgary to found the Federation.

Another CTF action which annoyed the Alberta Teachers' Association was the appointment of a general secretary without advertising the position.

Once more in 1959 the CTF annual conference was the scene of a confrontation between Ontario and the other provinces, particularly those of the west. Once more the basic issue seemed to be that the Ontario Teachers' Federation, consisting of five components, found its voting strength in the CTF far out of

[19]A. Kratzmann, "*The Alberta Teachers' Association: A Documentary Analysis of the Dynamics of a Professional Association*," unpublished doctoral dissertation, University of Chicago (1963), p. 154.

[20]*The ATA Magazine*, XXXVI, 2 (Oct. 1955), 47.

proportion to the number of teachers it represented, and to the levy, based on teacher membership, which it was expected to contribute to the national coffers. Once again those down-easterners attempted to gain by financial pressure the objectives which they were not able to achieve by exercise of their constitutional powers. The OTF presented three resolutions at the 1959 meeting, each of which would in effect have given any province a veto over the actions of the CTF. Each in turn was defeated. The Ontario federation reacted by refusing to pay more than $1 of the $1.25 per capita fee to the national body—"it was not the money, but lack of control over CTF affairs and lack of clarity of CTF functions, which prompted their actions."[21] The reaction of the ATA to such bullying was as might be expected—Ontario's membership in the CTF should be allowed to lapse if a commitment was not received by January 1, 1960, to pay its requisition in full. Apparently, as usual, the conflict was resolved, for Ontario did not withdraw, nor did it suffer the indignity of being expelled from the organization. Despite the tensions of the 1959 meeting in Halifax, the CTF did manage to reach a consensus on a number of matters. These included: approval of a Canadian Council on Educational Research; approval of a revamped policy on education, one that called for additional support at local, provincial and national levels; authorization for continued study of educational television; approval of support for the forthcoming 1962 Canadian Conference on Education.

The following year, ATA president A. D. G. Yates reported to its membership that this resolution had been commended to the CTF for consideration: "Whereas the prime objective of a federation is to provide services that strengthen and improve the administration of its constituent bodies, Be it resolved that the CTF embark on a programme of institutes and conferences dealing with, (*a*) teacher economics, (*b*) curricula, (*c*) magazines and publications, (*d*) association administration, (*e*) tenure, (*f*) pensions, (*g*) public relations, and (*h*) pensions."[22]

Yates went on to assess the effectiveness of the national body, something his predecessors had been doing periodically ever since the CTF was founded in 1920. In his opinion, ". . . the CTF has yet to move boldly into the area of promoting full cooperation and coordination among its constituent member

[21]*Ibid.*, XL, 2 (Oct. 1959), 55.
[22]*Ibid.*, XLI, 2 (Oct. 1960), 25-6.

associations. However ponderously, however reluctantly, the CTF is beginning to see a second aspect of its functions as a national organization."[23]

Perhaps as a result of the resolution quoted above, by February 1961 *The ATA Magazine* was able to announce that the Federation had sponsored a meeting at Toronto of executive secretaries of provincial teachers' associations, attended by people from Vancouver to St. John's.

In 1963 the CTF elected as its president another Albertan, ATA past president Inez Castleton. It also appointed another staff officer to fill the position of assistant secretary-treasurer. In February 1964 *The ATA Magazine* reported on the latest conference of secretaries of its affiliates, by now a continuing activity. It summarized six criticisms of teacher organizations presented to the gathering by J. M. Paton, former secretary of the Protestant Teacher of the Province of Quebec. These were:

1. They lack an educational philosophy which would enable them to act in the power structure of education and promote new developments.

2. The general public is unaware of the educational work and concerns of teacher organizations.

3. Teacher organizations have been unwilling to accept responsibility in teacher education and certification.

4. Teacher organizations demand more power instead of accepting more responsibility. The two are inseparable.

5. Teacher organizations lack over-all policy with respect to drop-outs, evening classes, etc.

6. "Teacher organizations have failed to present themselves to the public as experts who can speak on educational matters based on this expertise."[24]

The 1965 meeting, in Newfoundland, welcomed representatives of all provincial teachers' organizations in Canada except the Corps des instituteurs et institurices catholiques du Québec (later called the Corporation des enseignants du Québec), which sent observers. Work of the conference included revision of terms for the Federation's research division, and approval of a director of research and an advisory committee on research. An Alberta proposition for an international aid fund for teachers was accepted with contributions to be at the

[24]*The ATA Magazine*, XLIV, 6 (Feb. 1964), 34-6.
[23]*Ibid.*

discretion of the affiliates concerned. Fees had reached the figure of $1.75 per capita. In 1966 the Federation returned to Edmonton for a serious conference high-lighted by typical western hospitality and hoop-la—white cowboy hats from Calgary, Klondike Kate from Edmonton's very own Klondike, a western-style barbecue at Elk Island Park. The CTF approved the establishment of Canadian associations of teachers of science and of mathematics in 1966 and 1967, but for financial reasons turned down a proposal for a similar body for teachers of English. This turn-down could not be considered final, as the ATA was prepared to raise the matter again in 1968.

The CTF once again recommended establishment of a federal bureau of education, an idea which has been urged by many national bodies and is older than the twentieth century. An inherently more satisfying activity is the Federation's international project which the 1966 conference voted to continue. Dubbed Project Africa '66, this activity saw its 28 members assembled at CTF House in Ottawa during July for a three-day orientation session preparatory to departure for the Dark Continent. The purposes of the Project have been itemized as: "to help African teachers upgrade their certificates; to help African teachers strengthen their professional organizations; and to promote understanding and goodwill between African and Canadian teachers."[25]

The Federation also adopted as its centennial project the hosting of the World Confederation of Organizations of the Teaching Profession in Vancouver. The CTF, after almost a half-century of existence, formally recognized the dual-language nature of Canada by deciding to expand the Federation into a bilingual and bicultural organization within the limits of its constitution. This decision was probably inspired by a realization that the CTF membership of almost 170,000 included teachers from every provincial organization except that of the 55,000 French-speaking Roman Catholic teachers of Quebec. The roster even included 318 teachers from the North-West Territories. Outside the French-speaking organization, the only sizeable body of teachers remaining without the Federation consisted of Indian Affairs' cadre of some 1,500 members.

CTF Barkis is willin'. It remains to be seen whether the Corporation des enseignants du Québec is willing to play the part of Pegotty.

[25]R. McIntosh in *The ATA Magazine,* XLVII, 3 (Nov. 1966), 23.

Postlude

John Walker Barnett, LL.D.

The citation in conferring posthumously the Honorary Degree of Doctor of Laws on the late Mr. John W. Barnett was given by the Chancellor of the University of Alberta, Dr. G. Fred McNally, at the Fall Convocation, October 18, 1947, in Convocation Hall.

"The Senate of this University, at its February meeting, granted the Degree of Doctor of Laws, *honoris causa*, to John Walker Barnett, for many years General Secretary of The Alberta Teachers' Association. I had the privilege and honour of informing Mr. Barnett's action and of formally inviting him to accept the degree. On two other occasions only did I see him so deeply moved. In a voice filled with emotion, he said he would be happy to accept the honour, realizing that in honouring him the University wished to pay a tribute to the great profession to which he had given his life.

"In the meantime his work has been completed and he has gone from us.

"John Walker Barnett was born in Grantham, Lincolnshire, sixty-seven years ago. He came of vigorous north country stock and of a family of teachers. Not so long ago his oldest brother retired after a distinguished career as a headmaster. After training at Westminster College, he was certified and entered upon his teaching career. He taught for some time in the Army College at Aldershot and at Surbiton before coming to Canada. In 1911 he came to Alberta and at once began work as a teacher. He brought with him first-hand knowledge of the work of the National Union of Teachers and soon reached the conclusion that teachers in this country were handicapped by the lack of a similar organization. When the Alberta Teachers' Alliance came into being, it was natural that Mr. Barnett's knowledge, experience, enthusiasm and faith should be enlisted in the direction of the infant organization. From that time, the history of the Association was largely a history of the activities of John W. Barnett. In journeyings, often in peril of floods, in perils of the wilderness. in perils of dirt roads or no roads, he carried on. Though progress was slow, indifference great, and opposition powerful, no one ever heard John Barnett complain or say a disloyal word to those he had set out to serve.

"He was largely instrumental in the formation of the Canadian Teachers' Federation, the national organization. He persuaded Legislatures to make important changes in The School Act, and played an important part in drafting such legislation as The Teachers' Retirement Fund Act and The Teaching Profession Act. He served on the Department's Liaison Committee on Teacher Training, which later evolved the plan of Teacher Education now in effect in this Province. As a member of the Survey Committee which was responsible for our present University Act, and later as a member of the Senate of this University, he played his full part.

"So then, as an able teacher, as a man of great courage and singleness of purpose, as a fearless fighter, as a champion of the weak and defenceless, as a matchless leader and as a gallant and upright gentleman, we honour his memory and confer on him posthumously the honorary degree of Doctor of Laws."

Appendices

Appendix I

OFFICERS OF THE ALBERTA TEACHERS' ALLIANCE AND THE ALBERTA TEACHERS' ASSOCIATION

1917-18
(Provisional)

President	*Dr. G. D. Misener*
Vice-President	*C. E. Leppard*
General Secretary-Treasurer	*J. W. Barnett*

1918-19

President	*Dr. G. D. Misener*
Vice-President	*Mr. Long*
General Secretary-Treasurer	*J. W. Barnett*
Member	*T. E. A. Stanley*

1919-20

President	*T. E. A. Stanley*
Past President	*Dr. G. D. Misener*
Vice-President	*John Scoffield* resigned, term completed by *H. C. Newland*
Members and the following co-opted advisors:	*Miss Kate Chegwin* *C. E. Peasley* *H. B. Dobson* *J. M. Roxburgh*
General Secretary-Treasurer	*J. W. Barnett*

1920-21

President	*H. C. Newland*
Past President	*T. E. A. Stanley*
Vice-President	*Charles E. Peasley*
General Secretary-Treasurer	*John W. Barnett*
Edmonton	*Miss Kate Chegwin*
Calgary	*W. W. Scott*
Southeastern Alberta	*Claude Robinson*
Southwestern Alberta	*W. Crawford*
Northern Alberta	*W. S. Brodie*

1921-22

President	*H. C. Newland*
Past President	*T. E. A. Stanley*
Vice-President	*Charles E. Peasley*
General Secretary-Treasurer	*John W. Barnett*
Edmonton	*Miss Kate Chegwin*
Calgary	*W. W. Scott*
Southeastern Alberta	*J. T. Cuyler*
Southwestern Alberta	*S. R. Tompkins*
Northern Alberta	*Miss Ada I. Wright*

1922-23

President	*Charles E. Peasley*
Past President	*H. C. Newland*
Vice-President	*J. E. Somerville*
General Secretary-Treasurer	*John W. Barnett*
Edmonton	*Miss Kate Chegwin*
Calgary	*Miss M. B. Tier*
Southeastern Alberta	*D. M. Sullivan*
Southwestern Alberta	*W. S. Brodie*
Northern Alberta	*Miss Ada I. Wright*

1923-24

President	*J. E. Somerville*
Past President	*Charles E. Peasley*
Vice-President	*F. D. B. Johnson*
General Secretary-Treasurer	*John W. Barnett*
Edmonton	*H. C. Newland*
Calgary	*Miss M. B. Tier*
Southeastern Alberta	*Miss Marie J. Goudie*
Southwestern Alberta	*Mr. Goldon L. Woolf*
Northern Alberta	*Miss Ada I. Wright*

1924-25

President	*W. W. Scott*
Past President	*J. E. Somerville*
Vice-President	*S. R. Tompkins*
General Secretary-Treasurer	*John W. Barnett*
Edmonton	*H. Leonard Humphreys*
Calgary	*Fred Parker*
Southeastern Alberta	*C. Riley*
Southwestern Alberta	*John Stevenson*
Northern Alberta	*James McCrea*

1925-26

President	*Fred Parker*
Past President	*W. W. Scott*
Vice-President	*C. Riley*
General Secretary-Treasurer	*John W. Barnett*
Edmonton	*A. Waite*
Calgary	*Dr. H. E. Smith*
Southeastern Alberta	*Charles E. Peasley*
Southwestern Alberta	*K. P. Stewart*
Northern Alberta	*James McCrea*

1926-27

President	*A. Waite*
Past President	*Fred Parker*
Vice-President	*H. D. Ainlay*
General Secretary-Treasurer	*John W. Barnett*
Edmonton	*Dr. C. B. Willis*
Calgary	*Miss Annie Campbell*
Southeastern Alberta	*C. E. Peasley*
Southwestern Alberta	*H. C. Sweet*
Northern Alberta	*A. J. Powell*

1927-28

President	*H. C. Sweet*
Past President	*A. Waite*
Vice-President	*R. D. Webb*
General Secretary-Treasurer	*John W. Barnett*
Edmonton	*Dr. C. B. Willis*
Calgary	*F. Speakman*
Southeastern Alberta	*Miss Mary Fowler*
Southwestern Alberta	*R. E. Hicken*
Northern Alberta	*James McCrea*
Central Alberta	*F. L. Tilson* retired in Dec., term completed by *Dr. C. Sansom*

1928-29

President	*H. D. Ainlay*
Past President	*H. C. Sweet*
Vice-President	*Dr. C. Sansom*
General Secretary-Treasurer	*John W. Barnett*
Edmonton	*C. G. Elliott*
Calgary	*E. B. Asselstine*

Southeastern Alberta	*Mrs. A. M. White*
Southwestern Alberta	*George Watson*
Northern Alberta	*J. Steele Smith* until Sept., term completed by *A. J. H. Powell*
Central Alberta	*J. E. Simpson*

1929-30

President	*A. J. H. Powell*
Past President	*H. D. Ainlay*
Vice-President	*C. G. Elliott*
General Secretary-Treasurer	*John W. Barnett*
Edmonton	*C. O. Hicks*
Calgary	*Miss J. McColl*
Southeastern Alberta	*Mrs. J. M. Jakey*
Southwestern Alberta	*W. L. Irvine*
Northern Alberta	*Leslie Robbins*
Central Alberta	*Miss E. Catherine Barclay*

1930-31

President	*R. D. Webb*
Past President	*A. J. H. Powell*
Vice-President	*C. O. Hicks*
General Secretary-Treasurer	*John W. Barnett*
Edmonton	*George Clayton*
Calgary	*M. W. Brock*
Southeastern Alberta	*A. J. Heywood*
Southwestern Alberta	*Miss Olive V. Haw*
Northern Alberta	*M. D. Meade*
Central Alberta	*J. F. Swan*

1931-32

President	*C. O. Hicks*
Past President	*R. D. Webb*
Vice-President	*D. L. Shortliffe*
General Secretary-Treasurer	*John W. Barnett*
Edmonton	*George Clayton*
Calgary	*H. G. Beacom*
Southeastern Alberta	*A. J. Heywood*
Southwestern Alberta	*George Watson*
Northern Alberta	*A. H. Clegg*
Central Alberta	*J. E. Appleby*

1932-33

President	*M. W. Brock*
Past President	*C. O. Hicks*
Vice-President	*D. L. Shortliffe*
General Secretary-Treasurer	*John W. Barnett*
Edmonton	*G. A. Clayton*
Calgary	*Miss Grace H. Robinson*
Southeastern Alberta	*Miss S. M. Gordon*
Southwestern Alberta	*H. H. Bruce*
Northern Alberta	*H. A. Kostash*
Central Alberta	*J. E. Appleby*

1933-34

President	*George A. Clayton*
Past President	*M. W. Brock*
Vice-President	*E. J. Thorlakson*
General Secretary-Treasurer	*John W. Barnett*
Edmonton	*G. G. Harman*
Calgary	*H. E. Panabaker*
Southeastern Alberta	*Miss S. M. Gordon*
Southwestern Alberta	*Miss Effie R. Reid*
Northern Alberta	*H. A. Kostash*
Central Alberta	*W. K. Gish*

1934-35

President	*E. J. Thorlakson*
Past President	*George A. Clayton*
Vice-President	*Dr. Alex B. Currie*
General Secretary-Treasurer	*John W. Barnett*
Edmonton	*G. G. Harman*
Calgary	*H. G. Beacom*
Southeastern Alberta	*E. C. Ansley*
Southwestern Alberta	*Miss Edna J. Scott*
Northern Alberta	*William Tomyn*
Central Alberta	*W. K. Gish*

1935-36

President	*G. G. Harman*
Past President	*E. J. Thorlakson*
Vice-President	*H. A. Kostash* became Inspector in Sept., term completed by *E. C. Ansley*
General Secretary-Treasurer	*John W. Barnett*

Edmonton	*H. C. Clark*
Calgary	*H. T. Robertson*
Southeastern Alberta	*E. C. Ansley* became Vice-Pres., term completed by *H. W. Bryant*
Southwestern Alberta	*M. G. Merkley*
Northern Alberta	*William Hayhurst*
Central Alberta	*Raymond Shaul*

1936-37

President	*E. C. Ansley*
Past President	*G. G. Harman*
Vice-President	*Dr. M. E. LaZerte*
General Secretary-Treasurer	*John W. Barnett*
Edmonton	*H. C. Clark*
Calgary	*H. T. Robertson*
Southeastern Alberta	*H. W. Bryant*
Southwestern Alberta	*M. G. Merkley* left to complete education for University degree. *Solon E. Low* took over post till Jan., when chosen as Provincial Treasurer leaving post vacant till next AGM election
Northeastern Alberta	*F. Hannochko*
Northwestern Alberta	*R. A. Peterson*
Central Alberta	*Raymond Shaul*

1937-38

President	*Dr. M. E. LaZerte*
Past President	*E. C. Ansley*
Vice-President	*Raymond E. Shaul*
General Secretary-Treasurer	*John W. Barnett*
Edmonton	*H. C. Clark*
Calgary	*Miss Isabel Breckon*
Southeastern Alberta	*H. W. Bryant*
Southwestern Alberta	*W. S. Brodie*
Northeastern Alberta	*F. Hannochko* became Inspector in Dec., term completed by *W. E. Kostash*
Northwestern Alberta	*H. T. Sparby*
Central Alberta	*J. A. Smith*

1938-39

President	*Dr. M. E. LaZerte*
Past President	*E. C. Ansley*
Vice-President	*Raymond E. Shaul*
General Secretary-Treasurer	*John W. Barnett*
Edmonton	*Gordon G. Harman*
Calgary	*W. C. Frickelton*
Southeastern Alberta	*Frank J. Edwards*
Southwestern Alberta	*H. G. Teskey*
Northeastern Alberta	*W. E. Kostash*
Northwestern Alberta	*H. T. Sparby*
Central Alberta	*J. A. Smith*

1939-40

President	*Raymond E. Shaul*
Past President	*Dr. M. E. LaZerte*
Vice-President	*Dr. C. Sansom*
General Secretary-Treasurer	*John W. Barnett*
Edmonton	*Gordon G. Harman*
Calgary	*W. C. Frickelton*
Southeastern Alberta	*Eric C. Ansley*
Southwestern Alberta	*H. G. Teskey*
Northeastern Alberta	*W. E. Kostash*
Northwestern Alberta	*H. T. Sparby* resigned in June, term completed by *H. C. Melsness*
Central Alberta	*Lynn G. Hall*

1940-41

President	*Raymond E. Shaul*
Past President	*Dr. M. E. LaZerte*
Vice-President	*James A. Smith*
General Secretary-Treasurer	*John W. Barnett*
Edmonton	*T. D. Baker*
Calgary	*W. R. Eyres*
Southeastern Alberta	*Eric C. Ansley*
Southwestern Alberta	*Sydney White*
Northeastern Alberta	*W. E. Kostash*
Northwestern Alberta	*H. C. Melsness*
Central Alberta	*A. A. Aldridge*

1941-42

President	*James A. Smith*
Past President	*Raymond E. Shaul*
Vice-President	*Dr. Herbert E. Smith, Major* resigned, military duties, Dec., *T. D. Baker* completed term
General Secretary-Treasurer	*John W. Barnett*
Edmonton	*T. D. Baker* became Vice-Pres., term completed by *Miss A. Mina Johnston*
Calgary	*L. A. Daniels*
Southeastern Alberta	*R. A. Morton*
Southwestern Alberta	*Sydney White*
Northeastern Alberta	*L. L. Kostash*
Northwestern Alberta	*H. C. Melsness*
Central Alberta	*A. A. Aldridge* resigned Sept., term completed by *L. R. McLeay*

1942-43

President	*James A. Smith*
Past President	*Raymond E. Shaul*
Vice-President	*T. D. Baker*
General Secretary-Treasurer	*John W. Barnett*
Edmonton District	*Miss A. M. Johnston*
Calgary District	*L. A. Daniels*
Southeastern Alberta	*E. C. Ansley*
Southwestern Alberta	*Sydney White*
Northeastern Alberta	*L. L. Kostash*
Northwestern Alberta	*H. C. Melsness*
Central Alberta	*L. R. McLeay*

1943-44

President	*Dr. C. Sansom*
Past President	*James A. Smith*
Vice-President	*H. C. Melsness*
General Secretary-Treasurer	*John W. Barnett*
Edmonton District	*Miss A. M. Johnston*
Calgary District	*T. N. Roche*
Southeastern Alberta	*E. C. Ansley*
Southwestern Alberta	
Northeastern Alberta	*L. L. Kostash*

Northwestern Alberta	*W. A. Kujath*
Central Eastern Alberta	*L. A. Broughton* became Inspector, term completed by *M. R. Butterfield*
Central Western Alberta	*D. A. Ure*

1944-45

President	*Dr. C. Sansom*
Past President	*James A. Smith*
Vice-President	*H. C. Melsness*
General Secretary-Treasurer	*John W. Barnett*
Edmonton District	*G. C. French*
Calgary District	*T. N. Roche*
Southeastern Alberta	*E. C. Ansley*
Southwestern Alberta	*W. A. Rea*
Northeastern Alberta	*L. L. Kostash*
Northwestern Alberta	*W. A. Kujath*
Central Eastern Alberta	*M. R. Butterfield*
Central Western Alberta	*D. C. Dandell*

1945-46

President	*H. C. Melsness*
Past President	*Dr. C. Sansom*
Vice-President	*Dr. H. E. Smith*
General Secretary-Treasurer	*John W. Barnett*
Edmonton District	*T. D. Baker*
Calgary District	*F. J. C. Seymour*
Southeastern Alberta	*E. C. Ansley*
Southwestern Alberta	*W. A. Rea*
Northeastern Alberta	*L. L. Kostash*
Northwestern Alberta	*L. E. Kelly*
Central Eastern Alberta	*A. O. Aalborg*
Central Western Alberta	*E. T. Wiggins*

1946-47

President	*H. C. Melsness*
Past President	*Dr. C. Sansom*
Vice-President	*Dr. H. E. Smith*
General Secretary-Treasurer	*John W. Barnett* retired Sept., post filled by *Eric C. Ansley*
Edmonton District	*F. J. C. Seymour*
Calgary District	*T. D. Baker*

Southeastern Alberta	*J. R. Johnston*
Southwestern Alberta	*M. Holman*
Northeastern Alberta	*L. L. Kostash*
Northwestern Alberta	*L. E. Kelly*
Central Eastern Alberta	*A. O. Aalborg*
Central Western Alberta	*E. T. Wiggins*

1947-48

President	*Dr. H. E. Smith*
Past President	*H. C. Melsness*
Vice-President	*E. T. Wiggins*
General Secretary-Treasurer	*Eric C. Ansley*
Edmonton District	*Marian Gimby*
Calgary District	*Douglas Norton* died Aug. 14, term completed by *W. R. Eyres*
Southeastern Alberta	*J. R. Johnston*
Southwestern Alberta	*M. Holman*
Northeastern Alberta	*G. Kolotyluk*
Northwestern Alberta	*F. C. Toews*
Central Eastern Alberta	*A. O. Aalborg*
Central Western Alberta	*A. R. Patrick*

1948-49

President	*Edgar T. Wiggins*
Past President	*Dr. H. E. Smith*
Vice-President	*A. O. Aalborg*
General Secretary-Treasurer	*Eric C. Ansley*
Southeastern Alberta	*J. R. Johnston*
Southwestern Alberta	*M. Holman*
Northeastern Alberta	*G. Kolotyluk*
Northwestern Alberta	*F. C. Toews*
Central Eastern Alberta	*L. Olson*
Central Western Alberta	*A. R. Patrick*

1949-50

President	*F. J. C. Seymour*
Past President	*Edgar T. Wiggins*
Vice-President	*Marian Gimby*
General Secretary-Treasurer	*Eric C. Ansley*
Southeastern Alberta	*N. A. Wait*
Southwestern Alberta	*Marguerite Esplen*
Northeastern Alberta	*G. Kolotyluk*

Northwestern Alberta	*H. Dewar*
Central Eastern Alberta	*L. Olson*
Central Western Alberta	*A. Allen*

1950-51

President	*F. J. C. Seymour*
Past President	*E. T. Wiggins*
Vice-President	*Marian Gimby*
General Secretary-Treasurer	*Eric C. Ansley*
Edmonton District	*F. J. Edwards*
Calgary District	*E. G. Callbeck*
Southeastern Alberta	*N. A. Wait*
Southwestern Alberta	*N. A. McNair Knowles*
Northeastern Alberta	*G. Kolotyluk*
Northwestern Alberta	*Harry Dewar* retired Nov., term completed by *Mary Gray*
Central Eastern Alberta	*Selmer Olsonberg*
Central Western Alberta	*Arthur Allen*

1951-52

President	*Marian Gimby*
Past President	*F. J. C. Seymour*
Vice-President	*Lars Olson*
General Secretary-Treasurer	*Eric C. Ansley*
Edmonton District	*Frank J. Edwards*
Calgary District	*W. Roy Eyres*
Southeastern Alberta	*Edwin McKenzie*
Southwestern Alberta	*Robert A. Kimmitt*
Northeastern Alberta	*Nicholas Poohkay*
Northwestern Alberta	*Mary Gray*
Central Eastern Alberta	*Selmer Olsonberg*
Central Western Alberta	*H. L. Larson*

1952-53

President	*Marian Gimby*
Past President	*F. J. C. Seymour*
Vice-President	*Lars Olson*
General Secretary-Treasurer	*Eric C. Ansley*
Edmonton District	*F. J. Edwards*
Calgary District	*W. Roy Eyres*
Southeastern Alberta	*Edwin McKenzie*
Southwestern Alberta	*Robert A. Kimmitt*

Northeastern Alberta	*Nicholas Poohkay*
Northwestern Alberta	*W. D. McGrath*
Central Eastern Alberta	*Kenneth W. Sparks*
Central Western Alberta	*D. A. Prescott*

1953-54

President	*Lars Olson*
Past President	*Marian Gimby*
Vice-President	*F. J. Edwards*
General Secretary-Treasurer	*Eric C. Ansley*
Edmonton District	*H. J. M. Ross*
Calgary District	*I. K. Castleton*
Southeastern Alberta	*Dorothy Benjamin*
Southwestern Alberta	*G. S. Lakie*
Northeastern Alberta	*Michael Skuba*
Northwestern Alberta	*W. D. McGrath*
Central Eastern Alberta	*K. W. Sparks*
Central Western Alberta	*D. A. Prescott*

1954-55

President	*F. J. Edwards*
Past President	*Lars Olson*
Vice-President	*G. S. Lakie*
General Secretary-Treasurer	*Eric C. Ansley*
Edmonton District	*H. J. M. Ross*
Calgary District	*Inez K. Castleton*
Southeastern Alberta	*Dorothy Benjamin*
Southwestern Alberta	*R. B. McIntosh*
Northeastern Alberta	*Michael Skuba*
Northwestern Alberta	*W. D. McGrath*
Central Eastern Alberta	*M. W. McDonnell*
Central Western Alberta	*D. A. Prescott*

1955-56

President	*G. S. Lakie*
Past President	*F. J. Edwards*
Vice-President	*H. J. M. Ross*
General Secretary-Treasurer	*Eric C. Ansley*
Edmonton City	*W. E. Kostash*
Edmonton District	*R. F. Staples*
Calgary City	*Inez K. Castleton*

Calgary District	*L. R. Workman*
	died Oct., term completed by
	Ralph L. McCall
Southeastern Alberta	*Dorothy Benjamin*
Southwestern Alberta	*R. B. McIntosh*
Northeastern Alberta	*N. J. Andruski*
Northwestern Alberta	*W. D. McGrath*
Central Eastern Alberta	*M. W. McDonnell*
Central Western Alberta	*D. A. Prescott*

1956-57

President	*H. J. M. Ross*
Past President	*G. S. Lakie*
Vice-President	*Inez K. Castleton*
General Secretary-Treasurer	*Eric C. Ansley*
Edmonton City	*W. E. Kostash*
Edmonton District	*R. F. Staples*
Calgary City	*Eva Jagoe*
Calgary District	*Ralph L. McCall*
Southeastern Alberta	*F. M. Riddle*
Southwestern Alberta	*R. B. McIntosh*
Northeastern Alberta	*N. J. Andruski*
Northwestern Alberta	*W. D. McGrath*
Central Eastern Alberta	*M. W. McDonnell*
Central Western Alberta	*D. A. Prescott*

1957-58

President	*Inez K. Castleton*
Past President	*H. J. M. Ross*
Vice-President	*W. D. McGrath*
	became superintendent, term completed
	by *R. F. Staples*
General Secretary-Treasurer	*Eric C. Ansley*
Edmonton City	*A. D. G. Yates*
Edmonton District	*R. F. Staples*
	became Vice-Pres., term completed by
	H. C. McCall
Calgary City	*Eva Jagoe*
Calgary District	*R. L. McCall*
Southeastern Alberta	*F. M. Riddle*
	became superintendent, term completed
	by *G. Chopey*

Southwestern Alberta	*R. B. McIntosh* resigned Sept., term completed by *T. F. Rieger*
Northeastern Alberta	*A. J. Shandro*
Northwestern Alberta	*R. E. Bean*
Central Eastern Alberta	*J. D. McFetridge*
Central Western Alberta	*D. A. Prescott*

1958-59

President	*Inez K. Castleton*
Past President	*H. J. M. Ross*
Vice-President	*R. F. Staples*
General Secretary-Treasurer	*Eric C. Ansley* till Oct., then *L. C. Hyndman* became Acting GST till Jan., then *Dr. S. C. T. Clarke* appointed
Edmonton City	*A. D. G. Yates*
Edmonton District	*H. C. McCall*
Calgary City	*Elizabeth W. Duff*
Calgary District	*N. P. Bragg*
Southeastern Alberta	*J. A. McDonald*
Southwestern Alberta	*T. F. Rieger*
Northeastern Alberta	*A. J. Shandro*
Northwestern Alberta	*R. E. Bean* by-election Nov., *E. J. L. Guertin* elected
Central Eastern Alberta	*J. D. McFetridge* became Exec. Assistant, May term completed by *Mrs. Jean Saville*
Central Western Alberta	*D. A. Prescott*

1959-60

President	*R. F. Staples*
Past President	*Inez K. Castleton*
Vice-President	*A. D. G. Yates*
General Secretary-Treasurer	*Dr. S. C. T. Clarke*
Edmonton City	*Frank Loewen*
Edmonton District	*H. C. McCall*
Calgary City	*Elizabeth W. Duff*
Calgary District	*N. P. Bragg*
Southeastern Alberta	*J. A. McDonald*
Southwestern Alberta	*T. F. Rieger*
Northeastern Alberta	*A. J. Shandro*

Northwestern Alberta	*E. J. L. Guertin*
Central Eastern Alberta	*Jean Saville*
Central Western Alberta	*D. A. Prescott*

1960-61

President	*A. D. G. Yates*
Past President	*R. F. Staples*
Vice-President	*J. A. McDonald*
General Secretary-Treasurer	*Dr. S. C. T. Clarke*
Edmonton City	*L. Jean Scott*
Edmonton District	*H. C. McCall*
Calgary City	*E. W. Duff*
Calgary District	*N. P. Bragg* died Sept., term completed by *Edison F. Bardock*
Southeastern Alberta	*Lucy I. M. Milne*
Southwestern Alberta	*T. F. Rieger*
Northeastern Alberta	*A. J. Shandro*
Northwestern Alberta	*E. J. L. Guertin*
Central Eastern Alberta	*Jean Saville*
Central Western Alberta	*D. A. Prescott*

1961-62

President	*J. A. McDonald*
Past President	*A. D. G. Yates*
Vice-President	*H. C. McCall*
General Secretary-Treasurer	*Dr. S. C. T. Clarke*
Edmonton City	*L. Jean Scott*
Edmonton District	*William Moysa*
Calgary City	*Elizabeth W. Duff*
Calgary District	*E. F. Bardock*
Southeastern Alberta	*Lucy I. M. Milne*
Southwestern Alberta	*T. F. Rieger*
Northeastern Alberta	*Frank Shymko*
Northwestern Alberta	*E. J. L. Guertin*
Central Eastern Alberta	*M. W. McDonnell*
Central Western Alberta	*D. A. Prescott*

1962-63

President	*H. C. McCall*
Past President	*J. A. McDonald*
Vice-President	*T. F. Rieger*
General Secretary-Treasurer	*Dr. S. C. T. Clarke*

Edmonton City	*L. Jean Scott*
Edmonton District	*William Moysa*
Calgary City	*Elizabeth W. Duff* resigned Dec., term completed by *F. W. Hoskyn*
Calgary District	*E. F. Bardock*
Southeastern Alberta	*Lucy I. M. Milne*
Southwestern Alberta	*R. I. Stonehocker*
Northeastern Alberta	*Frank Shymko*
Northwestern Alberta	*F. J. Dumont*
Central Eastern Alberta	*M. W. McDonnell*
Central Western Alberta	*D. A. Prescott*

1963-64

President	*T. F. Rieger*
Past President	*H. C. McCall*
Vice-President	*L. Jean Scott*
General Secretary-Treasurer	*Dr. S. C. T. Clarke*
Edmonton City	*B. T. Keeler*
Edmonton District	*Wm. Moysa* by-election Oct., *Harold G. Ross* elected
Calgary City	*F. W. Hoskyn*
Calgary District	*E. F. Bardock*
Southeastern Alberta	*Lucy I. M. Milne*
Southwestern Alberta	*R. I. Stonehocker*
Northeastern Alberta	*Frank Shymko*
Northwestern Alberta	*F. J. Dumont* by-election Oct., *Garfield Potvin* elected
Central Eastern Alberta	*M. W. McDonnell*
Central Western Alberta	*D. A. Prescott*

1964-65

President	*L. Jean Scott*
Past President	*T. F. Rieger*
Vice-President	*M. W. McDonnell*
General Secretary-Treasurer	*Dr. S. C. T. Clarke*
Edmonton City	*Dr. B. T. Keeler*
Edmonton District	*Harold G. Ross*
Calgary City	*Frank W. Hoskyn*
Calgary District	*E. F. Bardock*
Southeastern Alberta	*E. R. Hadlington*
Southwestern Alberta	*R. I. Stonehocker*

Northeastern Alberta	*Frank Shymko*
Northwestern Alberta	*E. J. L. Guertin*
Central Eastern Alberta	*Marjorie Knapp*
Central Western Alberta	*I. P. Stonehocker*

1965-66

President	*M. W. McDonnell*
Past President	*L. Jean Scott*
Vice-President	*F. W. Hoskyn*
General Secretary-Treasurer	*Dr. S. C. T. Clarke*
Edmonton City	*Dr. B. T. Keeler*
Edmonton District	*H. G. Ross*
Calgary City	*J. W. Carlton*
Calgary District	*E. F. Bardock*
Southeastern Alberta	*E. R. Hadlington*
Southwestern Alberta	*R. I. Stonehocker*
Northeastern Alberta	*F. Shymko*
Northwestern Alberta	*G. Potvin*
Central Eastern Alberta	*Marjorie E. Knapp*
Central Western Alberta	*I. P. Stonehocker*

1966-67

President	*F. W. Hoskyn*
Past President	*M. W. McDonnell*
Vice-Presidents	*A. M. Arbeau and Dr. B. T. Keeler*
General Secretary-Treasurer	*Dr. S. C. T. Clarke*
Edmonton City	*W. S. Bailey*
Edmonton District	*A. O. Jorgensen*
Calgary City	*J. W. Carlton*
Calgary District	*R. S. Woolsey*
Southeastern Alberta	*E. R. Hadlington*
Southwestern Alberta	*R. I. Stonehocker*
Northeastern Alberta	*F. Shymko*
Northwestern Alberta	*G. Potvin*
Central Eastern Alberta	*Marjorie E. Knapp*
Central Western Alberta	*I. P. Stonehocker*

1967-68

President	*Dr. B. T. Keeler*
Past President	*F. W. Hoskyn*
Vice-Presidents	*A. M. Arbeau and R. I. Stonehocker*
General Secretary-Treasurer	*Dr. S. C. T. Clarke*

Edmonton City	*W. S. Bailey*
Edmonton District	*R. V. Mundell*
Calgary City	*J. W. Carlton*
Calgary District	*R. S. Woolsey*
Southeastern Alberta	*L. P. Cluff*
Southwestern Alberta	*V. D. Van Orman*
Northeastern Alberta	*H. J. Leskiw*
Northwestern Alberta	*G. Potvin*
Central Eastern Alberta	*L. A. Strandberg*
Central Western Alberta	*I. P. Stonehocker*

Appendix II

HONORARY LIFE MEMBERS OF THE ALBERTA TEACHERS' ALLIANCE AND THE ALBERTA TEACHERS' ASSOCIATION

*William Aberhart
Harry Dean Ainlay
*John Walker Barnett
*Herbert Daniel Cartwright
Mary Roberta Crawford
*Samuel Henry Crowther
Donalda James Dickie
*Frank J. Edwards
Olive M. Fisher
*William Edward Frame
Lloyd Garrison
Cedric Oliver Hicks
Eva Osyth Howard
Milton Ezra LaZerte
Murray MacDonald
Jessie Winnifred Maxwell
*Hubert Charles Newland
Lars Olson
Harold Edward Panabaker
*Gilbert C. Paterson
Charles Edgar Peasley
Arthur Joseph Howson Powell
Chester Ronning
*Arthur Edward Rosborough
*H. J. McKim Ross
*Clarence Sansom
*Frederick John Charles Seymour
*Thomas Edwin Adelbert Stanley
*Harry Charles Sweet
Clara Tyner
*Allan James Watson
George Watson

*Deceased

Appendix III

THE ALBERTA TEACHERS' ASSOCIATION
CODE OF ETHICS
(Approved by resolution of 1962 Annual General Meeting)

The Code of Ethics shall apply to all members, and the term "teacher" as used in this code includes all members of The Alberta Teachers' Association. A complaint of violation of this code made to the Association by any person or group shall be regarded by the Executive Council of the Association as a charge of unprofessional conduct under the *By-laws Relating to Discipline* of the Association. Excessive or flagrant violation of the Standards of Professional Conduct by any member of the Association may also lead to discipline charges being laid against that member.

1

The teacher studiously avoids unfavorable criticism of an associate except when made to proper officials, and then only in confidence and after the associate has been informed of the nature of the criticism.

2

No group of teachers nor any teacher purporting to speak on behalf of such group makes representations to the government, its members or officials, or to the officials of the University of Alberta on matters affecting the interest of teachers generally or advocating a change in educational policy without the knowledge and consent of the Executive Council of the Association.

3

The teacher, on request of proper authorities, presents relevant testimonials and documents and makes full and complete disclosure of relevant matters which affect his engagement or advancement with an employer.

4

The teacher adheres to collective agreements negotiated by his professional organization.

5

The teacher respects and fulfills his contractual obligation until released by mutual consent or according to law.

6

The teacher does not apply for, nor accept, a designated position before such position has become vacant.

7

The teacher does not divulge information received in confidence or in the course of professional duties, except as required by law, or where, in the judgment of the teacher, it is in the best interests of the child.

8

The teacher does not accept pay for tutoring his own pupils in the subjects in which he gives classroom instruction.

9

The teacher does not use his professional position for personal profit by offering goods or services to his own pupils or their parents.

Appendix IV

THE ALBERTA TEACHERS' ASSOCIATION STANDARDS OF PROFESSIONAL CONDUCT

(Approved by resolution of 1962 Annual General Meeting)

The Standards of Professional Conduct shall apply to all members, and the term "teacher" as used in this statement of standards includes all members of The Alberta Teachers' Association. This statement does not attempt to define all items of acceptable conduct. These items are minimum standards of professional behavior which members are expected to observe. Excessive or flagrant violation of the Standards of Professional Conduct by any member of the Association may lead to a charge of unprofessional conduct under the *By-laws Relating to Discipline* of the Association.

IN RELATION TO PUPILS

1

The teacher speaks to and acts towards pupils in a respectful and dignified manner.

2

The teacher's demands upon pupils take into account their ability and their work load in other courses.

IN RELATION TO THE GENERAL PUBLIC

3

The teacher does not engage in gainful employment outside of his regular contract where the employment affects adversely his professional status or impairs his standing with students, associates, or community.

4

The teacher works constantly to improve education through study and constructive criticism.

5

The teacher conducts himself at all times in such manner as to maintain the prestige of the profession so that no dishonor or disgrace may befall him or his profession through his actions.

IN RELATION TO EMPLOYERS

6

The teacher does not accept a position with an employer whose relations with the professional organization are unsatisfactory without first clearing through head office of The Alberta Teachers' Association.

7

The teacher intending to terminate his employment with a school authority gives notice of his intention as early as possible.

8

The teacher notifies all boards to which he has sent applications as soon as he has accepted a position.

9

The teacher does not accept without protest assignment of duties nor the existence of working conditions which make it difficult or impossible to render professional service.

IN RELATION TO COLLEAGUES

10

The teacher does not undermine the confidence of pupils in other teachers.

11

The teacher submits to the Association all disputes arising from professional relationships with colleagues which cannot be resolved by personal discussion at the local level. (The Association may refer the matter to the Professional Relations Commission or to the Discipline Committee.)

12

The teacher notifies any other teacher whose pupils he proposes to tutor.

13

The teacher observes a reasonable and proper respect for the authority of school administrators and recognizes the duty to protest through proper channels, administrative policies and practices which he cannot in conscience accept; and further recognizes that if administration by consent fails, the administrator must adopt a position of authority.

14

The teacher as an administrator respects staff members as individuals and provides continuous opportunities for staff members to express their opinions and bring forth suggestions regarding the administration of the school.

IN RELATION TO THE ASSOCIATION

15

The teacher adheres to Association policy and seeks to change such policy only through the proper channels of the Association.

16

The teacher accepts as a professional obligation service to the Association at the local and provincial levels.

17

The teacher who has requested the Association to represent him in any dispute honours commitments made on his behalf by the Association.

IN RELATION TO PROFESSIONAL GROWTH

18

The teacher strives constantly to attain standards of qualification accepted by the Association.

19

The teacher strives constantly to improve his educational practices through professional development activities.

Appendix V

THE ALBERTA TEACHERS' ASSOCIATION
EDUCATIONAL PLATFORM

1

Official recognition of The Alberta Teachers' Association as the organization representing the teaching profession of the province,
(a) by the government,
(b) by the school boards, and
(c) by all other groups.

2

Fullest possible co-operation between The Alberta Teachers' Association and
(a) the Department of Education,
(b) school boards, and
(c) all other organizations interested in education.

3

The right of The Alberta Teachers' Association to have representation on all boards of inquiry having under consideration the efficiency or conduct of a teacher(including summary dismissals and transfers).

4

Promotion on the basis of seniority, all other qualifications being equal.

5

Increased government grants.

6

Equality of educational opportunity: free adult education, extension of high school and university privileges to rural districts.

7

Provision for special instruction of talented children.

8

Provision for special instruction of handicapped children.

9

Province-wide medical and dental inspection of schools

10

Elimination of juvenile labour.

11

A tightening of the truancy law and release of the teacher from the duty of informing.

12

Higher professional training for teachers

13

Equal pay for equal professional education and teaching experience.

14

A limit of 25 students per class or room for proper work in a modern school system.

Index

www.ingramcontent.com/pod-product-compliance
Lightning Source LLC
LaVergne TN
LVHW090803070826
844660LV00022B/1066

* 9 7 8 1 4 4 2 6 3 9 0 4 1 *